THE MADNESS OF BELIEVING

THE MADNESS OF BELIEVING

A Memoir from Inside Alex Jones's Conspiracy Machine

JOSH OWENS

GRAND CENTRAL

New York Boston

The Madness of Believing is a work of memoir. It is a true story, based on the author's personal experiences and recollections. Portions of dialogue have been re-created in accordance with the author's best memory of actual conversations and events. In some cases, names and identifying details have been changed.

Copyright © 2026 by Josh Owens

Cover copyright © 2026 by Hachette Book Group, Inc.

Hachette Book Group supports the right to free expression and the value of copyright. The purpose of copyright is to encourage writers and artists to produce the creative works that enrich our culture.

The scanning, uploading, and distribution of this book without permission is a theft of the author's intellectual property. If you would like permission to use material from the book (other than for review purposes), please contact permissions@hbgusa.com. Thank you for your support of the author's rights.

Grand Central Publishing
Hachette Book Group
1290 Avenue of the Americas, New York, NY 10104
grandcentralpublishing.com
@grandcentralpub

First Edition: April 2026

Grand Central Publishing is a division of Hachette Book Group, Inc. The Grand Central Publishing name and logo is a registered trademark of Hachette Book Group, Inc.

The publisher is not responsible for websites (or their content) that are not owned by the publisher.

The Hachette Speakers Bureau provides a wide range of authors for speaking events. To find out more, go to hachettespeakersbureau.com or email HachetteSpeakers@hbgusa.com.

Grand Central Publishing books may be purchased in bulk for business, educational, or promotional use. For information, please contact your local bookseller or the Hachette Book Group Special Markets Department at special.markets@hbgusa.com.

Print book interior design by Marie Mundaca

Library of Congress Cataloging-in-Publication Data

Names: Owens, Josh author
Title: The madness of believing : a memoir from inside Alex Jones's conspiracy machine / Josh Owens.
Description: New York : GCP, 2026.
Identifiers: LCCN 2025048742 | ISBN 9781538757321 hardcover | ISBN 9781538757345 ebook
Subjects: LCSH: Owens, Josh | Jones, Alex, 1974- | Infowars.com | Television producers and directors—United States--Biography | Internet television—Production and direction—United States | Television—Production and direction—United States | Conspiracy theories—United States | LCGFT: Autobiographies
Classification: LCC PN1992.9236.O94 A3 2026
LC record available at https://lccn.loc.gov/2025048742

ISBNs: 978-1-5387-5732-1 (hardcover), 978-1-5387-5734-5 (ebook)

Printed in the United States of America

LSC-C

Printing 1, 2026

To Lacey

CONTENTS

Prologue 1

PART ONE: BELIEF

1. The War Room 7
2. Idiocracy 27
3. The Doomsday Machine 41
4. A Cure for Tyranny 48
5. Spies Like Us 62

PART TWO: MADNESS

6. In Camelot 75
7. Fukushima, California 89
8. Bow Tie 107
9. Inheritance 116
10. Madman 133
11. The Crossing 140
12. Men in Beige 151

13. Why Do the Heathen Rage? 167
14. The World Beneath Her 178
15. Everything That Rises Must Converge 192
16. Virgil at the Gates 206

PART THREE: DISBELIEF

17. Waking Up 229
18. A Good Man Is Hard to Find 240
19. Monsters 255
20. Made in America 265

Acknowledgments *273*

You have to quit confusing a madness with a mission.

—Flannery O'Connor, *The Violent Bear It Away*

PROLOGUE

The sign above the door read BIRDS OF A FEATHER. I pushed it open and took a seat on the couch, next to a wooden shelf with two small porcelain canaries in mid-flight. The room felt hotter than usual. I removed my jacket and draped it over the arm of the sofa as my therapist sat down across from me. Anne was in her early fifties, radiating an enviable air of confidence. I, on the other hand, was twenty-nine, diffident and calculated, terrified of being perceived as an unreasonable, unlikable conspiracy junkie.

"How are you?" she asked.

"Good," I said.

This was how we began every session: a simple question resulting in a simple answer. It felt performative but always had the intended effect of setting the conversation in motion.

I was struggling with how I'd spent the past four years of my life. The scams I'd contributed to. The lies I'd helped spread. The people I'd harmed. The guilt clawed at me, insistent and unyielding. I had been a cog in a monstrous machine, a part of something I had once believed, in earnest, to be valiant. Often in these sessions, I sat in silence, unsure of where to start, but Anne's x-ray vision cut through my taciturn moments.

"Why is this room called 'Birds of a Feather'?" I eventually asked.

"It's a reference to the saying, about people forming groups around similar interests," she said. "Really, though, each room in this office just has an animal theme."

I looked back over at the canaries on the shelf, the porcelain swan on the table between us, the macramé tapestry of crane silhouettes. After months in that room, I'd never considered the deliberate motif. Or the symbolic coincidence.

"Maybe that's part of my problem," I said, "the whole 'birds flock together' thing. Without a partner encouraging me to think or feel differently, I probably wouldn't have left; I certainly wouldn't be on this couch."

Anne relaxed into her chair. "You might be right," she said, "but before you can understand any of this, you have to acknowledge what you've gone through." Reaching into her bag, she pulled out a notepad. "I've been thinking you might need to see someone who specializes in trauma or PTSD." She hesitated before saying those last four letters—an acronym typically ascribed to those who've witnessed, firsthand, the horrors of humanity. "I can give you some names."

"The place I worked *was* called 'Infowars,'" I said, joking, dismissive, "but despite my militaristic boss, I never saw combat."

I thought back to the chaos of protests, the burn of tear gas, the anger that hovered over everything. The sharp crack of gunfire, laughter that cut through the tension, friendships built on defiance and uncertainty, the proximity between the fantastic and the hateful. It all merged into a confusing monolith of fear, disillusion, and madness. I knew what I'd experienced—it's what filled most of the hour-long conversations we had in that room—but I didn't feel comfortable shifting from offender to victim. So I resisted.

"I *chose* to be there," I said, turning those memories inward.

Anne paused for a moment. "Yes, at first you chose to be there," she replied, leaning forward. "You also chose to leave."

Part One
BELIEF

1
THE WAR ROOM

I pulled up to a red-brick office building, convinced I had taken a wrong turn. In my naïve fantasies, I pictured the office downtown, alive among bustling city streets, sidewalks filled with tepid locals, spirited tourists, sharply dressed commuters navigating their frenetic lives.

Instead, the highway became a frontage road that curved through an underpass, crossing industrial warehouses, semiconductor plants, and a flat, balding field, overgrown and enclosed by a chain-link fence. Smoke from nearby factories filled the sky with ashen clouds. A cool breeze flitted through oak saplings as I pulled into an empty parking spot and noticed, only then, the blacked-out windows and conspicuous lack of signage on the maroon office building. Maybe this *was* the perfect location, I thought, reconsidering my initial doubt, seeing it then as a cloak-and-dagger operation straight out of a movie.

The first door I tried was locked. The second, while also bolted shut, had a small intercom positioned by the handle. I pressed the white button and peered at the dark windows, unable to see anything but my own reflection.

This was my first time in Austin, my first time in Texas. I had traveled a thousand miles for a job I knew little about. A year earlier, on a whim, I submitted a video to an online contest and was offered a position as a camera operator and editor. I knew accepting that role would break my monotonous routine in film school, hoped it would lead to other opportunities, but I had no idea where that decision was taking me, the darkness I was inviting into my life, the ruinous effects of crossing that threshold. On that May morning in 2013, I only recognized the immediate: I was stuck outside a locked door, desperately trying to get in.

I knocked once, twice, but no one answered. From behind me came the subtle scrape of shoes against pavement—slow, deliberate, like someone trying to be discreet. Turning, I spotted a scowling man coming toward me from the parking lot. He was middle-aged, wearing a vertical-striped silk shirt tucked into cargo pants with a leather fanny pack snapped tightly around his waist. Above the belt he looked like a mobster's errand boy; below it, a gelded father enduring a family vacation to Disney World. I smiled as he approached.

"Who are you?" he said, eschewing all formality.

I introduced myself and told him I was looking for Free Speech Systems, the company name stamped on the letterhead of my job offer. I'd been warned to keep the location private—an address I'd been given only a few days prior after my background check cleared. During the interview I was told it remained undisclosed to keep "crazy people" from showing up unannounced, and so I avoided giving the stranger further details. "This is my first day," I said. "It's possible I'm at the wrong place."

The man sighed as if we'd had this conversation before and he was irritated by the repeated inconvenience. He unzipped his waist bag and pulled out a cell phone. At first, I thought he was making a call, but he just stood there, staring down at the screen. That's when I realized I'd seen him before. He had been in the background of a video I'd watched online, one associated with the company who'd hired me.

"I'm looking for Infowars," I said, watching his face for a reaction.

He glanced up from his phone. "Infowars?"

"Yeah," I said, hoping my candor would warrant a response. "Alex Jones."

The man returned to his phone and shrugged his shoulders. "Never heard of him."

I stood there confused, wondering if this was some sort of test. Suddenly, static exploded through the intercom and a woman's voice bellowed out like the gatekeeper in *The Wizard of Oz*. I stepped back toward the door. "Hi...um...I'm looking for Free Speech Systems."

There was a pause before she responded. "Is this Josh?" She sounded friendlier this time, the tonal shift revealing her thick Texas accent. I leaned forward, relieved, confirming my identity. The man behind me slid his phone in his pocket and pulled out a fistful of keys, scraping them together until he found the plastic among the brass. "Apologies," he said, waving the key fob near the handle and opening the door. "Sometimes crazy people stop by, looking for Jones, so we have to be careful."

I uttered a half-hearted affirmation. The weight of the moment heaved at my insides, causing a queasiness I couldn't ignore. I had quit film school in my third year, moved halfway across the country with no savings, and convinced my girlfriend of four years to uproot her life and join me. But instead of making a good first impression at a place that claimed to expose lies, I had just been duped by a guy wearing a fanny pack.

As I stepped inside the office, the man who had accosted me introduced himself as Raymond, still eyeing me with suspicion. As the door sealed shut behind me, everything went dark. Pitch-black. I couldn't see anything, accentuating the bitter scent of burnt coffee and spent cartridge toner lingering in the air. "Wait here," I heard Raymond say, his voice trailing off in the distance. The office was frigid and murky like a cave. Black aluminum blinds covered the windows, blocking out the glaring Texas sun. It took a moment for my eyes to adjust. A row of fabric partition panels blocked my view of the space, and I could hear distant footsteps, the low hum of a printer, the erratic shuffling of paper nearby.

A squat woman with kind eyes appeared around the corner. "I'm Michelle," she said, her voice a match for the one I'd heard on the intercom. She beckoned me to follow her. As we made our way through the office, I was surprised at how messy it was. Instead of an impressive headquarters, what the lead-in to Jones's radio show described as the "central Texas command center deep behind enemy lines," the space looked more like an unkempt college media department. Cables were strewn across the floor, desks were heaped with disassembled broadcasting equipment, and stacks of printed news articles cluttered every surface.

"Where are you from again?" she asked as we moved down a long corridor. The walls stood bare except for a few oil paintings. One was a crude copy of Hokusai's woodblock print *The Great Wave off Kanagawa*, and the other a grotesque futuristic humanoid towering over a Technicolor mountain. Both looked as though they were painted by a child.

"I grew up in Georgia," I said, taking note of the wooden sign at the end of the hallway, scrawled with the words LIBERTY OR DEATH as an ominous warning.

Michelle was from Texas, though she didn't specify which part, and had worked for Infowars a few years after her brother, the operations manager, got her a job. She leaned in close and lowered her voice as she spoke. "It's a crazy place," she said with a raised eyebrow, gauging my reaction. I must've looked nervous, perhaps wondering why the word "crazy" had already been used numerous times during my brief interactions with employees. "Don't get me wrong," she clarified, attempting to sound enthusiastic, searching for the right descriptive word, "it can also be... exciting."

The carpeted floors turned to concrete as we entered the shipping department. Walls were lined with steel wire shelves crammed full of DVDs, stickers, and an array of custom-designed T-shirts. On the ground was a large wooden pallet, stacked four feet high with Infowars magazines. That month's issue: *A History of False Flags*.

"Here's our warehouse," she said. "I work in the building across the street—we just got the extra space so there's only a few of us over there." I watched the workers, all young men, rhythmically pulling merchandise from the shelves, wrapping delicate items in packing paper, and placing them into cardboard boxes before taping them shut. They all wore headphones and seemed to be in a trance. "I handle customer service," she said with a smile. "At least that's what they call it. I answer emails and phone calls from listeners of the show." She chuckled, cupping her hand to her mouth, and whispered, "Speaking of crazy..." There was that word again.

As we made our way out of the warehouse and into another hallway, I heard laughter in the distance. The conversation was muddled but I could make out a familiar voice—the gravelly, unmistakable declarations I'd grown accustomed to hearing online, over the radio, and in documentary films for the past five years.

It was Alex Jones.

He sounded jovial and relaxed, speaking to the voiceless others. Much like the location of the office, and the disorder therein, this was unexpected. Jones was renowned in fringe circles for his fiery histrionics, his long-winded rants, his keen ability to weave grand, often outlandish theories with news headlines to convey, in equal measure, his cinematic and apocalyptic worldview.

One of my biggest concerns accepting the position at Infowars was how Jones's mercurial on-air personality translated into the workplace. Young and unsure of myself, I was a shifting panorama of contradictions: vain and self-deprecating, adversarial and submissive, misanthropic, inexperienced, and in the throes of admiration and financial dependence, prone to bootlicking. However, based on the sounds emanating from the room at the end of the hallway, it seemed entirely plausible that Jones's on-air persona was just that: a persona, an exaggeration, a clever facade deployed to attract a greater audience to his ideas. In any other circumstance the duplicity would have bothered me, but since I was an employee, it was the best-case scenario.

The hallway led to a large studio with walls covered in black curtains that stretched from floor to ceiling. On the right side was an office that looked out onto the main parking lot. I can't recall what the men were discussing, but I remember that Jones, as I entered the room and saw him in person for the first time, was smiling.

"This is Josh," Michelle said, motioning me inside.

Jones extended his hand. "Great to meet you, buddy." He was shorter and thinner than I had expected, dressed in a well-fitted dark blue button-up shirt with short sleeves. His hair was slicked back and still damp, as if he had just stepped out of the shower, the parallel lines from the tines of a comb leading to a touch of gray at his temples. Before I could respond, he reached up and grabbed the collar of my blue nylon windbreaker. "Look at that jacket," he said, his meaty hand lingering near my throat. "You look like a fighter in the Rebel Alliance."

I had spent the past two years in film school watching and studying the work of some of the greatest filmmakers in the world: Ingmar Bergman, Akira Kurosawa, Agnés Varda, Yasujirō Ozu, David Lean,

Stanley Kubrick. But I had never seen a *Star Wars* movie. I laughed at Jones's comment, trying not to reveal my ignorance. For fear of being perceived as a fanboy, I tried to focus on something other than Jones, but it was difficult. Everything felt heightened, his bull-necked presence exerting a strange kind of gravity. It was unsettling to be in such proximity to him, as if he possessed some kind of hypnotic power that made the rest of the world fade away.

The spell was broken when I realized the two other men in the room were the ones who'd conducted my job interview a month earlier. Rob Dew was a news producer and Marty Tillman a video editor. "Good to finally meet you in person," Dew said. Tillman seconded his civility. He was an older man, maybe in his fifties, with salt-and-pepper hair and a neatly trimmed beard. Next to him, Dew looked more like the kind of person I expected to encounter in Austin—an earthy, free spirit that embodied the slogan "Keep Austin Weird." He was a tall, shaggy-haired dead ringer for The Dude in *The Big Lebowski*, wearing knit shorts, open-toed sandals, white socks, and a lime green Primus T-shirt.

Jones asked if I liked Austin so far, but before I told him I'd been there only two days and most of that time had been spent in my hotel room nauseous with anxiety, he continued, "There are a lot of trendies here." He sounded apologetic, as if these interlopers were somehow an atrocious reflection on himself. "Trendies" was a word he often used on his show referring to young liberals. To him, they were emblematic of a shallow, conformist mindset, driven more by the desire to appear progressive than by any true conviction.

Tillman chimed in, assuring me he would recommend the least "hippie" establishments so I could avoid "running into people like Dew." He laughed as Dew responded with a middle finger.

"Gentlemen," Jones shouted, sliding between them, "you can't fight in here; this is the War Room!" Everyone erupted in laughter, which fueled his performance. "'Mr. President, this lousy commie rat was taking pictures of the big board!' 'The whole point of a Doomsday Machine is lost if you keep it a secret.' 'Boys, I reckon this is it—nuclear combat toe-to-toe with the Ruskies!'" Jones continued quoting lines as I stood there, shocked. I wasn't so much surprised by the cheerful, welcoming atmosphere as I was by the familiarity of Jones's references. He was quoting from the film *Dr. Strangelove*, a fictional Cold War–era story of paranoia, catastrophic misjudgment, and military bureaucracy during the nuclear arms race. The film would serve as my gateway to Jones's conspiratorial world five years earlier.

In 2008, a television screen in a living room that wasn't my own flickered with the black-and-white images of *Dr. Strangelove*. I was in a fragile emotional place, having just graduated from high school and struggling to pursue my dream of being a musician. My girlfriend at the time had a cousin who lived in the Florida Panhandle, and we were visiting her and her boyfriend for a long weekend. One night as we strolled on Destin Harbor, Royce, the boyfriend, said that Stanley Kubrick had used an aerial shot of the beaches we were walking on in *Dr. Strangelove*, prompting a rewatch of the film back at their apartment. When we got to the scene where Sterling Hayden's character, Brigadier General Jack D. Ripper, launches into a manic tirade about the dangers of water fluoridation, Royce reached for the remote and hit pause. He turned to me, his face lit by the frozen frame on-screen, and asked a question that would change the trajectory of my life. "Have you ever heard of Alex Jones?"

Jones, he told me, was a small-time radio show host out of Austin who focused on conspiracy theories. The phrase "conspiracy theories" conjured up memories of watching Oliver Stone's *JFK* and a brief teenage fascination with UFOs sparked by my love of *The X-Files*. Royce jumped out of his seat and ran to the bathroom, returning with a tube of toothpaste and reading the warning label out loud: "'If more than used for brushing is accidentally swallowed, get medical help or contact a Poison Control Center right away.'" He looked at me like he'd just pulled the curtain back on reality, that even mundane toiletries revealed horrible truths. I didn't know what fluoride was, and until he told me, I didn't realize it was added to the water supply to help prevent cavities. He asked me to explain why swallowing a pea-sized amount of fluoride in toothpaste warranted a call to poison control, while drinking an unknown amount from the tap was of no concern. I had no explanation, but according to Royce, Alex Jones did. Jones claimed studies proved fluoride caused lower IQ levels and the elite used it to dumb down the population. He had a theory, based on his supposed deep research, that the elite needed subdued humans so they could maintain dominance and control, like the plot of *The Matrix*.

That night, after retiring to the guest room, I looked up Alex Jones for the first time—an online search that yielded far fewer results than it would today. The first Alex Jones who appeared was a Pulitzer Prize–winning *New York Times* journalist; the next, a British playwright; followed by a woman finalist for the Eurovision Young Dancer's Competition. Finally, I found the one I was looking for: "American radio host and filmmaker, best known for his promotion of conspiracy theories."

Jones had begun his career in Austin with a cable access show, later transitioning to radio on a local FM station. After refusing to broaden his conspiratorial topics, he was fired and began broadcasting a hybrid radio and online video show aptly named *The Alex Jones Show*. In late 2008, his notable guests included the actor Ed Asner, Professor Noam Chomsky, film director David Lynch, writer Gore Vidal, and actor Charlie Sheen. Jones had won Best Public Access Show and tied for Best Radio Show in an annual poll for the alternative local newspaper the *Austin Chronicle*. He had also acted in two Richard Linklater films, playing versions of himself in *Waking Life* and *A Scanner Darkly*.

Eventually I was directed to his website: Infowars.com. A bizarre maze of headlines filled the screen, predicting that the Chinese yuan would reign as the new global currency and asserting the US government used insidious psychological tactics to control and manipulate the masses. And then there was the scathing article accusing then US Senator Barack Obama of being a "Marxist" front man for the bankers. What struck me most was the unwavering certainty behind these claims—there was no room for doubt. This was not just speculation or theory, it was reality, and anyone who dared question it did so at their own peril.

I glanced over at the clock. Hours had gone by without my even realizing it. Some of the articles I read were confounding, but the overarching mystery kept me engaged. I wanted this all to be real. In just a few hours, life already felt more exciting. As I ventured further, an image caught my eye. It was a thumbnail showing grainy hooded figures gathered around a towering stone statue. A shiver went down my spine, baiting me to click on the video. *Dark Secrets Inside Bohemian Grove*, one of Jones's earlier documentaries, focused on the Bohemian Club. It claimed it was a private, all-male group of leaders from around the world including prime ministers, chancellors, presidents, governors, heads of media, industry, banking, and academia that had existed for over a hundred years. They gathered annually at Bohemian Grove—a secluded 2,700-acre redwood grove in Northern California—to take part in "bizarre, ancient Canaanite, Luciferian, Babylon mystery religion ceremonies." A young Alex Jones sat at a desk, addressing the viewers of his documentary. "All throughout history," he said, "spanning back into the mists of the beginnings of civilization, we see world leaders, from the empires of old, from the Aztec kings and priests to Babylonian leaders, to Ancient Rome, engaging in twisted behavior. Could it be," Jones posited, "that when you have all the power, and all the women and all the money and all the land and all the art, you have to do something new. You have to go against the basic grain of humanity."

He sounded like a mad David Attenborough. His wife had come with him, along with his cameraman, Mike Hanson, and they met up with two people who Jones referred to as "The Redcoats." British journalist Jon Ronson and his camera operator had come to accompany Jones. Over the span of a few days, they crept through the California redwoods, spoke to eccentric locals, and infiltrated the grove, capturing on film the Cremation of Care—a dramatic performance in which a body was burned in effigy at the base of the owl statue as an allegory for the banishment of worldly concerns.

At the time, Ronson was working on his own documentary series and accompanying book, *Them*, detailing his encounters with conspiracy theorists, though this wasn't made clear in Jones's documentary. It wasn't until years later, after a chance encounter, that I read Ronson's book and heard his version of events. He described Bohemian Grove as an "overgrown frat party," and the Cremation of Care as nothing more than a play, a metaphor. Jones, however, was convinced he had captured a satanic ritual on camera, insinuating that the body they burned could've been real.

As the documentary ended, I sat back, my mind reeling. I had my own complicated past with religion. I was raised by evangelicals in the Bible Belt and had struggled with my beliefs for years before dropping religion altogether. The idea of satanists gallivanting in the woods didn't scare me. The rational part of my brain insisted it was just conspiracist delusion, a confused mash-up of *The Blair Witch Project* and *Eyes Wide Shut*, but a smaller, more stimulating voice began to wonder if Jones was right. What if, behind the veil of power, dark rituals and darker motives guided the course of world events?

In that moment something began to shift inside me; the dullness of everyday existence parted to reveal a more vivid world beneath the surface. Suddenly, I was no longer a bored, directionless kid staring at a computer screen. I was Fox Mulder combing through the X-Files, Rod Serling opening a door to the Twilight Zone, Rosemary Woodhouse convinced that the neighbors were members of a ritualistic cult.

Back in the War Room, Jones hustled out after he'd finished displaying his ability to recall and quote entire movie scenes verbatim. His show began at 11 a.m. and he only had a few minutes before he had to be in studio across the building. Before leaving, he asked Dew to make sure the radio crew had a specific video ready for a segment. This led to a drastic shift in Jones's demeanor, the playfulness replaced by an exasperation that spread throughout the room. "When I ask for it, they won't know what I'm talking about," Jones said, breathless. "Nobody's bad, I just, I just... I need you to go over and make sure they have the clip because last week I got the deer in headlights look from them and I can't handle it anymore."

Dew jumped up from his seat and assured Jones he would take care of it, running out of the room at full speed as Jones ambled down the hallway after him, muttering under his breath. I settled into an empty chair and surveyed the room. A framed poster of Richard Linklater's *Waking Life* hung on the wall, featuring a rotoscope animation of Jones yelling into a microphone. Beside it, another poster displayed chaotic lines connecting logos, images of corporations, banks, and world leaders, culminating in a pyramid topped with an all-seeing eye. Above a white board filled with indiscriminate writing and a yellow Gadsden flag was a nameplate with DEWCIFER written in a font of dripping blood. Tillman noticed me staring. "It's a nickname," he said, shaking his head in amusement. "A well-earned nickname."

Dew came back into the room, incensed and out of breath, with a fire on his tongue that gave credence to the devilish moniker on the wall. "Those fucking guys," he said, throwing himself in the chair. "I warned them they better have the clip ready to go or Jones was going to lose it. And, of course, they just stared forward, dead-eyed." He turned to face me, seizing the moment to impart some hard-earned wisdom. "It's good you're hearing this. If Jones asks for something, just do it, don't act like those idiots over there. Get yourself a notebook, and anytime he says something, anything, write it down. A day, a week, sometimes even a month later, he's going to ask for whatever it is, and you better have it."

"Trust us," Tillman said, warning me Jones's playfulness could turn on a dime. "He may seem like he's goofing around and not paying attention, but he never forgets anything, and you don't want to make him angry."

I took their warning seriously. A pen and paper were on the desk next to me, so I grabbed them and wrote down the words "GET NOTEBOOK ASAP" in bold letters, folded the paper, and stuck it in my pocket.

The main building was divided into two sections: the radio side and the production side. On one end, writers were busy creating content for Jones's website, churning out original articles and reposting stories from other outlets, while the radio crew produced his flagship program. The other side housed the production department, where reporters focused on Jones's newfangled nightly news show and produced special reports for the website.

Infowars was in a liminal state. Jones wanted to expand his small operation into a full-fledged 24-hour news network. He had just hired four reporters and was in the process of building a new studio, one to rival the looks of mainstream outlets like CNN or Fox News. Dew took me on a brief tour of the office, introducing me to the reporters and giving me a glimpse of the wardrobe room, filled with memorabilia and costumes Jones had worn in parody videos. There was a Gorn mask from *Star Trek*, a Cobra Commander outfit from *G.I. Joe*, along with robes and pitchforks and light sabers. It was a treasure trove for geeks. Hanging on the wall, behind glass, was the actual Wolverines letterman jacket Charlie Sheen wore in the 1984 movie *Red Dawn*, gifted to Jones by Sheen himself. According to Jones, the two had become friends over their shared belief that the US government had perpetrated the September 11 attacks.

Dew led me into what would become the new studio—a giant room filled with coiled cables and drywall. "How long before it's finished?" I asked, not spotting anything that resembled a professional studio.

"Who knows?" Dew said. "A year, maybe less."

We made our way to the other side of the building, where Jones recorded his live radio show. It was a much smaller room, like a closet compared to what they were constructing. There were four men in the control room, pushing buttons and adjusting audio levels in front of a large glass window peering into the studio, where Jones was seated behind a desk covered in articles. These were the "idiots" Dew had referred to earlier. I could see Jones gesturing to the camera, but I couldn't hear him through the soundproofed room until Dew handed me a pair of wireless headphones. Jones's voice buzzed to life. "People say Alex Jones is crazy," he said. "He thinks there are armored vehicles, billions of bullets, and citizen spies."

Jones continued, "We're on an express elevator to hell. Let me tell you something, even if somebody is bigger and badder and meaner than you, when they're attacking you, they're not in the right. And they don't have the energy. And even if they are three times stronger than you, and better trained than you, if you kick and bite and snap and poke and punch and just turn loose your human power, you will stomp their butt nine times out of ten."

Jones often used physical violence as a metaphor for his work. He believed he was in an information war—hence the name of his organization—and he seemed to be obsessed with justice and retaliation and proving his physical strength, making sure the audience knew he could take on his perceived enemies if push came to shove.

Dew tapped me on the shoulder, motioning for me to follow him. Next to the studio was the writers' room, where three writers were seated at small desks, glowering at their computer screens. "They're next to the studio so Jones can pop over during a break and have them change a headline or write a story," Dew said. They appeared busy, drained of energy, and none of them acknowledged our presence. We continued down the same hallway I'd been in earlier, where Dew noted the hanging artwork had been painted by Jones. It was a hobby he'd picked up for relaxation, though it didn't last long.

Dew led me to the other building for the next phase in the orientation process: completing the new-hire paperwork. I sat in a conference room, alone, thrumming my fingers on the lacquered wood, waiting for Lydia, the office accountant. At the time there was no human resources department so she alone would be handling my onboarding. Lydia walked in carrying a stack of papers and placed the first packet, the employee manual, in front of me. The next packet was thinner, and she handled it delicately, like it could explode. She explained that this was the non-disclosure agreement and emphasized the importance of reading it thoroughly. I opened the employee manual, flipping to the first section.

WELCOME TO OUR COMPANY!

We're very happy to welcome you to Free Speech Systems, LLC. Thank you for joining us! We want you to feel that your association with the company will be a mutually beneficial and pleasant one. You have joined an organization that has established an outstanding reputation for quality products and services. Credit for this goes to every one of our employees. We hope you too, will find satisfaction and take pride in your work here.

Fight Tyranny, Love Liberty and be Happy.

I scanned through the sections and then pulled out the NDA. It was eight pages long and most of the document went over my head. I didn't care. *There's no way I need to concern myself,* I thought before signing my name and dropping the paper off at Lydia's desk.

As I walked back into the War Room, someone new was seated at the desk next to Dew. He looked busy, working on a 3-D model of President Obama on his computer when he noticed me and removed his headphones. Heavy metal music poured out into the room. Carlos was different than the other people in the office. He had a sense of ease about him and a kindness that felt out of place. The interactions I'd had with Jones's employees thus far were welcoming on the surface, but I got the feeling they were all hiding something.

My work computer hadn't come in, and I didn't have a desk yet, so I pulled up a chair and sat down next to him. Carlos, in his all-black attire with steel hoop earrings that pulled on his earlobes, was a video editor and producer for the nightly news. Since I had nothing else to do, he offered to show me how to turn news articles into graphics for Jones's videos. He explained that if the source was a mainstream outlet like the *New York Times* or the *Wall Street Journal*, we were to highlight it prominently, but to hide it if it came from a random website. I realized I had never noticed that Jones's videos often omitted sources. Carlos added that if Jones mentioned a source to support one of his theories, I had to at least attempt to find an article to back it up, emphasizing that the content itself didn't matter. What counted was the headline.

In the corner of the room a television played Jones's live show. The audio was low so I couldn't make out what he was saying, but I could see he was interviewing the Libertarian activist Adam Kokesh. Tillman asked Dew what he thought of Kokesh.

"There's something odd about him," Dew said. He rolled his chair to the TV and pointed at Kokesh's beard, noting how it tapered to a point beneath his chin. According to Dew, this was a style used by devil worshippers to signal their allegiance to dark forces. He elaborated, describing how Kokesh's head resembled an upside-down star, with his hair forming the bottom two vertices, his ears the sides, and his beard completing the shape.

"I've never heard that," Tillman said, sounding skeptical.

"It's definitely a thing," Dew said. "The upside-down star is also a goat's head, like Baphomet."

So that was it, I thought to myself, *all it took was the shape of someone's head to stir suspicion?* Even if he *was* a "devil worshipper," what secret message was he sending to Jones's audience? It reminded me of the absurd fears I heard from evangelicals growing up, about Pokémon cards or Harry Potter hiding satanic messages. I suddenly felt self-conscious in the room. Slowly and inconspicuously, I smoothed out my facial hair and made sure there were no inadvertent shapes to give off the wrong idea.

After the show ended, Jones came back to the War Room and beelined to the corner door, which turned out to be his private bathroom. I could hear a muffled jangling sound, intense grunting, and then a flush, lasting all of thirty seconds. When he came out, he stood in the middle of the room, buttoning his pants, staring at the television playing a rebroadcast of his show. Once *The Alex Jones Show* ended, the three-hour stream restarted in a continuous loop until the next live broadcast.

"Somebody shut this off," Jones said. "I can't stand seeing my giant pumpkin head on-screen." Dew grabbed the remote and hit the power button. Jones pulled an empty chair next to me and sat down, wiping sweat from his brow.

"I bet you weren't expecting to learn on your first day that it takes Alex Jones thirty seconds to take a shit," he said, laughing. He leaned back in the chair and asked if I was married. I told him I had a girlfriend, who would be moving to Austin after graduating college in a few months. "What's her degree?" he asked with a long sigh. When I mentioned she was earning a BFA in painting, he made a face like I'd said she was majoring in tiptoeing or cloud-watching, the perceived frivolity diminishing his interest. "That's good," he said, his eyes glazing over as he sat forward, scrolling through the computer screen. "Don't get married," he said, his voice carrying a hint of sadness. "Women start expecting more from you and it ruins everything." It was an odd statement coming from someone who boasted about his family life publicly, but I could sense the weight of regret in his words.

The room grew still and tense. Jones shifted in his seat, restless, and broke the silence, groaning about not wanting to go home that evening. After another deep sigh, he sat upright, like an idea had just struck him, a desperate attempt to escape whatever demons were lurking in his mind. "Let's go see a movie."

We arrived early to an Austin chain of dine-in theaters called Alamo Drafthouse. Movie theaters were one of my favorite places to be. There was something profound about taking in an entire world in one sitting, not having to engage or impose yourself onto the story, but simply being an inactive participant in a crafted narrative. I was the sort of kid who walked around as an open vessel, impressionable and willing to attach my identity to something that attracted me in the moment. Having no desire to become like my parents, teachers, or friends, I craved the excitement and complexity of the characters I saw on-screen.

Jones gestured toward a cocktail lounge attached to the theater, and we followed him in. There were six of us in total, just enough to fill the small bar. He offered to cover dinner but insisted on limiting each of us to two drinks. "I don't want you guys getting a DUI tonight," he said, pushing the menu away and addressing the bartender. "I'll take a double vodka soda, and—" He glanced over, waiting for my order. I scanned the menu and asked for a paloma, which was listed as their specialty drink. Jones scrunched his face in disgust. "No, no... order a real drink," he said. "A man's drink."

I wasn't much of a drinker, and my tastes leaned toward Joy Williams over Charles Bukowski, romance over action, *Harold and Maude* over *First Blood*. I wasn't dominant or aggressive, and I had no qualms about showing my emotions. I didn't need to order a specific drink to validate my identity, but I also lacked the confidence to push back against Jones. I ordered an old-fashioned, and Jones seemed satisfied.

We lost track of time at the bar and the previews had already begun when we made it inside the theater. I was the last to enter and Jones forced the others to move down, insisting I sat next to him. "You like cheeseburgers?" he asked.

"Sure," I said.

"I'll order for you, then," he said, repeating the menu item aloud as he wrote it down. "The... Royale... with... Cheese."

An informational video played on-screen, warning of the theater's low tolerance for cell phone usage. Throughout the movie, Jones kept pulling out his phone, scrolling through the Infowars website. Ushers asked him repeatedly to put his phone away before threatening to remove him from the theater. Jones briefly complied, but he couldn't help himself. Eventually, he had to walk out into the hallway. After a few minutes, he came back and took his seat. "Did I miss anything?" he whispered.

I told him nothing important had happened, but the truth was, I hadn't paid the slightest attention to the movie. My body was in the theater, but my mind was elsewhere, distracted by how suddenly and profoundly my circumstances had changed.

2
IDIOCRACY

After the first day, I moved to an alcove in the hallway. The L-shaped desk was surrounded by partition panels facing a window with a view of the parking lot. Mornings, I watched Jones speed up in his Dodge Charger Hellcat with reckless abandon. He seemed free of the sort of nervous concerns that engulfed my mind—what if a cop saw me speeding, what if I accidentally hit someone walking to their parked car, what if I wrecked into a tanker full of gas and was burned alive? His was a pure expression of self-centered freedom, a defiant assertion of his own whims, seemingly unconcerned with how his actions affected others, and on occasion, even himself.

Some mornings, Jones emerged from his muscle car with a bounce in his step, soaking wet from his early swim at a spring-fed pool downtown. Others he appeared irritated and exhausted, slamming doors as he made his way through the office. But on this Tuesday morning, he strolled in belting out the words to "Mother" by Danzig, attempting his best imitation of the deep, dramatic vocals.

> *"Mother, tell your children not to walk my way,*
> *Tell your children not to hear my words, what they mean,*
> *what they say."*

The song was dark and defiant, but Jones sang like he was in a karaoke contest after a few too many drinks. His voice trailed off, disappearing into Dew's office as he closed the door behind him. I was glad to be in the hallway by myself, a spectator more than a participant.

The door to the War Room swung open and Jones marched out, his discordant sounds coming to a halt behind me. "We've got big plans tonight," he said, leaning on the partition. "Dew will fill you in on the details but it's important and I want my best guys on it." As he walked off, I pondered the phrase "best guys." Jones hadn't seen any of the work I'd done that past week. All he had to go on were my written credentials, and while no one was aware of it, I had lied on my résumé. I didn't know how to operate the cameras they used and was just skilled enough at editing to convincingly fake it. It was true that I had worked on short films in college, even shooting and directing a few of my own, but those projects were with friends, and we had time to figure things out at our own pace. This job was different. If I couldn't hook up a microphone or adjust camera settings on the spot, I suspected Jones would lose patience.

Dew asked me to follow him to the equipment closet to help pack for the shoot. "We're interviewing Mike Judge tonight," he said, watching my face for a reaction. My eyes widened when I heard the name, and I tried to control the grin tugging at the corners of my mouth. I grew up on Mike Judge's work, from *Beavis and Butt-Head* to *King of the Hill* and *Office Space*.

The equipment closet was nestled in a corner on the radio side of the building. There were shelves and cabinets and drawers, each labeled to hold the necessary tools of production—cameras, lenses, microphones, lights, tripods—but nothing had been returned to its respective area. The only thing that appeared orderly was the top shelf, where megaphones were lined up, the handles protruding for easy access. Otherwise, it looked as though a tornado had blown through.

I was overwhelmed by the mess, but Dew didn't seem bothered. "We had a system," he said, "but it fell apart." We weren't meeting Judge until later, so we gathered in the War Room after everyone else had gone home for the day, biding our time before we had to leave.

Jones sat at a computer, punching each key with a single digit, searching for something on YouTube. He stared at the screen in bewilderment. "How do you get sound out of this thing?" he asked, fiddling with the knobs on the interface connecting the external speakers. "I don't understand why I pay for this complicated shit; it's like disarming a bomb."

"Try unplugging the headphones," Dew said.

Jones ripped the cord out of a small box beneath the monitor and audio exploded into the room. It was a clip from Jones's earlier days in broadcast, back when he had a more noticeable Southern accent. He beamed, watching a younger version of himself on-screen talking about deceptions and cover-ups. I rolled my chair closer to get a better look. The video of Jones cut to a shaggy-haired man in what looked like a basement, responding to the previous clip. "I couldn't have said it better myself..." He gave a long pause before referring to Jones as "Mr. Hicks." Jones burst into laughter, pounding his fist on the desk as an image of the comedian Bill Hicks appeared on-screen. The video cut to side-by-side comparisons of Jones's and Hicks's teeth and hands, followed by separate audio clips to compare their vocal patterns. Jones fostered an environment of suspicion and paranoia where even he had become a part of the conspiracy.

The theory, which had been around for years by that point, suggested that the comedian Bill Hicks, known for his biting social commentary and dark humor, had faked his death from pancreatic cancer in 1994 at the age of thirty-two and reappeared months later as a twenty-one-year-old Alex Jones on Austin's public access. Both men were born in Texas, loud and prone to rants on government corruption and the distrust of state power. They discussed conspiracy theories like the assassination of President John F. Kennedy and the Waco Siege, and despite their almost twelve-year age difference, Jones looked a decade older than he claimed to be, adding more fuel to the conspiratorial fire.

The idea that Jones was a character played by Bill Hicks required a suspension of disbelief so profound that it defied logic. It overlooked the fundamental differences in their appearance, voice, and personality, and it ignored the logistical challenges of faking one's death and the improbability of such an elaborate deception being carried out without any credible evidence surfacing. It, like many conspiracy theories, was easy to dismiss for its sheer implausibility. And yet, at the time, none of us saw the irony in mocking the man in the video while indulging in our own fantasies.

Jones continued scrolling through YouTube. He clicked on a clip from C-SPAN, an interview with Jon Ronson, shot a few years after they infiltrated Bohemian Grove together. The interviewer asked Ronson his opinion of Jones, if he'd listened to his show before they met up in California.

"Yeah, I've listened," Ronson said. "He's fantastic. I mean, if he wasn't so crazy, he'd be the new Bill Hicks—"

"Oh god," Jones said, rolling his eyes in amusement, "now Ronson is in on the conspiracy. Next, he'll claim he watched me turn into a reptoid or something."

Jones turned up the volume as Ronson continued. A few weeks before the 2004 interview we were watching, a man attempted to break into Bohemian Grove armed with a rifle and several rounds of ammunition.

His target was the members of the Bohemian Club, spurred on by the conspiracy theories made public by Jones's film. Ronson brought up the incident, describing a moment that happened between him and Jones after they left the grove. "I remember at the time—because, you know, Alex is an intelligent man—I remember saying to him, 'Alex, you know that what you're saying about Bohemian Grove isn't true. You're playing with fire here.' And Alex said, 'Yeah, but I'm not going to tell my listeners that.'"

Jones stopped the video, his face twisting into a nervous smirk as he tried to downplay Ronson's comments. "He knows that's not true," Jones said, "but I get it, he chose to play their game. Now he's got the book deals and the Hollywood films..." The color drained from his face, and he pushed the keyboard away as the room grew quiet. I couldn't tell if Jones felt guilty, or his feelings were hurt because he thought they were friends and the interview had been a betrayal. Either way the fun was over.

We arrived at Mike Judge's residence in Austin, a modern Georgian-style home at the dead end of a residential neighborhood. On the ride over, Jones informed us that even though they had recently become friends, it took some convincing before Judge agreed to the interview. "I don't know how political he'll want to get on camera," Jones said, "but we hung out last night and he basically agrees with me on everything."

Jones led the way as we lugged our equipment through an iron gate, down a winding path to the portico. Judge answered the front door and invited us in. Through the foyer, we were led into a large room filled with musical instruments—a mahogany grand piano, pedal steel, upright bass, and a custom Gibson double neck electric with *Beavis and Butt-Head* written in pearl inlays along the fret board. "We *have* to get this in the shot," Jones said, plucking the strings.

"Whatever you want," Judge said. On the surface, he seemed approachable and laid-back, but as our interview began, I sensed a hint of discomfort. It was almost as if he felt obligated to participate as a friend.

Judge discussed his early years, his initial interest in sketch comedy and animation, and told Jones that Dale, a character he wrote for the series *King of the Hill*, was inspired by Jones's early days on public-access television. Dale was conspiracy obsessed and fixated on grand ideas while oblivious to his own reality, like the fact that his wife was openly cheating on him. To me, this wasn't a compliment, but Jones radiated with pride.

Keen to keep the focus on himself, Jones brought up his infamous appearance on Piers Morgan's CNN show earlier that year. Morgan had invited Jones on after he started a petition to have Morgan deported for his aggressive calls for increased gun control in light of the tragic shooting at Sandy Hook Elementary School. The segment was intended to highlight the differing opinions on gun regulation, but the appearance had become infamous for Jones's intense, erratic response, which overshadowed any substantive discussion about gun policy.

"I was thinking, 'Hey, right on, Alex, go for it,'" Judge said. "And everything you were saying was true too. I mean, the clip that *I* saw." He then attempted an impression of Jones, repeating the threat he made to Morgan on his program. "Hitler took the guns, Stalin took the guns, Mao took the guns, Fidel"—Judge started laughing, and then continued imitating Jones's voice—"and if you try to take our firearms, 1776 will commence again!"

I peered at Judge through the camera, remembering the first time I saw clips of the CNN appearance months earlier, amazed not by the information, but by Jones's visceral intensity on national television. He ranted and raved and mocked Morgan's British accent, eventually challenging him to a boxing match on air. For me, this was part of Jones's appeal. It wasn't so much what he said, but how he said it.

A month before their debate, as the harrowing news of the Sandy Hook massacre unfolded, I was anxiously awaiting Dew's response about whether I'd gotten the job. Much like Jones's religious perspective, I didn't agree with everything he said. I didn't believe Sandy Hook was a staged event to push for gun control, just like I didn't believe that God revealed the secrets of the universe to Jones while he ate chicken fried steak at a diner (a story he often recounted on his radio show). But in my willful ignorance, it was easy to brush off these fever dreams as eccentricities and excesses—not the heart of Jones's operation. To Jones, the label "false flag" was a perennial response to every mass shooting, a grim ritual that no longer held any shock value. In his twisted universe, where everything was a carefully constructed lie, Sandy Hook was simply another chapter in a desensitizing narrative, one that would eventually and deservedly come back to haunt him.

The term "false flag" dates back to naval warfare in the seventeenth century, referring to ships flying the flag of a different, often friendly, nation to deceive enemies and launch surprise attacks. Over time, the term evolved to encompass any deliberate act of deception with significant political consequences, like the Reichstag Fire of 1933, or the Gulf of Tonkin incident in 1964. Now, especially in the context of online conspiracy theories, the term "false flag" has become a rhetorical weapon, an all-encompassing accusation whenever something disrupts a preferred narrative.

For Jones, every tragedy, every disaster, every horrific act of violence, whether it be mass shootings or terrorist attacks, was framed as a false flag. But what made the constant invocation so insidious was how it bypassed critical thinking and replaced it with paranoia. The false flag implied that every official account was suspect, that all explanations were somehow part of the deception. Mass shootings? False flags. Public health emergencies? False flags. The sheer volume of these accusations created a climate of constant fear, a sense that nothing could be trusted.

And in that confusion, Jones could use the news of tragedies like Sandy Hook, the Boston Marathon bombing, and the September 11th attacks as a gateway into his worldview, reducing real, devastating events, and turning human suffering into fodder for ideological warfare.

At the end of the interview with Mike Judge, Jones asked him one last question: "You don't have to if you don't want, but could you give us some of the voices?"

Judge took a deep breath. It was obvious he'd been asked to do this numerous times throughout his career and wasn't fond of it. "What do you want me to say?"

"Give us something we can use for the radio show," Jones said.

Judge took a moment to get into character. "Hello, this is Hank Hill," he said in that iconic Texas drawl, "and I'm telling you what, you need to listen to Alex Jones." Then he switched over to the apathetic, teenage slacker, Butt-Head. "Yeah, yeah! Hm!" he grunted, in a pitch-perfect performance, "Infowars.com! Hm! Hm! Heh!"

A broad, almost bashful, smile spread across Jones's face. It was as if getting Mike Judge to say his name in character was the impetus for the entire conversation. Jones shot out of the chair, thanked him for his generosity, and ended the interview.

When we wrapped, I expected a quick exit, but Judge asked if we wanted to join him for a drink. His friends were playing at a dive bar outside of town, and he'd promised to be there. We met up with him at a small shack somewhere out in the woods with dim lighting and a bustling atmosphere. Since we had all our equipment in the car, he asked if we would be willing to film a music video for his friends. We ran the cameras while Judge directed it, guiding us through the room as the band motioned playing the same song repeatedly to a pre-recorded track.

As the night wore on, I tried to take it all in. Here I was, in Austin, working a camera for a last-minute music video directed by

Mike Judge. It felt surreal, validating. If I'd told myself this was where I'd end up when I worried over quitting film school, the decision would've been much easier to make.

The following day, while seated at my desk, I overheard a heated conversation coming from the War Room. Most of the voices were muffled behind the closed door, but as Jones got louder, I heard him repeatedly ask, "Is this guy a fucking idiot?"

After a few minutes, the office door swung open, and Jones stomped down the hallway. Dew followed close behind and stopped at my desk. "You're in trouble," he said, grinning as he rubbed his hands together. My throat tightened. Dew claimed I'd turned off one of the cameras early and we'd lost part of Mike Judge's interview. I hesitated, not wanting to sound defensive, but I was sure that wasn't the case. I even recalled keeping the recording going after Jones and Judge had left their seats.

I asked which camera it was, hoping to prove my innocence. Carlos, Dew, and I had rotated positions throughout the interview, but I remembered where I was standing at the end.

"Not sure," Dew said.

"What do you mean you're not sure?" I asked. "How can you not be sure?"

"Think of it as an initiation," he said, ignoring that he or Carlos could've been at fault and framing it as a favor. "Everyone fucks up at least once... now you've gotten it out of the way."

I laughed, perplexed at his absurd rationale. "That's bullshit," I said, no longer concerned with appearing defensive.

"Carlos didn't do it, and I know I didn't, so it had to be you," he said, staring down at me. "Don't get so upset. Jones isn't even that mad." He turned and walked back to his office. It was clear he and Carlos had thrown me under the bus. The phrase I'd overheard through the door replayed again and again in my head: *Is this guy a fucking idiot? Is this guy a fucking idiot? Is this guy a fucking idiot?*

I imagined what it would be like to return home—without a job, without a place to live, without my dignity—explaining to my friends and family that I had been fired from my position all because someone accidentally flipped a quarter-inch piece of plastic on a camera.

Jones had been led to believe I was to blame, and protesting would only make the situation worse. So instead of rattling off excuses or getting angry at Carlos and Dew, I owned up to it. After Jones got off the show, I pulled him aside and apologized for the mistake.

"I fucked up," I said, meeting his gaze head-on. "It won't happen again."

His eyes, sharp and calculating, made my stomach turn, and I braced for an explosion of anger. But his mouth curled into a smile. It wasn't warm, exactly, but it wasn't the feral snarl I had anticipated either. "No one around here admits anything they've done," he said, his voice becoming low and conspiratorial. "Most of these guys are potheads. They don't know what planet they're on half the time." He took a step closer into my personal space, and I fought the urge to step back. "You don't smoke pot, do you?"

"No," I said, shifting uncomfortably. "I tried it once, years ago, and got so stoned I thought demons were dragging me to hell."

It was an alarming experience, but it typically elicited a laugh from anyone I told. Jones, however, wasn't laughing. A paranoid glint surfaced on his face, the wheels turning behind his flared eyes. "Demons? That sounds like PCP or something. Not that I've ever done PCP." The last part he added quickly, a disclaimer that sounded like a lie.

"I guess it's possible," I said, wishing I hadn't mentioned it. "But I never tried it again."

"Well, that's why I stopped," Jones said, his sharpened features softening into something akin to camaraderie. "I'll maybe test it out once a year, just to monitor its strength. But it's gotten out of control." He turned and made his way to the other side of the building. "Look," he shouted over his shoulder, "don't stress about the interview, buddy!"

But it was too late. No matter what he said, I'd been saddled with the first impression of incompetence, one that led Jones to ask, behind closed doors, if I was a fucking idiot.

After that, I became obsessed with correcting his view of me, unaware that this would become a constant, ever-shifting struggle, impossible not only for me, but for anyone, to achieve. From that day forward, I would drag the proverbial lamb to the slaughter in the form of capitulation, a ritual to appease and maintain favor. It would be years before I realized that absolution was unattainable in Jones's world. You were only ever as good as your last sacrifice.

The following week Jones began flying in guests for an upcoming documentary, a sequel to his previous movie, *The Obama Deception*. The first person to visit the office was the political activist Larry Pinkney, a former member of the Black Panther Party and the Republic of New Afrika, a Black separatist movement in the United States. Despite the most recent incident, it was my job to set up and film these interviews. Dew insisted I needed only a single memory card and one additional battery on hand. During the Pinkney interview, I scrambled back and forth between the cameras, staring at the battery level, sweat pouring into my eyes.

At the twenty-nine-minute mark, I noticed each camera had stopped recording, realizing, only then, that there was a maximum continuous capture time of thirty minutes. Jones asked open-ended questions and Pinkney gave long, drawn-out answers, leaving almost no pauses, so I had to interrupt him to restart the cameras. Jones looked annoyed. After a few minutes, a notification appeared that the card in one of the cameras was full. Again, I had to stop Pinkney, apologize profusely as Jones's eyes grew wide, and run to the other side of the building for additional cards.

When I returned and replaced them, we began rolling again. Before I noticed, the power signal began flashing red on one of the cameras. I waited as long as I could before I had to interrupt his thought for a third time. "I'm so sorry," I said, watching as Jones jerked toward me, looking furious. I replaced both batteries and started recording again.

Before the interview was over, this happened two more times.

Afterward, Jones followed me into Dew's office, enraged. But instead of directing his anger at me, he focused in on Dew. "What the fuck is going on with our equipment?" he shouted, pacing around the room, talking over Dew when he attempted to explain the camera's limitations. "I can't handle this shit anymore," Jones said.

Neither of them acknowledged my presence, so I crept out of the room and slunk back to my desk. "This is unacceptable, unprofessional, and it can't fucking happen again," Jones said, his voice echoing through the hallway.

Jones had calmed down by the time he left Dew's office, stopping at my desk to give one last directive. "I want you to buy ten more cameras and fifty more memory cards," he said before leaving for the day.

I had purchased a Moleskin notebook to keep track of my assignments and anything Jones said to me. The pages were filled with the events of those first few weeks, ending in a quickly scribbled note: *Buy 10 more cameras. Buy 50 more cards.*

We didn't end up buying the additional cameras after Dew said Jones would be even angrier if we spent that much money, but we did purchase extra memory cards and batteries. I spent the first few weekends combing through the equipment manuals, learning everything I could to avoid similar disasters in the future. Each interview went smoother than the last, and with newfound confidence in my ability to operate the equipment, Jones asked me to start accompanying reporters in the field.

The first assignment was in town. Lee Ann McAdoo, one of the newly hired reporters, had arranged for us to interview the president and chair of the Austin Center for Peace and Justice, delving into the topic of mandatory labeling laws for genetically modified foods. We would also be covering the Food is Free Project, a local nonprofit dedicated to promoting community gardening and providing free food to those in need. Jones, however, didn't seem too enthused about the assignment.

"There's some hipster farm Lee Ann wants to report on nearby," he said. "Use the place as a backdrop for the real stuff. Make sure she talks about *Ecoscience*, fertility rates, depopulation..." He waved his hands vaguely as if planting invisible seeds of wisdom in the air around us.

Jones was referring to the book *Ecoscience*, co-authored by Paul Ehrlich, Anne Ehrlich, and John Holdren, the director of the White House Office of Science and Technology Policy during Obama's administration. He claimed this book supported his assertion that the government was pursuing a form of eugenics, attempting to "soft-kill" the population by deliberately introducing harmful chemicals into the food and water supply. In reality, the authors of *Ecoscience* emphasized the need to address overpopulation and environmental degradation, advocating for informed policy decisions grounded in scientific understanding, but they never suggested harming the population or endorsed eugenics in any form.

Jones continued by questioning McAdoo's intelligence, and I worried she might hear us through the paper-thin walls. "I'm sure she's got it covered," I said. Jones raised his eyebrows and peered at me, looking deep into my eyes as he asked, out of nowhere, if my mother had breastfed me as a child.

The question hung in the air, absurd and unexpected. *What did he just say?* I thought to myself, feeling the idiotic smile stretched too thin on my face as I searched his expression for any sign of jest. But Jones wasn't joking—he wanted an answer.

"Uh... I'm not sure," I said, "I never thought to ask."

"Well, you should. It's designed for us. It carries nutrients all the way back from the mitochondrial DNA. Did you know that?"

I shook my head, the action more reflexive than communicative. The concept of mitochondrial DNA hadn't been on my radar prior to this moment—why would it?—but it felt as though Jones was imparting knowledge that should have been obvious to me. His gaze remained locked onto mine. "I know when someone hasn't been breastfed," he said. "Nine times out of ten they have a perceptibly lower IQ." His voice was grave, as if discussing a matter of national security rather than the personal feeding choices made by a mother decades ago. "You're a smart guy," he finally said, I assume determining my stupidity was at least hidden. "I'm sure you were breastfed."

He patted me on the shoulder, seeming relieved to have had this conversation, and walked away. I remained seated, hands hovering over the keyboard without purpose, trying to make sense of what just happened. The conversation clung to me like static, making it hard to shake off the sensation that reality had skewed off-kilter. The rational side of my brain searched for some semblance of logic in Jones's questions. First, it was about marijuana use, then my infant feeding habits, like he had a mental checklist to assess my character. I couldn't shake the feeling I was being sized up, observed, examined for how well I might fit into his strange orbit. The thought yanked me back to the present, to the report downtown, and I rushed to pack up the equipment.

3
THE DOOMSDAY MACHINE

Most of my nights and weekends were spent driving around Austin, looking for a place to live. Jones had agreed to cover an extended stay for a month while I found something more permanent, but transient living was taking its toll. I was alone, lonely, and anxious for my girlfriend to pack up our two dogs and head west. She was still in Georgia, graduating from college and finishing up a public art project that had been commissioned in our hometown. I'd been helping her build wooden frames and paint glass for a mosaic she'd designed when I got the call from Dew offering me the job. When I told her, tears welled in her eyes.

After four years together, I had thrown a curveball into our lives. It wasn't that she didn't want to move with me, but she had no job prospects and didn't know anyone who lived in Austin. Throughout our relationship she'd supported my shifting ambitions—deciding to be a screenwriter after watching *In a Lonely Place*, a documentary filmmaker after watching *Vernon, Florida*, and even a chef (that eventually became a memoirist) after reading Anthony Bourdain's *Kitchen Confidential*. She didn't know much about Jones or his show, but she appreciated that I was pursuing my passions rather than sitting around incessantly complaining about my film classes and the people in them.

Lacey and I started dating in 2009, two years after I had graduated from high school. We grew up in the same small town in north Georgia, an insular community in the foothills of the Appalachian Mountains, lined with pine trees, carpet mills, and evangelical churches. She was a year younger than me, and we only knew each other tangentially. After high school, I played guitar in a band no one had ever heard of, with hopes of turning it into a career. When the other members gave up and went off to college, realizing we were never going to make it, I was stuck, unsure of my future and angry at myself for refusing to have a contingency plan.

Lacey had moved to the coast to attend the Savannah College of Art and Design. After reading a short story I'd written, she reached out to say she enjoyed it. That message sparked a connection. We soon began emailing each other and having long conversations over the phone about our lives and families and all the things we hoped to accomplish. In high school, Lacey was class president, a member of the National Honor Society, in the art club and the theater club. She spent her free time volunteering for nonprofits and community programs. I, on the other hand, was a punk who thought school was a waste of time, instead choosing to live vicariously through the books and films that consumed my life. But somehow, it seemed to work. We had a similar sense of humor, a mutual respect and admiration for one another, and a shared curiosity about life beyond the small-town culture we'd grown up in. Lacey was burned out from years of perfection, and I was determined to shed my feigning indifference. We were both in search of something new. I began driving as often as possible to the coast once she returned to school, and not long after, applied and got accepted into the film program at SCAD.

At first it was stirring to be in the cobblestoned streets of Savannah, living near Flannery O'Connor's childhood home, attending film premieres, getting to hear talks with people like James Gandolfini and Lily Tomlin. But after a few years I grew restless and bored.

That's when I heard about a reporter contest Alex Jones was putting on. At twenty-three, I was vulnerable, entitled, and looking for a path forward, so I decided to give it a shot. Lacey and I traveled to Jekyll Island—birthplace of the Federal Reserve—and I attempted to recite the lines I'd written for the report as she held the camera.

"On November 22, 1910, a group of seven men holding as much as one fourth of the world's wealth took a secretive trip to The Jekyll Island Club Hotel, which you can see behind me," I said to the camera. "This hotel was the hunting retreat for American banker, and first-class scumbag, J. P. Morgan—"

Lacey scoffed, her expression hardening into a look of amusement and pity.

"What?" I asked, defensive.

"Nothing," she said. "Sorry, keep going."

"No, what is it?"

"It's just... 'scumbag.' Why call him that?"

"Because he's a scumbag," I said, not understanding the problem. "The guy was the fucking epitome of financial imperialism with the railroads and steel and—"

Lacey put a hand up, trying to save me from my own blustering enthusiasm. "It just doesn't sound like something a reporter would say," she offered. I tried to explain this wasn't your run-of-the-mill reporter job. Jones was always screaming and hurling insults—it was, you know, more real. She didn't quite get the cult of Jones, but she liked that I was excited about something again.

Out of what Infowars said were thousands of submissions, my video—a half-witted, conspiratorial glance at the creation and function of the Federal Reserve—made it to the final round. Jones was unconvinced I could cut it as a reporter. According to Dew, Jones didn't think my personality was aggressive enough, so instead, he offered me a full-time position as a video editor. I told Lacey I wouldn't accept the job if she didn't want to move, but she said we had to at least try, knowing if I turned down the offer, I might spend the rest of my life wondering what could have been.

A few weeks after the Mike Judge interview, I arrived at the office and heard a howling in the distance. Screams reverberated from across the building. The only discernible word echoing through the warehouse was "motherfucker." This came from Jones with no audible response. Suddenly, I heard a loud crash, then footsteps: each one louder than the last. He darted through the hallway into the back office and slammed the door behind him.

After his live show began, I walked over to the other side of the building. On the ground, in front of where the water cooler used to be, the carpet was soaked, surrounded by beige and crystal blue shards of plastic. According to an employee who witnessed the incident, Jones had noticed the drip tray had mold growing in it the week before and asked for someone to clean it out. That morning, it still hadn't been touched, so in a fit of rage he grabbed a large knife from the kitchen, stabbed the plastic base wildly, and smashed it to pieces on the ground.

Later, I overheard Jones telling Dew that he'd been more stressed than usual. He complained about his wife, giving no specifics, and said that he'd decided to take the rest of the week off. The plan was for him to spend time with his kids downtown, kayaking on Lake Austin, but even *that* set him off. "It's really a river that's been dammed up, but they call it a lake. Why not?! These people are fucking liars," he shouted.

The next day, while seated at my desk, I heard what sounded like a loud, roaring engine outside. The office windows began to rattle, and one of the writers ran through the hallway claiming that military helicopters were flying overhead. "Grab a camera!" Dew shouted in a panic, running past my desk to the back lot.

I walked outside and looked up. The sky was clear blue, not a single helicopter or even a cloud in sight. To get a better view, I stepped out into the middle of the drive and above the office, on the rooftop, I spotted Dew. He had attached a telephoto lens on the camera and was aiming at something in the distance.

Back inside, he was out of breath. "I got it," he said.

"A helicopter?" I asked.

"No," he replied, still trying to catch his breath. "It was a plane."

A plane? Who cares about a plane? Just as I was about to express this thought out loud, Dew's phone began to ring.

"I just saw a plane downtown, flying level with the skyscrapers," Jones said, frenzied. "This is 9/11 all over again! The plane was a Boeing E4B. It's only brought out during doomsday scenarios. There's stealth helicopters and more military aircraft, green C130s. I think this is some kind of invasion!" Dew had Jones on speakerphone as he held his cell out in front of him, listening intently. "I'm telling you," Jones continued, sounding more focused, yet shifting through incongruous ideas. "I'm telling you, it's a way to reinvoke 9/11 and test the public. I saw the metal rivulets glinting in the sun. My adrenals are completely shot right now. This is the military conditioning us that they are God. It's like *War of the Worlds*. This will be the biggest news story by tomorrow."

David Knight, a reporter who had also been hired through the same contest I entered, was hosting the live show. Jones called in and repeated, almost verbatim, what he'd said over the phone. He also directed the crew live on the air, detailing how he wanted the story rolled out. My job was to take the footage Dew had captured of the plane and edit in an image of an E4B aircraft to prove Jones had identified it correctly, and then include some clip Jones referenced of Anderson Cooper on 9/11. The video was to be titled "Low Flying Doomsday Plane Buzzes Austin." Jones then commissioned an accompanying article from the writers, referencing an incident that occurred in 2009 where Air Force One circled Lower Manhattan for a photo op, frightening citizens of New York and New Jersey. Jones claimed that this incident lent credence to his theory that the Austin flyover was a government psychological operation to reinvoke the fears of 9/11.

Twenty-four hours later the story had scrolled off the front page of the Infowars website. I looked online and saw that KUT, a local news station, had reported it was a plane from Tinker Air Force Base performing a standard touch-and-go operation—a common exercise in which a pilot lands and takes off again without stopping.

When Jones returned to the office the following day, he made no mention of the plane, acting as though nothing out of the ordinary had happened. It felt like I was living in a Franz Kafka story, like I'd woken up in bed and found myself transformed into a giant insect. Only a day prior, the incident was a watershed moment in history, gripping the entire nation, but by the next morning, I wasn't sure he even remembered it.

I didn't know how to make sense of the extreme highs and lows, the reaction and conviction that disintegrated just because the story didn't go viral. Jones must have noticed a slight change in my demeanor, because one evening he stopped by my desk and asked if I wanted to go to the movies with him and a few other employees from the office. This felt like an obvious attempt at boosting morale after his recent chaotic behavior, but I could either go see a movie with him or sit alone in my hotel room that evening, so I said yes.

The film Jones chose was Nicholas Winding Refn's *Only God Forgives* starring Ryan Gosling, a neon-soaked noir about the blurred lines of justice and vengeance, brutality, and retribution. Afterward, we lingered in the parking lot discussing our differing interpretations. Jones was animated, hyperfocused on trying to decipher the film, like it had deeper implications for him personally. He seemed affected by the story and, a few weeks later, booked the director as a guest on his show. They talked about the religious subtext of the film, the nature of fear, cruelty, love, and kindness. It was a strange conversation for Jones, not only because he shied away from discussing current events or political narratives, but because he seemed vulnerable.

When Refn talked about how he saw filmmaking as an addiction, constantly chasing the high of the process, Jones nodded along as if it had unlocked something within him. "It's the same with news and politics," Jones said, his voice tinged with a rare humility. "The more you learn, the more you realize how little you know. It becomes this endless cycle where you can't stop thinking, and your brain gets rewired. You start to see the world in layers that are so complex, it's hard to express them clearly."

I looked at him—really looked at him—for the first time that day. The person defined by grandiose statements and fearmongering, who saw a low-flying airplane and instinctually constructed a doomsday scenario in his mind, was also someone who seemed to be struggling with the nature of reality, mired in the complexities of forcing every moment into a box, like sitting in a movie theater, frustrated, trying to impose rigid meaning onto a story he couldn't quite understand.

4

A CURE FOR TYRANNY

Two weeks after the "doomsday incident," a former producer and camera operator from Jones's public access days (including the Bohemian Grove documentary) visited the office. Mike Hanson was a burly man who appeared a bit older than Jones—a difficult approximation, given Jones looked closer to fifty than his actual age of thirty-nine. Hanson behaved more like an old friend, an unwavering admirer, than a one-time employee.

He arrived at the studio with an armload of framed photos, newspaper clippings, and memorabilia from the infancy of Jones's career. "There he is," Jones said, brimming with nostalgic joy as the two men nearly collided in the hallway. It was strange to see Jones so happy. He wore a childlike grin, which tempered his usual imposing demeanor.

"Eighteen years ago, we worked out of your dining room, now look at this place," Hanson said, laying the objects on the ground and motioning to his surroundings. Though the hallway had nothing more than a set of dark leather chairs pressed tightly against the empty white wall, his sentiment was clear.

"It *has* changed quite a bit," Jones said, looking around as if he, too, was viewing his accomplishments through Hanson's eyes. It struck me as odd that Hanson, once so intertwined with Jones and his business, hadn't visited the new space.

Hanson had purchased his grandparents' estate in Gonzalez, Texas, after they passed away, and he decided to relocate, leaving Jones to continue building his empire without him. Though ten years had passed, and their experiential gap had widened, the two self-professed patriots fell right back into old habits.

"Remember when somebody broke into our hotel room?" Jones asked.

"And then"—Hanson raised his hands in the air with a perplexed look—"it just so happened that *guy* drove from Texas and met us in Florida."

"And he jumped out of the bushes," Jones said.

"He was a provocateur," Hanson said.

"No, he was a Navy Seal," Jones corrected him.

Hanson bent down and flipped through the items on the floor. "Then he followed us to Waco," he said in a strained voice, lifting a framed copy of the *Waco Tribune-Herald* from 1998 and handing it over. On the cover, under the headline DAVIDIAN CHAPEL GROUND BROKEN, a young Jones posed next to an empty wheelbarrow: a single foot planted forward with a hand resting on his knee, giving him a Washington-esque look of gallantry.

Five years before this picture was taken, the Bureau of Alcohol, Tobacco, Firearms and Explosives raided David Koresh's Branch Davidian compound in Waco, leading to the deaths of over 80 people, including 22 children. Though the unprecedented 51-day standoff was widely criticized, Jones's disapproval went far beyond the mainstream. To him, the Waco tragedy was evidence of an illegitimate, tyrannical government prepared to attack and kill its own citizens. And he wasn't alone. Many right-wing anti-government militias, and so-called patriot groups, adopted similar beliefs, including Timothy McVeigh, who carried out the 1995 Oklahoma City Bombing in part as a direct response to Waco. These two tragedies, along with the World Trade Center bombing in 1993, provided Jones with a significant level of cultural fear to propel his nascent career. He rallied his audience, raised $92,000 to help rebuild the Branch Davidian Church, and with the media attention this received, gained a national profile.

Jones stared down at the fifteen-year-old picture in the paper. "My god, look how thin I was," he said, rubbing his stomach. "I didn't know you were bringing all this stuff."

"You said we were going over old times," Hanson said, placing the frame back at his feet with the other items. "What you need to do—and I've told you before—is take all this and open a museum."

"That's not going to happen, Mike." Jones sounded equally decisive and disappointed, as if he knew it wouldn't happen but wished, deep down, it would.

"I'm serious," Hanson said. "I remember the exact day I saw you on access TV." He pointed at Jones; his eyes narrowed with conviction. "I said, 'That guy's gonna be a star!'"

"Knock it off, Hanson!" Jones snickered, embarrassed, affected, struggling to hide his delight. It became clear why Jones had looked so uncharacteristically happy that morning. Hanson held Jones in the highest esteem, treating him like a hero. And even though Jones pretended to abhor the attention, it was obvious he believed, under all the self-loathing and false modesty, that he deserved it. "Mike," he said with unaccustomed sincerity, "I really missed you. I'm so glad you're here."

Later that evening, Jones called me into the War Room, where he and Dew were having a conversation. "I might need you to drive over to Hanson's place in Gonzalez to get a box of old VHS tapes," he said, looking up at me with tired eyes.

"Tonight?" I said, standing in the doorway.

"Next week, maybe. Mike said his guy might drive them up here, but who fucking knows. We'll have to wait and see." The cheerfulness had faded and was replaced by the burden of irritation. "Hanson has all the old tapes from my access shows; he's got footage back when I protested the Klan on the courthouse steps in Waco and when I predicted 9/11 months before it happened. I've got *Esquire* writing a piece on me and they're trying to fact-check but I don't have any way to prove certain things." He leaned back in the chair, clasped both hands behind his head, and let out a deep sigh. I wasn't sure whether Jones wanted me to leave or not, so I stood there, listening as he continued, "Hanson is sitting on millions," he said. "Maybe even tens of millions. His grandfather's property was on the Eagle Ford Shale, and I'm telling you, he's raking in money from that oil lease." Jones pursed his lips and scratched his clean-shaven jaw. "They call him the 'Slumlord of Gonzales.'"

Earlier that day, I noticed Hanson's shirt: a short-sleeved burgundy polo with the words GONZALEZ RENTAL PROPERTIES stitched in white. It seemed plausible that, at the very least, he was in some way affiliated with a property management company in Gonzalez. As to his millionaire status, this felt more like an exaggeration by Jones, an excuse to talk about his own money concerns.

"I'm surprised he didn't cut you in," Dew said.

"He tried to get me to invest in some property down there, but I told him I don't invest. I put everything back into the business." Jones stared up at the ceiling with a look of defeat. "That might've been a mistake. We're bleeding money and I can't even get the damn reporters to do any work. If I didn't have to handle the business side of things, I'd be churning out content nonstop." He looked over at Dew, perched on the edge of his chair. "You remember when I'd shoot an iPhone video driving to work and it would get, like, half a million views?"

"People love the candid stuff," Dew said.

"I'm not bitching," Jones said, lowering his voice, "but it's like they don't realize the audience we have here. They could sit in front of a camera and talk about literally anything: July Fourth, NSA surveillance, hell, I told them I'd pay for movie tickets if they'd shoot a report outside the theater afterwards. Have they done it? They just sit around gossiping and obsessing over planning the nightly news. And that's a total waste of—look, I know we're trying to build something there, but the nightly news doesn't make money. They could spend less time shooting a video at their desk—as long as it's dynamic and interesting—throw some graphics over it and boom, they'd get a million views like that—" He snapped his fingers together.

At the time, Jones's YouTube account had a little over six hundred thousand subscribers. The twenty to thirty videos uploaded per day received anywhere from ten to fifty thousand views each. On occasion, a report would draw over a hundred thousand views, but at the time, only five videos on Jones's channel had reached over a million. The videos that drew the most attention had incendiary headlines like TROOPS ORDERED TO KILL ALL AMERICANS WHO DO NOT TURN IN GUNS; or PROOF! BOSTON MARATHON BOMBING IS STAGED TERROR ATTACK. Other top reports accused Obama of "fake crying" after the Sandy Hook shooting, one promised to expose the dangers of additives in the food supply, and the most watched video on Jones's channel, with over three million views, was of actor Charlie Sheen requesting a meeting with Obama to reopen the 9/11 investigation.

The sharp edge of the door frame dug into my shoulder, but I stood still, lifeless, not wanting to draw attention. Jones's dissatisfaction wasn't directed at me, but it seemed that all it would take was a sideways glance, or a misinterpreted look, before I found myself in the crosshairs. Jones must have noticed my discomfort because he spun his chair around to face me.

"What do you think?" he said. "I mean, you're around the reporters during the day, you see the work they're putting out. It's basically nothing, right?"

To me, it appeared the reporters were always busy working on something. But I didn't want him to redirect blame onto me: the most recent addition to his company's payroll.

"They do seem to spend an inordinate amount of time fiddling over writing scripts and picking stories for the nightly news," I said.

Dew gave me an angry look, likely because he was the nightly news producer and responsible for the reporters. "The host might be focused on picking stories," he said, "but no one scripts the show."

That was the case for Jones—he never preplanned anything—but I had seen multiple reporters writing and memorizing their lines for the nightly news. Some of them had even complained, asking for a teleprompter. But Jones had always used the fact that he was "teleprompter-free" to prove that he was somehow outside of the establishment. It didn't matter if the reporters already wrote and recited their own scripts, a teleprompter had become a symbol, and Jones would never allow one in his building.

"Everyone is doing a good job, for the most part," Jones said, cutting the tension in the room. "I'm not mad at anyone, but if you guys knew how much it cost to run this place... It's ridiculous. We're bringing in about seven million dollars a year right now and spending every bit of it. I haven't been paid in eight months, and it looks like I won't be paid for the year. I've got some emergency backup set aside to fund things for a few months, if we get shut down or something, but that's it." Jones took a deep breath and stood up; the chair squeaked beneath him as he pushed it under Carlos's desk and headed for the door. "Hanson is over in Gonzalez like Boss Hogg and here I am spending more money than I bring in, having to beg my employees to do their job. Pretty soon, I'll be a pauper."

Jones took the rest of the week off to go fishing with his children. I overheard him, after the conversation the previous evening, ask Knight if he would take over hosting duties. "There's so much to do here, so much news to cover, but I have to see my kids," Jones said. "I used to work, like, eighteen hours a day and I didn't spend any time with my first two, but I actually know my third child a lot better." I couldn't tell if Jones believed his work was that important, or if he was simply more comfortable in front of a camera than living his actual life.

In his absence, Jones gave Dew the task of conveying his disappointment to the reporters. According to Jakari Jackson—the first-place winner of the reporter contest—the meeting consisted of Dew telling them that Jones was unsatisfied with their output and expected more. More content published to his website and social media platforms; more reports to reference during his live show; more dynamic material to enrich the nightly news program. In no uncertain terms, for Jones to justify their employment, they would have to make substantial changes.

"What's the proposed solution?" I asked, making sure Jakari sensed my sarcasm. I didn't want him to think I supported Jones's blanket dissatisfaction, even though I'd thrown them under the bus the day before.

"We have a quota now," he said, grimacing. "One report a day, no exceptions, not including the nightly news. Other than that, no real information. Dew just kept shouting 'Churn and burn! Churn and burn!'" This was the motto Jones threw around often. Instead of the phrase's original meaning—a union-busting tactic to bring in new, non-union workers to diminish the power of the union in a workforce—Jones used it to refer to the creation of endless content. "Churn" out reports, squeeze as much material from a given story, and "burn" it by rapidly moving on to the next newsworthy item, replicating to death any story or concept that went viral, and chucking what didn't. This was the operating system of Infowars, the only mission statement I was ever made aware of. Quantity, not quality.

The subsequent reports were the video equivalent of clickbait—shocking at first glance but, for the most part, devoid of substance. Often the more incendiary content came from Jones, like traveling with McAdoo to Saint Louis to cover an anti-Obama protest or accompanying Jakari to an active shooter drill at a Texas elementary school to ascertain whether the Department of Homeland Security was somehow involved.

Ultimately, none of these reports garnered substantial views, and Jones grew more irritated by the day. It wasn't until Jakari arrived at the office one morning with an unintentional prototype that I began to understand what Jones was looking for. Hours earlier, in the dead of night, Jakari overheard a commotion in the hallway outside his apartment. When he looked out the peephole he spotted cops in SWAT gear, holding assault rifles, towering over two people lying face down on the ground. Jakari grabbed his camera and opened the door. The officer shouted for him to go inside but Jakari insisted he *was* in his apartment. The officer stepped over without saying a word and slammed the door in Jakari's face.

That was it. That was the entire video. But when Jakari came into the office that morning with the footage, Jones was ecstatic. It wasn't newsworthy, especially without context, but Jones was able to use that short clip as a launching point for his ideas on the looming police state. It was also exciting, dangerous, and more interesting than anything the reporters had done previously. Jones didn't just want content; he wanted controversy.

After work one evening, Dew invited me to watch his friend's experimental band perform at a club in downtown Austin. I hadn't spent much time with anyone outside of the office, so I agreed to go. We convened in the parking lot, where I climbed into Carlos's dented SUV as he plucked the remains of a joint from the console ashtray and extended it toward me. I declined, trying to mask my unease.

On the ride to the venue, I noticed a child's car seat in the back of the SUV. Surprised, I asked him if he had children. "I do," Carlos said, laughing as he rolled his window down and lit the joint, mocking my apparent assumptions. "I'm also married, own a house, and pay my taxes."

I cringed, aware how judgmental I sounded. "No, no, that's not what I meant. I just didn't expect—"

"I'm only teasing," Carlos interrupted, saving me from further embarrassment.

I forced a laugh, uncomfortable in the realization that I sounded like the conservatives I'd grown up around, implying Carlos was a deadbeat because he was in his late thirties, wore heavy metal T-shirts, had thick-gauged hoop earrings, and smoked pot. "How long have you worked for Jones?" I asked, desperate to change the subject.

"A little over two years," he said, elaborating on the evolving landscape of the office with new studios and employee turnover. He took a drag and held the smoke in his lungs. "Tell me if the smoke bothers you," he said, exhaling toward the open window. I mentioned Jones's complaints about money, wondering aloud what it could mean for the company's future. According to Carlos, one way Jones intended to assuage his financial woes was by getting into the health and wellness industry. He was previously involved with Youngevity, a multi-level marketing retailer that sold supplements advertised for health and weight management. Around the time I started, Dew asked if I would be interested in joining his tier, saying it provided him with a nice supplemental income and maybe it could do the same for me. All I needed to do was pay a $50 fee and purchase a $500 welcome kit. I passed on the offer.

Carlos said Jones planned to continue his relationship with Youngevity but also wanted to get involved with a company that could make him more money. Initially, the idea came from Joe Rogan. He and Jones had been friends since 1998, and as Rogan had successfully hawked supplements on his own podcast, he encouraged Jones to do the same. This wouldn't have been the first time Rogan and Jones were business associates. Kevin Booth, the comedian Bill Hicks's production partner, founded a company called Sacred Cow Productions. This outfit released Rogan's first standup special in 2001, *Live from the Belly of the Beast*, which began with Jones and Rogan wearing Bush masks, getting high, and wandering around the Texas State Capitol. Sacred Cow also produced Jones's film *Martial Law 9/11: Rise of the Police State* in 2005.

Carlos claimed that Jones had been in the process of signing a deal to promote Rogan's brand Onnit but something happened and the contract fell apart. A few months prior to my employment, Rogan had invited Jones and some of his crew to an Onnit event in Austin to get him to promote Onnit products on Infowars.

"So we're all getting pretty drunk at this event," Carlos said, "and Jones, just fucking around, tells Nathan that all the women at the party are prostitutes."

"Who's Nathan?" I asked.

"He used to work here," Carlos said. "Anyway, Jones makes this joke, and that idiot takes it seriously. Later, Nathan is talking to a woman at the bar and asks her about pricing. Like 'How much for a blow job? How much for sex?'" Carlos cackled as he turned into the venue parking lot. "And that's not even the best part. Turns out, she was an executive at Onnit, the person Jones was supposed to talk to about signing the deal."

"Jesus," I said, unlatching my seat belt and reaching for the door handle.

"Needless to say, Nathan didn't work here long after," Carlos said. The whole incident soured Jones's relationship with Onnit and the deal fell through. But according to Carlos, Jones had found another connection and was planning to develop his own supplement brand.

We stepped out of Carlos's SUV and walked into the venue. It was dark and, like most grimy bars, smelled of stale beer and urine. The band was already onstage, and crunchy guitars rang out, accompanied by piercing bursts from a saxophone. I spotted Dew dancing in the sparse crowd, flailing his body along with the rhythm of the drums. It was strange to see him so unencumbered. In the office he could be uptight and short-tempered—his nickname was "Dewcifer" after all—but here he seemed like just another carefree, tie-dye-clad hippie.

Not long after, in early September, Carlos's claims were proven correct. Jones announced his plan to roll out the first Infowars-labeled supplement—an iodine tincture marketed as a "shield" against nuclear fallout—and I was asked to film the initial advertisement.

I stood behind the camera as Jones stepped into the frame. Next to me was a guy around my age named Anthony Gucciardi, who was recently brought in as a contractor. Gucciardi had created a health website—which Jones acquired after hiring him—and had contacts in the wellness industry. He was there to develop the supplements, find manufacturers, bring in a doctor to endorse the products, and make sure Jones followed FDA guidelines.

While filming the ad, Jones claimed the iodine supplement was FDA approved and had helped people detox from fluoride poisoning.

"Let's pause for a second," Gucciardi said, stepping in front of the camera. "We can't say the product is FDA approved."

"You told me it was," Jones fired back.

"It comes from an FDA-approved facility," Gucciardi said, "but we can't say the product itself is approved." He looked down at the script he'd written for the ad, which Jones wasn't following. "We also can't say it's a detox for fluoride."

Jones threw his copy of the script on the ground. "The establishment is obsessed with natural supplements," he said. "The FDA literally exists so pharmaceutical companies can get away with killing people. It's pure evil!"

Gucciardi stood in silence, his confidence deflated. I stared at the camera's screen pretending to adjust the focus, the exposure, the audio levels, anything to distance myself from the confrontation. Jones took a deep breath, rubbing his forehead, and continued his spiel, improvising the full ad in one take. He left out the FDA claim, but still mentioned fluoride detox. When finished, he pulled the microphone off his lapel.

"Good?" he asked, the tension gone in his voice.

"Perfect," Gucciardi said, stressed, seemingly aware he was no match for Jones's insistence to say what he wanted, when and how he wanted to say it.

At Jones's request, the ad started with a shot of the Fukushima Daiichi nuclear power plant as it exploded. I doubled the sound of the explosion, adding a glitch filter and sirens in the background for dramatic effect. After the radio show ended, Jones stood over my shoulder as I edited. "This is great," he said. "See if you can find flyover footage of Chernobyl as well."

On September 26, 2013, four months after I started working there, Jones premiered the iodine ad and began selling his first product under the banner "Infowars Life." He had Dr. Edward Group on his show to promote the iodine supplement. With his blond, shoulder-length hair, Dr. Group looked like a villain in a B-list action movie. "He has so many doctorates behind his name, I can't even go over all of them," Jones said on his live show. Dr. Group spent the interview dancing around claims about the product and its efficacy against certain illnesses. "Iodine is extremely effective against cancer," he said, specifying that doctors had used iodine to treat breast and ovarian cancer. He also claimed to have treated members of the royal family and that the reason prostate cancer was on the rise was due to a lack of iodine.

After the show, Dr. Group stayed to be interviewed by McAdoo for the nightly news. McAdoo, poised with a notepad, asked if he recommended everyone take iodine. He did, expounding on the critical role of supplements and emphasizing the equally important aspects of diet. He detailed his own regimen, referring to himself as a fruitarian. "I'll mix some nuts and seeds in every now and then," he said, "but mostly I just eat raw fruit."

He cited the silverback gorilla as an example of a strong animal thriving on a predominantly vegan diet. "We don't really need as much protein as people think," he said. "In fact, I've been studying breatharianism for the past ten years, which is remarkable."

"Breatharianism?" she said skeptically.

"There are sixty to seventy thousand people in the world, right now, living off air alone," Group said. "You have pollen that you're breathing in, the water in the air—there's a lot of evidence that we don't need anything but air to survive."

I sat at my desk, eavesdropping on their conversation, wondering what the fuck Dr. Group was talking about. If we could live off air alone, then why did twenty-five thousand people die every day of hunger? After a few minutes of searching his name online, I discovered that Dr. Group wasn't even a medical doctor; he was a chiropractor and a naturopath. I wondered if Jones had deliberately lied about this, if Group had misled him, or (blinded by my own gullibility) if he had simply made a mistake. No matter what the answer, the audience didn't seem concerned about Group's credentials. According to Jones, the iodine supplement, the first in a long line of products he hoped would solve his financial concerns and pave the way for Infowars to become a media juggernaut, was scheduled to sell out in the next three days.

5

SPIES LIKE US

Following the success of the supplements, Jones sent me to Utah with Gucciardi and Dalton, the Infowars warehouse manager, to visit the manufacturing facility. It was a mom-and-pop operation, offering private labeling services in addition to selling their own liquid herbal concoctions online. Gucciardi had brokered the relationship between Jones and the company, and my job was to film the procurement process and gather B-roll for future ads. The trip would have been uncomplicated, but true to the "churn and burn" ethos, Jones had one more stop in mind.

Four months earlier, the *Guardian* and the *Washington Post* broke a major story on the release of top-secret documents concerning the National Security Agency's role in global surveillance. The classified information, leaked by former NSA contractor Edward Snowden, revealed that the US agency was conducting sweeping surveillance of American citizens: from forcing Verizon to hand over the phone records of millions of Americans, to the Prism program allowing access and collection of data from companies like Facebook, Google, Apple, and Microsoft.

"I told you sixteen years ago exactly how the spying worked, who was doing it, and what was being set up," Jones said to his audience. He had also accused the "New World Order" of using weather weapons to manipulate natural disasters for political gain, of using the impending Y2K collapse to impose martial law, and of regularly feasting on newborn babies who had been spit roasted and wrapped in edible gold leaf. Much like the idiom "A stopped clock is right twice a day," Jones, too, occasionally provided correct information, even if only by accident.

Months after the Snowden leaks, the NSA was set to open a $1.5 billion facility to assist in their data storage needs. The location, codenamed Bumblehive, required enough electricity to power sixty-five thousand homes, spanned one million square feet, and was located on an Army National Guard base a few hours away from the manufacturing facility in Utah.

"While you're there," Jones said, before we were set to leave, "you should go to the new NSA Data Center."

"You mean file a report with the center in the background?" Gucciardi said with a confused look.

"No," Jones said. "Anyone can use a building as a backdrop. I want you to drive up to the compound and confront them. Hell, just walk right inside." I assumed he was joking but his stern appearance said otherwise. Gucciardi tried to stammer a response, but Jones cut him off. "If they can spy on *us*, we can spy on *them*."

I glanced over at Dalton and Gucciardi, relieved that we all shared a similar expression of unease.

Jones had performed his version of gonzo journalism many times before. In 1998 he interrupted then Governor George W. Bush during a campaign rally, demanding the abolishment of the Federal Reserve and the Council on Foreign Relations. In 2007 he crashed Geraldo Rivera's live Fox News program while screaming "9/11 was an inside job," and was arrested for operating a megaphone without a permit. In 2011 he stormed the Texas Capitol, leading a group of angry protesters after the Senate pulled a bill criminalizing invasive airport security searches by federal TSA agents. In each instance—and many others—Jones heavily promoted his website as a sort of brand militancy, turning aggressive confrontation into avaricious capitalism.

This time, Jones would be leading the charge from afar. Sending us as proxies and orchestrating the stunt from the comfort of his studio. "I'm not saying you guys do anything crazy," Jones sneered, dumbfounded by our lack of enthusiasm. I nodded, appearing to acquiesce without having to give a verbal commitment in case someone had the guts to push back. But no one did. Instead, we stood there, trancelike, distracted by the notion that forcing our way into the country's biggest spy center located on a military base, during a fierce public debate on national security, was somehow a reasonable request.

Without the vibrant expressions of approval Jones was used to receiving from his employees, he grew incensed. "Look," he said, glaring at us. "If you infiltrate the NSA, it'll be national news! If security stops you, confront them. Look confident, don't cower. And if you get arrested, even better!"

Jones was the boss, and this was what he wanted.

It was my first time in Utah. I marveled at the jagged cerulean skyline, the steep Wasatch Range to the east and the Oquirrh Mountains to the west. Dalton drove the rental car through the peaks and canyons thirty minutes to Park City, where we checked into three separate suites at the Waldorf Astoria and grabbed dinner at a nearby steakhouse. Gucciardi and Dalton were of the mind that if Jones wanted us to risk our safety, he would have to foot an exorbitant bill.

"Won't he be upset about all of this?" I asked, tipping my glass of Belle Glos to the Niman Ranch porterhouse surrounded by an array of shaved black truffle and parmesan dusted sides. They both laughed, assuring me that since the iodine supplement went on the market, Jones was bringing in so much money, he wouldn't notice. A few weeks earlier he claimed he hadn't paid himself in eight months; now we were charging thousands of dollars to the company credit card like we'd won the lottery.

The following morning, we drove two hours east through the winding mountain roads to meet the owners of the supplement company. We arrived at a quaint log cabin in the middle of nowhere surrounded by lush gardens. The owners, Vincent and Cheryl, were a husband-and-wife team, both in their late fifties with a rustic, free-range look that matched the landscape.

After an interview with Vincent, I wandered the property, capturing footage of the idyllic countryside as Gucciardi and Dalton sat down with the owners to discuss Jones's product needs. It didn't take long before we were given directions to the manufacturing facility, where we would meet the operations director for the company, who also happened to be their son. He, according to the father, was the "real scientist in the family."

It was a thirty-minute drive from their cabin to the factory. The sun had set, and the mountains were shrouded in darkness.

"Jones is going to be so pissed," Gucciardi said from the passenger seat. The conversation with the owners hadn't gone as expected. Jones had sent us there to strong-arm them into producing and shipping more of the iodine supplement, but it turned out this wasn't possible.

"It's a load of shit," Dalton said. "Three months to produce what we need? If that's the case, we'll have to find somewhere else."

"I'll piss in bottles before I tell Jones we'll be sold out for three months," Gucciardi said.

"Maybe if we get arrested by the NSA tomorrow, he won't be so upset," Dalton said sarcastically. I laughed from the back seat, and he glanced over his shoulder. "You good with that?"

"Sure," I said, matching his sarcasm. "Anything to keep the boss happy."

We drove down a long, empty highway until a small, flickering light appeared in the distance. "Is this the right place?" I asked. It was a lone, tin-sided structure, about the size of a two-car garage, and I started to understand why they were having trouble keeping up with Jones's demand. We knocked on the hollow aluminum door. A short man in his thirties answered wearing a white lab coat. "I'm Jason," he said with a stolid expression, welcoming us in, staring at the camera in my hand.

On the back wall of the lab were shelves of semitransparent plastic barrels filled with liquids of varying colors, each labeled with a corresponding herb tincture. Jason explained that the barrels were still in development and off-limits for filming, which was fine with us since we were only there to get footage of the iodine. His demeanor shifted as he pointed to a black curtain covering the entrance to another room. The iodine procurement took place behind the curtain and was proprietary, meaning we couldn't film that either.

"You're kidding," Gucciardi said. But he wasn't. The more Gucciardi argued with him, the quieter Jason got. He tried to look austere, but the oversized lab coat wasn't helping. Instead, he resembled a child playing dress-up.

I peered around the room and spotted a typewriter-size machine on a steel table. It was a labeler for the supplements, positioned next to a box of amber-colored dropper bottles and a package of InfowarsLife Survival Shield labels. Desperate for something to film, I suggested to Gucciardi that we capture footage of the labeling process.

Gucciardi agreed and, with a puckish grin, asked Jason if he could borrow his lab coat for the shot. Jason sighed and removed his coat, reluctantly handing it over. I filmed Gucciardi labeling the bottles in his ridiculous knee-length smock, and on the ride back to the hotel, realizing how little we'd achieved on this trip, I accepted that visiting the NSA Data Center was the only possible hope of accomplishment.

The next morning, I stood outside, waiting for Gucciardi and Dalton, hoping the crisp air and lukewarm hotel coffee would mitigate my lack of sleep. It was quiet and serene. Other than the valet, I was alone, standing in front of a stone fire pit, hypnotized by the dancing hues of orange and yellow. My mind was elsewhere, filled with dread, still reasoning my way out of Jones's futile plan. Gucciardi and Dalton stepped out of the hotel just as our rental car arrived and I could no longer distract myself from reality.

The Utah Data Center was in the sand-dusted town of Bluffdale, nestled in a bowl-shaped valley and slightly obscured from the main highway. As we approached, the sprawling facility came into view. The structure itself was modern and dreary looking; the concrete-walled buildings and massive power generators stood out among the rolling foothills flecked with sagebrush. Both sides of the road were lined with barbed wire fencing and NO TRESPASSING signs.

I received a call from the radio producer. The live show was about to begin, and Jones wanted to make sure we were ready to go. I pulled out the company iPhone, attached the audio cables Dew had given me before we left, and attempted to connect. It didn't work. I tried again. Nothing. Frantically, I restarted the phone, reconnected the cables, and tried to troubleshoot with the crew back in Austin, but the cell signal kept dropping.

Just as the memory of Jones's gravelly voice roared to life in my head—"Is this guy a fucking idiot?"—Gucciardi was able to connect to the streaming platform on his personal phone. There was a slight delay in audio, so we had to regroup: Dalton would man the live video stream, Gucciardi would call into the show for audio, and I would use my camera to capture everything in high definition to be uploaded in a full report later.

"I'm taking you live," the producer said.

After a few seconds, I heard Jones in my earpiece. "You guys are doing a great job," he said on-air. "What the NSA is doing is illegal. This is a command center to run the technocracy during the shutdown of America. It might as well be an alien mothership that has landed in Utah to run operations against us."

As we approached the data center, there were numerous signs along the side of the road, clearly telling us to stop doing what we were there to do.

> DO NOT FILM
> NO UNAUTHORIZED VEHICLES
> PRIVATE PROPERTY
> VIOLATERS WILL BE PROSECUTED

We pulled into a parking spot and exited the vehicle. Gucciardi handed the live-streaming phone to Dalton and put on a black blazer. I spotted an NSA officer at the guard post, staring at us. "Who knows?" Gucciardi said. "Maybe they're fans of the show."

Jones cackled in my ear. "Oh, they're definitely watching," he said. "Stay right there, guys. We're going to break, and we'll be right back."

The timing made no sense. Did Jones expect us to wait? We were trespassing on a restricted military base and had already been spotted. Just then, we heard a voice in the distance. "... The! ... Off! ... Now!"

It was the NSA officer, but we were too far away to make out more than a few words. The closer we got, the easier he was to hear. "Turn the cameras off!" he shouted. "Right now!"

The officer stepped inside a white unmarked Ford Explorer, slammed the door, and floored it in our direction. Gucciardi and Dalton looked excited, accepting the situation with equanimity. I, on the other hand, was terrified, steeling myself for a hostile confrontation. As we stood there, watching the vehicle barrel toward us, I thought of the last conversation I had with Jones before leaving Austin. He had shared a story from the late '90s—what sounded like a parable, though he insisted it was true. In this account, he and his cameraman Mike Hanson were confronted by Delta Force, the elite special operations unit of the US Army, while covering a military exercise at Fort Sam Houston in San Antonio. According to Jones, one of the soldiers approached them and instructed Hanson to turn off his camera.

"He wouldn't do it," Jones said with great pride. "So the soldier pulled out a Beretta, stuck it right to Hanson's chest, and said, 'I'm going to tell you one more time to give me that camera.'" Jones claimed that even with a gun to his chest, Hanson was resolute. The soldier eventually pried the camera from Hanson's grip, deleting the footage and therefore the evidence of this indelible altercation. Jones's point was clear: No matter what happened in Utah, even if it meant taking a bullet, I had to keep the camera rolling.

When the officer arrived, he stepped out of the vehicle and asked us, again, to turn the cameras off. As he approached, he rested his right hand on the gun holstered at his side.

"We just want to have an interview," Gucciardi said. "We're trying to find a representative."

"Nope. I will not do an interview with you," the officer said, motioning to me and Dalton. "I need you to turn those off."

Gucciardi name-dropped the First Amendment, but the NSA officer was unfazed. He warned us that we were on federal property and threatened to confiscate our equipment if we didn't comply.

"I mean, listen," Gucciardi said, "we just want to ask a few questions. We're wondering—" He abruptly stopped and looked off into the distance. None of us had discussed the details beyond the initial confrontation, and he struggled to think of a single question to ask.

"Turn the camera off," the officer said again, now looking at me. "I'm not going to answer any questions until you turn the cameras off."

"Why not?" Gucciardi said with a smug grin. "We're just journalists. We just want to talk, we don't want to have any trouble at all, we just want to ask you a few questions."

"I don't want any trouble either, so please turn them off." The officer was calm, and nicer than I'd expected, but it was clear his patience was waning.

Suddenly, I heard a song begin to play. War drums pounded as brass rang out. It felt like I was watching a movie—the NSA Data Center towering above, the officer demanding trespassers shut off their cameras and leave—all of it accompanied by a suspenseful, dramatic score. After a moment of confusion, I realized the sound was coming through my earpiece. I was listening to the bumper music—"Anvil of Crom" from *Conan the Barbarian*—at the end of the ad break on Jones's show.

I snapped back to reality when an unmarked Chevrolet Tahoe sped through the parking lot and stopped in front of us. An officer and a lieutenant exited the vehicle and asked us to turn the cameras off.

"Alex, they're calling in their buddies," Gucciardi said into the phone. "They're about to confiscate all our cameras right now."

The lieutenant approached Dalton, yanked the cell phone from his hands, and switched off the live stream. Jones's story echoed in my mind. Any moment now, this lieutenant could draw his firearm and aim it in my direction. I'd never told Jones about my anxiety, the way I always imagined the worst-case scenarios, playing each anxious moment out to its inevitable, horrific end. Yet somehow, it felt like he knew. His odd questions, his mix of manipulative rage and disarming levity—it was as if all of it was designed to lower my guard and expose my vulnerabilities. What he didn't realize, though, was that my sense of fear far outweighed any loyalty I had to him. As a listener of his show, I was compelled by the gravity of his stunts, but being on the other side of the camera gave me a different perspective. There was no way I was going to risk my life for something so stupid. Nothing we did would affect the NSA spying program or make any difference whatsoever. I raised both of my hands in the air to signal my cooperation, but I kept the camera rolling. It was attached to a rig, perched on my shoulder. As I filmed the lieutenant fumbling with Dalton's phone, the first officer lunged forward and flipped the power switch on my camera. The screen went black.

We were disconnected from the show and no longer documenting the altercation. The officer confirmed my camera was off and then looked up at me. "Now," he said, folding his arms across his chest, "delete everything or I'll have to arrest you."

"We were streaming to *The Alex Jones Show*," Gucciardi said. "The footage is already out there."

"I've never heard of the show so that means nothing to me," he said. "But I *am* going to need him to delete what's on that camera."

I fumbled around for a minute, pressing buttons and scrolling through the digital screen while keeping an eye on the officer, who was standing uncomfortably close to me. I knew if I deleted the footage, Jones would be furious. But if I refused, we would be arrested.

I stalled for what felt like an hour, insisting I'd only recently been hired and was unfamiliar with the equipment. Finally, I surrendered. "All right," I said, hanging my head in defeat. "I emptied the card."

"Show me," the officer said, stepping behind me to look at the screen.

Once I'd scrolled through the camera and verified the footage had been deleted, the atmosphere shifted. Their physical demeanors became relaxed and amenable. One officer went to his vehicle and brought us an official NSA pamphlet with a DVD of footage from the facility that we could use.

After we stood around chatting for a moment, they allowed us to walk back to our vehicle. We'd streamed part of the confrontation on the live show, but the beginning was missing because Jones had cut to an ad break.

"Alex is going to lose it when he finds out we don't have the footage," Dalton said as he started the car.

I leaned forward and pulled a memory card from my shirt pocket. "Actually, I got it," I said. They looked back at me, puzzled. "I pretended I didn't know how to work the camera, and when the officer looked away, I swapped the card."

I might not have been willing to risk my life, or more realistically my freedom, but I still wanted Jones's approval.

Gucciardi pulled out his phone and called the studio. "Put me on with Alex," he said to the producer. In a matter of seconds, he was speaking to Jones on the show. "Alex, they're listening very closely to what we're saying right now," he whispered, acting as if the NSA were, at that very moment, spying on his call. "We're in the car and we maintained everything. Josh switched out the card and they couldn't erase it. We have the footage. We have it all."

Part Two
MADNESS

6

IN CAMELOT

It took less than a minute to clean out my desk. After six months, I hadn't brought in a single item to personalize my small corner of the office. No framed photos; no potted plants; not even a measly pencil cup. All I had was the black notebook for Jones's directives, a stack of office memos, and an Infowars coffee mug with a crudely designed image of a wolf chasing a sheep, which Dew had given me on my first day.

After our confrontation with the NSA, we flew back to Austin, where Jones instructed me to gather my things and move into the War Room. This was the inner circle of Infowars, where Jones spent most of his time; where Dew, Tillman, and Carlos were based, conveniently adjacent to Jones's private bathroom; and where I would now be stationed.

Jones was thrilled when he learned I'd tricked the NSA police. As we fled the scene and posted the full high-definition video of our altercation to his website, he ludicrously compared it to the Alamo during the Texas Revolution. "That's how the battle is won!" he howled. It wasn't a gun to the chest, but I couldn't deny the sense of pride I felt. After six months working to earn Jones's trust and proving I wasn't a fuckup, I had finally made my mark.

Jones planned to start sending reporters out into the field and wanted me on every trip moving forward. "I need somebody I can depend on," he said. "We're going to hire more reporters and cameramen and eventually be on the ground at every major news event in the world. But first, you'll be on the front lines, beta testing the whole thing."

Despite my relentless pursuit of Jones's approval, this was the last thing I wanted to hear. Lacey had just moved to Austin, and we'd settled into an apartment south of town. I chose a place far from the office after Dew pushed me to get one nearby. Initially, I spent all my time at work because I didn't have anything or anyone to go home to. I didn't even have a home. But now that Lacey was there, I wanted to get back to my life, to control how I spent my nights and weekends, to go out to dinner and take my dogs to the park and have some semblance of balance and dominion over my time.

The very idea of personal space was alien in Jones's world. He thrived on all-consuming obsession, demanding that everyone within his sphere match his intensity or risk unraveling the fabric of what he'd built. Like Tinker Bell in *Peter Pan*, the persona of Alex Jones would cease to exist without the belief of an audience, and there would be no audience without those of us willing to do his bidding. This happened with everyone who worked there. There was a direct correlation between proximity to Jones and lack of autonomy. I didn't realize it at the time, but by accepting the invitation into his inner circle, I was handing over my freedom on a silver platter.

Each morning, Jones would burst into the office, radiating whatever emotion gripped him in the moment—be it joy, rage, excitement, or disgust. He then retreated to the bathroom, where he would shower and make no attempt at discretion with his bowel movements, sometimes stepping out in only his underwear to continue conversations or hanging upside down on an inversion table, growling and screaming as his spine realigned itself with loud cracks and pops.

When he had ideas for new videos or needed someone to join him on an outing, I was the person he turned to. I worried the employees closest to Jones would feel replaced, but the opposite occurred—they seemed relieved to have a break from his obsessive compulsions. One day he asked me to accompany him and John McAfee—a figure both notorious and enigmatic—to a remote ranch to shoot guns. McAfee, the pioneering creator of antivirus software, had recently returned to the United States after fleeing arrest in Belize on suspicion of murdering his neighbor with a gunshot to the head. Jones, trying to capitalize on McAfee's infamy, brought along his two prized Barrett M82 rifles—their .50 caliber rounds designed to pierce military equipment—and they took turns firing them at trees in a field. McAfee's security guard, who claimed to be in the Mafia, flashed his gun at me, threatening to use it if I turned the camera on him. I made a point to shield him from the lens, searching his face for a smile or something to reveal his comment was a joke, but I saw nothing but a scowl. As dusk settled, McAfee insisted we leave immediately, saying he couldn't be out after dark because government assassins were trying to kill him.

The next day, I found myself at a Megadeath concert with Jones, mingling backstage with Dave Mustaine, the band's front man and a frequent guest on Jones's show. That night, Jones pulled me aside and thanked me for all my hard work, saying that hiring me was the best decision he'd ever made. He went on to joke about cloning me to replace his entire staff, a strange compliment that made me feel both gratified and uneasy.

A month after I'd settled into my new role, I was sent out on the road with Jones. It was the fiftieth anniversary of President John F. Kennedy's assassination, and the first time the city of Dallas planned to hold an official ceremony to commemorate the tragedy. Since Kennedy's murder by Lee Harvey Oswald in 1964, Dallas had been known as the "City of Hate," a hotbed for right-wing agitators. According to the mayor, the eyes of the world would be on Dallas, and he wanted to use the event not only to celebrate the life of the 35th president, but to once and for all shed that moniker.

This meant the small mob that descended on Dealey Plaza every year, chanting about conspiracies and cover-ups, would not be allowed to attend the official ceremony or hand out flyers. Jones, however, had no intention of adhering to such constraints. Where others saw boundaries, he saw challenges to overcome, and set about orchestrating his own spectacle.

Jones hired six pilots to fly over Dealey Plaza, trailing banners emblazoned with JFK TRUTH and INFOWARS.COM. He printed thirty thousand leaflets and two hundred posters, and purchased a small FM transmitter, commandeering an open Dallas radio station to broadcast his live show. From there, he urged his listeners to drive through downtown blasting the station from their speakers, creating a giant collective megaphone to drown out the ceremony and amplify his message. Jones would flood the city of Dallas with his conspiracy theories whether the mayor liked it or not.

Three days before the ceremony, we piled into vehicles and headed to Dallas. It was a three-hour drive and there were fifteen of us in total. Jones drove his Ford Raptor truck and brought along his father and ten-year-old son. I drove a rental SUV with Dew, and the rest of the crew were dispersed throughout our curious cavalcade as we journeyed north to the birthplace of one of the biggest conspiracy theories of all time.

My encounters with Jones's father were few and far between. David Jones was quiet, slinking through the office, speaking in his soft, raspy voice. He reminded me of a garden gnome—jolly, short, with balding curly hair and a thick beard. Most of what I knew about him came from Jones's stories. He claimed his father had been tested by the University of Texas as a high school junior and labeled the sixth smartest person in Texas. David had once been a member of the John Birch Society, giving anti-communist speeches in his youth. The conspiratorial books he kept around the house seemed to have had a formative influence on Jones, laying the groundwork for his worldview.

The more stories Jones told about his father, the more bizarre and fantastical they became, many resembling plotlines of *The X-Files*. He claimed that at sixteen, his father's intelligence led to a recruitment by UT's head of biology for a eugenics program aimed at sterilizing the US population. Later, as a dentist, he was supposedly approached by the CIA to work on a covert medical project. In the mid-1980s, after becoming one of the first dentists to perform oral implants, Jones said his father was recruited to work at an underground base on "biological androids"—humanoid creatures allegedly engineered with exoskeletons.

While I doubted the truth of these outlandish tales, one story seemed plausible: the reason his family moved from Dallas to Austin. At sixteen, Jones claimed he attended parties where sheriff's deputies dealt drugs to students. During a school assembly on drug testing, he accused one of the officers onstage of selling cocaine and ecstasy. Afterward, he was taken into an office, where the deputies slammed his head against the wall and threatened him, insisting he had to leave town. Concerned for his son's safety, Jones's father decided to relocate his dental practice and move the family to Austin.

Whenever Jones's motives were questioned, he would recount this story to portray himself as a truth teller, compelled to expose corruption. However, a few years later, I would discover this entire origin narrative was a lie.

Jones led the convoy, weaving through traffic and driving at least fifteen miles over the speed limit. About halfway to Dallas, as we neared the city of Waco, Dew's phone rang. Jones wanted to stop for food. I followed as he took a sharp curve and pulled into the parking lot of the first restaurant off the exit, a Texas Roadhouse. Inside there were no tables large enough to seat us all together, so we separated into multiple booths. Though it was his idea to stop for a meal, when the waiter came, Jones didn't bother ordering food. "Let me get a double vodka soda," he said. "Actually, make that two, we're in a hurry."

Once the rest of us ordered, Jones acknowledged that he'd been drinking more than usual. "Wife troubles," he said, lowering his voice, without elaborating, glancing over at his father and son, who were seated a few tables away, making sure they couldn't hear him. "I've decided, after this trip, I'm going to cut back."

It wasn't until I'd moved into the main office that I became aware of Jones's drinking habits. He slunk into the room every few days, an hour or two after he'd finished his radio show, and went straight for the metal cabinet next to my desk. It was around six feet tall, made of black alloyed steel, with two wing doors that clattered and echoed like thunder when opened. Inside, on the second-to-last shelf, was a tall bottle of Grey Goose Vodka with white Dixie Cups stacked beside it. Jones would pour the vodka without anyone making a comment—the sound of liquid splashing into an empty paper cup—and then disappear without a word. Any other time, Dew or Tillman would acknowledge his presence, taking any opportunity to ingratiate themselves further. But when it came to the bottle, everyone was silent.

The next day we had planned to walk around Dallas, broadcasting live as he showed the security measures put in place for the ceremony. However, that morning, Jones received a call letting him know the pilots he'd hired to fly banners over downtown Dallas were forced to cancel due to overcast skies. He also learned that military jets were scheduled to fly over the official ceremony, so even if the skies cleared, they wouldn't be able to take off until after the temporary no-fly zone had been lifted, long after the commemoration had concluded. To say he was angry would be an understatement. Jones was unskilled at managing his emotions, and his outbursts seemed like a means of catharsis, an auto-exorcism to rid himself of his reactionary rage. But once the wrath passed through, he was cleansed.

After his outburst, he spent the rest of the day in a spirited mood, prancing around the city, pestering every police officer he encountered. He resembled a court jester, an annoying child, a pesky fly impossible to swat away. Jones told random police on the street that he paid their salary, slapping them on the shoulder like they were old pals. He followed an officer through Dealey Plaza, asking, in a condescending tone, if he planned to arrest him for passing out flyers.

The following morning, we stepped outside to a forty-degree drop in temperature. It was in the mid-thirties, gray, and drizzling rain. Despite the weather, Jones coasted on his antics of the previous day, feeling invincible. His new plan was to force his way into the official proceedings. When we reached the media entrance, he attempted to stroll through the checkpoint, but without a press pass or ticket, the security guard turned him away. It was almost pitiful to see him scoff at the attendees who flashed their tickets and walked into the restricted area while he stood on the outskirts, where he always seemed to end up, yearning to get inside.

Jones insisted that had he been allowed access, he wouldn't interrupt the ceremony. But now that his exclusion was official, he had no other choice but to lead his audience in a full-throated rebuttal of the event.

We met around a hundred of Jones's fans at Belo Gardens. When we arrived, they rushed over to greet him. In their chaotic fervor, a few young men shoved me aside, ignoring the camera perched on my shoulder. "He's with me," Jones said as he reached through the horde, grabbed my raincoat, and pulled me back into the fold. Though he had been excluded from the ceremony, dismissed by the mayor, and laughed at by those who saw him as a silly conspiracy theorist, to the misfits and outcasts who tuned in to his show, he was a hero.

The entire trip had become less about free speech, and more about Jones winning against the police and the city. More than anything else, he wanted to be allowed inside the event, for his views to be accepted and praised. He had gone to great lengths to assure that his voice was part of the conversation that weekend. The problem, however, was that the weekend wasn't a conversation. It was a memorial.

As we made our way to the barricades, Jones gripped a megaphone, railing against what he perceived as the encroaching menace of globalism, his words painting vivid, dystopian images of a country dominated by an authoritarian regime. The crowd, energized by his impassioned speech, picked up the chant he initiated. "No more lies! No more lies!"

I followed Jones as he wedged his way through the crowd, inconsiderate of anyone's space but his own. We made it to the barricade and gathered behind a crane hoisting a flag emblazoned with an image of JFK. Jones asked those around him not to use their megaphones to interrupt the moment of silence, and they complied.

After the ceremony ended, the only people left outside were the protesters. Jones seemed tired and irritable, and he asked one of the police officers, standing on the other side of the barricade, when we would be allowed inside.

"That I'm not sure," the officer replied, "but for now you can't go in."

"Come on, man," Jones said. "The thing's over; we need to go in. The police department told us a week ago when we called them that after it was over at 2 p.m., we could go in for a moment of silence. COPA threatened a lawsuit. It's been in the *Dallas Morning News*. You guys know about that."

The police may very well have known what Jones was referring to, but it was my first time hearing it. A week earlier, a Washington DC–based nonprofit, the Coalition on Political Assassinations (COPA), had been told, after a year-long dispute with the mayor, that they would be allowed into Dealey Plaza once the ceremony had finished to observe their own moment of silence. But what shocked me most was they had also been given permission to hand out flyers. This meant that Jones was intentionally dishonest every time he claimed there was a total ban on distributing pamphlets. That hadn't been true for over a week, and I later found out that Jones had known the whole time.

It started raining harder. One officer told us to follow the fencing to our left until we reached another entrance; this, he said, was where we would be allowed to enter the area once it opened. When we arrived, another line of officers were waiting, creating a human hedge behind the barricade. Instead of getting angry, Jones reverted to his comedic persona. A stern-looking officer wearing a bright yellow raincoat and sporting a comically large walrus mustache walked up to the barricade.

"Oh my god, that guy is a rock star," Jones said. "I mean, that is spectacular! It's like the Russian czar. Come on over here, buddy. You know you want to show it off, it's why you got it." The officer ignored Jones as he cackled at his own joke.

Just then, a listener tapped Jones on the shoulder. "The police are coming for you," he said.

"They've got the reinforcements for the unruly crowd," Jones said sarcastically into the megaphone, unconcerned by the warning. "Why are there more police coming? Are we evil, or was it the joke about that guy's mustache?"

Since we'd arrived in Dallas, the police had managed Jones with a surprising level of passivity. Now that was over.

A band of sheriff's deputies rushed in and grabbed Jones by the collar, dragging him through the crowd, pushing all of us away from the ceremony. In the chaos, I got separated, though I could still hear him shouting about an officer who had just punched him in the stomach. Jones called out my name, wanting me to come over and capture the cop's face on camera, but I couldn't move. I struggled to even raise my arms to wipe the cold rain out of my eyes. It was like being caught in a rogue wave, unable to break free.

Next to me, an officer grabbed one of the protesters and pinned him against a metal kiosk on the sidewalk. This created a small open space, so I squeezed through and made my way over to Jones, who had been pulled farther ahead.

"You guys are a giant gang of wimp punks," Jones shouted. "Bring your biggest goon cop out here, have him stand up against me! I guarantee you're a bunch of damn cowards, and I hope you enjoy the lawsuits you get."

We were far enough away from the barricades at this point that the cops backed off and formed a line so we couldn't return to Dealey Plaza. I stood close to Jones, still filming, as his supporters circled us.

"If we would've resisted and beat their ass, they would've started shooting us and Tiananmen Square would've started," Jones said, panting. His humid breath billowed out like smoke into the cold air. "I'm telling you, 1776 almost kicked off, because if we would've started beating their asses, they would've started shooting people, including children."

As Jones ranted, I noticed two young kids standing nearby, holding on to their father's hands with tears in their eyes. At that moment, all I wanted was for Jones to walk away, to deescalate the situation so no one got hurt, but some of the protesters felt differently.

"Someone pushed a little girl!" a man from the crowd said, angling to spark a reaction in Jones. And it worked.

"That's it!" Jones shouted, harnessing all the justification he needed to reengage with the police. "You guys are fucking cowards."

He stormed back over to the troopers standing shoulder to shoulder. The crowd mirrored Jones's intensity and began screaming along with him. It seemed he wanted something catastrophic to occur. Two nights earlier, in a confrontational video where he hyped up the event, he expressed his desire to have his head blown off to mark the beginning of a revolution. I assumed he was being hyperbolic, but as I watched him scream at the row of police, I wasn't so sure anymore.

"You're fucking cowards!" he continued. "You're not cops, you're thugs and pieces of filth!"

Before long, Jones spotted the officer who he claimed had punched him in the stomach. "That's him!" Jones shouted, fighting to get through the line of police. "You think you can kick my ass? I'll take you and ten of your buddies on right now! Pull your armor off, put your gun down, and see what happens, punk!" The cop stood behind the row of police with a smirk on his face. "I'll check the tapes and sue your ass," Jones seethed. "You might beat the rap, but you won't beat the ride, pal. I'm going to get your Jet Skis and I'm going to get your bass boat. You better believe it!"

I stood behind him, amused by his audacity, and terrified he was going to get one of us shot. Luckily, Jones's histrionics were no match for his inability to focus on one thing for a prolonged period. He may have wanted to start a revolution, but he didn't quite have the stamina, so he turned his back on the police and walked away. His followers yelled out support, praising his bravado, trailing him down the street as he recounted the skirmish, asserting a violent revolution had almost begun. He eyed the crowd surrounding him in the middle of the road. "I literally just got radicalized ten more levels today."

I kept the camera trained on Jones as he continued milking the confrontation on his radio show. At one point, he snatched it and aimed it at me, asking for my take on the situation. I recounted the police's aggressive tactics with dramatic flair, mimicking Jones and reveling in the afterglow of the moment. Suddenly, he caught sight of a short, dark-haired woman behind me, and his entire demeanor changed.

"Did you hear about all the craziness?" he said, grinning wide.

"I was there," she replied in a British accent.

I turned and pointed the camera at her. She looked familiar but it wasn't until Jones began surreptitiously referencing certain films that I recognized her face. A year earlier, for a production class in film school, I had watched one of her documentaries. The woman standing in front of me was Vivian Kubrick, the daughter of the director of the film *Dr. Strangelove*, which had drawn me to Jones's world.

After a brief conversation, Jones invited Vivian, and the ten or so of his fans who had stuck around, back to the hotel and offered to buy them all dinner.

The bar was situated in the center of the eighteen-story atrium, under a wall of windows looking up at one of the city's most recognizable landmarks, the Reunion Tower.

"What would your dad—with his great artistic mind—think about what America has turned into?" Jones asked Vivian.

"My father was haunted by the factions on this planet that tried to manipulate humanity," she said. "But if you look at the films he made, they certainly address all the things you're talking about. *A Clockwork Orange*: thought control. All the anti-war films—"

"And *Dr. Strangelove*," Jones offered as an additional example.

"Uh, hello!" she said, her eyes growing wide. "But the fact is if you start to think for yourself, it all becomes clear."

Vivian told us stories about creating the score for *Full Metal Jacket*, building sets on *A Clockwork Orange*, and spending time with Jack Nicholson and Shelley Duvall during the filming of *The Shining*. It felt like a fever dream.

"It's kind of incredible that you're here," I said to Vivian.

"It's not, though," Jones interjected. "This is all providence; nothing happens by chance. All the decisions we make in life guide us to these moments."

"It's true," Vivian said.

In that moment, I couldn't help but believe them.

The next morning, I awoke with a searing headache, hungover from the night before. One by one the crew began to filter down to the lobby, each expressing their exhaustion and eagerness to get back to Austin. Jones was the last to arrive, looking disheveled as he wheeled his hard-shell suitcase behind him. As we waited in the lobby for the valet to bring our vehicles around front, Jones asked Dew if he'd seen his father and son. "I think they're waiting outside," Dew said. They had both been largely absent during the trip, lingering in the background as Jones wreaked havoc in his hometown. Jones told us he'd be right back.

The lobby pulsed with guests dressed in business attire, checking in and out at the front desk. I watched as they shouldered their leather bags and moved through the automatic sliding glass doors, offering a nod or a cordial smile to passersby. It felt odd that no one was shouting or trying to draw the ire of others or demanding the room's attention. What was considered normal behavior, the unwritten rules that defined acceptable and appropriate human interaction, were quickly becoming abnormal to me.

Jones reappeared at the top of the escalator, descending to the main lobby with a highball glass in hand. Somehow, even though the bar wasn't scheduled to open for a few hours, he had convinced someone to make him a drink. "I know, I know," he said, shaking his head. "I told you guys I'd slow down *after* the trip, not during." He squeezed a lime wedge over the clear liquid and tilted the drink back, watching through the rim of the glass as the valet approached with our keys.

7

FUKUSHIMA, CALIFORNIA

The weekend after we returned from Dallas, I awoke to a violent ring. It took a second before I realized it was coming from my phone on the bedside table. Through blurry eyes I watched Jones's name brighten and come into focus on the screen. He rarely called me back then, especially at 7 a.m. on a Sunday morning.

"Hey, buddy," Jones said, sounding chipper. "You get some rest?" I lied and said I had. "Good," he continued, "because—and don't be mad at me—I need you to come into the office today."

He wanted me to take the interview he'd done with Vivian Kubrick and edit it down to air on the Monday show—adding B-roll, clips from her father's films, headlines to substantiate Jones's claims, and when all else failed, stock footage of Hitler. As a video editor at Infowars, I always had World War II Nazi footage on hand to play over Jones's babbling. It was seldom, if ever, appropriate, but universally functional.

It also had the added benefit of effectively scaring the shit out of his audience. The JFK trip had been a success; Jones had stirred up enough controversy to draw attention not only *to* our videos but *from* the mainstream press. In this attention economy, the more we could take for ourselves, the happier Jones was.

"Sure," I said, trying to sound unbothered. I was exhausted from the trip and didn't want to spend my day off at the office.

"You have done well, Lord Vader," Jones said, in a convincing impression of Emperor Palpatine. Saying "thank you" didn't seem to come easy for him, so he showed his appreciation the only way he knew how... by quoting *Star Wars*.

Before I got started on the video, I went to the break room for coffee, noticing that the usual bags of whole beans were nowhere to be found. I remembered, as I searched the cabinets, that Jones was about to start selling his own private-labeled coffee and the first shipment had arrived before we left for Dallas. I walked over to the warehouse and found a row of boxes lining the wall. There were two options: the "Wake Up America Patriot Blend" (medium roast) and the "Wake Up America Immune Support" (with chaga mushroom powder). This was before the term "woke" became popular in right-wing vernacular to signify anything they disagreed with, like basic civil rights for minorities and a woman's bodily autonomy. The term had originated in the early twentieth century as a call for Black citizens to become more politically conscious, but somewhere down the line it was appropriated as a rallying cry for the conspiracy community. Back then, Jones used the phrase "wake up" to encourage his listeners to leave their dreamlike trance and begin seeing the world as he did. Those who were "awake" agreed with his worldview, and others, who were presumably asleep, didn't. (Jones eventually expanded his coffee offerings, selling an "Escape the Prison Planet Light Roast" and a "Tip of the Spear Dark Roast," each bag weighing in, per the label, at "one full pound of freedom.")

The original plan was to private-label his favorite coffee from an Austin roaster he frequented—the brand he previously kept stocked in the office—but according to him, they were unwilling to cooperate due to his political rhetoric, so he found where they sourced their beans and went directly to the supplier. I picked out a bag of the "Patriot Blend" and carried it with me into the break room.

A few hours later, Jones arrived at the office and came to my side of the building. He looked alarmed when he saw me. "What are you doing here?" he asked, walking past my desk and into his bathroom.

I thought he was joking so I responded in kind. "No days off when you're fighting tyrants," I said. He poked his head out of the bathroom. The vacant expression on his face indicated he was genuinely confused by my presence. My smile faded. "I'm working on this interview," I said, pointing to the screen, the brightness gone from my voice.

He glanced over my shoulder at the computer, then at me, then back to the computer. He stared for a moment, focusing on Vivian's face, and then, as if the past few seconds hadn't occurred, moved on. "How's it going?" he asked.

"Good," I said, tacitly agreeing to ignore the previous moment, even though I'd lost my one day off, was exhausted, and had just realized he didn't care enough to remember.

He disappeared into the bathroom. The sound of urine echoed through the open door, splashing into the toilet water and then going silent, as he hit either the seat or the floor. "Shit," I heard him say, righting his stream back into the bowl. This was followed by a flush, running water, and the flick of a light switch as he walked back out. He never said anything else to me directly about the video, though he complained on the show the following day that I hadn't cut enough of his stammering.

Before leaving the room, he reminded me that the holidays were approaching and promised that when it came time for Christmas bonuses, my hard work would be rewarded. The offer, much like his performative plea of "Don't be mad at me," was, I suspected, a dangling carrot to stave off resentments.

A few days later, I received an email from Lydia asking me to come to her office. When I arrived, she handed over a check informing me, without elaborating, that Jones had decided to forgo bonuses that year, but he'd instructed her to make an exception. "You must be doing something right," she said, avoiding eye contact. "I've been here for years, and we've always gotten *something* over the holidays."

I glanced down at the check, spotted four figures, and slid it back into the envelope, trying to maintain a stolid expression. "Thank you very much," I said.

"Don't thank me," she said dryly. "I just do what I'm told." Lydia had a way of making you feel like an inconvenience. I wondered, given how long she'd been there, if candor was her means of survival, if that's what it took to be a woman working for someone like Jones.

"Also," she said, reaching for her coffee cup, "make sure you keep this to yourself. We don't want anyone getting their feelings hurt." I nodded, tucking the check deep into my jacket pocket as I left the room.

When I returned to my desk, Tillman was waiting for me. He glanced down the hallway, making sure no one was coming, and spoke in a whisper. "We always get bonuses on Christmas... but not this year." His sarcasm was matched only by his anger. "And with the fucking money Jones has been bringing in with these supplements? Of course, we don't get compensation for our part."

I could feel the check, rigid in my jacket pocket, as I tried to look appalled. Tillman continued, pacing the room, expressing his frustrations about having to watch Gucciardi park his new "yuppie car" in the parking lot. "How is that not a stab in the back?" he asked. "Some of us have worked here for years. He's been here a few months and already he's making enough money to buy a BMW!"

I nodded along, wishing I could tell him about my conversation with Lydia. Not to gloat, but because I agreed with him. It was unfair. In Utah, Gucciardi told me Jones had paid $800,000 to bring him in as a contractor and obtain exclusive rights to his supplement contacts. On top of the initial payment, Gucciardi also claimed he was getting a percentage of the supplement sales, which I imagined were significant since it was proving to be the most profitable endeavor of Jones's career. Though part of me sympathized with Tillman, another part was relieved to be an exception to Jones's unfairness. I had convinced myself that by playing the game—doing as Jones asked, never questioning his motives, keeping my dissatisfactions at bay—I, too, would reap similar rewards.

Two weeks later, I woke up in a hotel off the Pacific Coast Highway, outside of San Francisco, in a pool of my own sweat. It was January, the air conditioner had been disabled, and the room was stifling despite the fifty-degree temperatures outside. There were three of us, sharing two adjoining rooms, each sent with a specific responsibility—Jakari was the reporter, Adan the writer, and I ran camera and edited video reports. Jones expected this expedition to net significant returns, deciding, before we left, that we would break nationwide news, and he wanted to make sure we had every angle covered.

This trip had come together less than twenty-four hours before we left. By *come together*, I mean Jones watched a viral YouTube video, devised a skeletal plan in a matter of seconds, and had Dew pass along the details. Our instruction was to fly to California, rent a vehicle, and drive the full length of Highway 1, stopping every ten miles to check radiation levels on the coast, and to post reports, in real time, detailing the severity of our findings. None of us knew when we'd return.

The YouTube video that sparked Jones's limited imagination consisted of a nameless, faceless man, walking along Surfers' Beach in Half Moon Bay, holding a Geiger counter. The numbers ticked up, reaching five times the normal level of radiation. This video, coupled with unrelated reports of melting starfish in the Pacific Ocean and conjoined gray whale calves in Mexico, was enough to convince Jones that we would be entering a radioactive wasteland in California. Not only was he certain of the outcome, but he also claimed to know the source. Jones believed the radiation was fallout from the disaster at the Daiichi nuclear power plant in Fukushima, Japan. (The same incident he'd instructed me to include in the first ad I made for his flagship supplement four months earlier.)

Jones didn't conjure this idea out of thin air. NBC News had published an article five months prior with the headline, FUKUSHIMA'S RADIOACTIVE OCEAN PLUME DUE TO REACH US WATERS IN 2014. But since Jones failed to read the contents of the article, which clearly stated that the radioactive particles had been diluted to well below the World Health Organization's safety levels, he continued to warn his audience that debris and toxic chemicals were drifting through the water and air, and the disaster was nearing its event horizon in the States.

The viral YouTube video had also garnered the attention of the California Department of Public Health, and they had already confirmed the radiation at Surfers' Beach wasn't related to the disaster in Japan. If the particles on the beach had been caused by the nuclear meltdown in Fukushima, they would have to be cesium 137, and they were not. An analysis by county and state officials found the radiation was the result of naturally occurring minerals. But this didn't dissuade Jones. Rather, it strengthened his conviction.

"We saw the government say the dust from the collapsed towers on 9/11 was safe," Jones said on his radio show the day before we left. "We saw them come out and say Agent Orange wasn't bad for people. They knew the entire time exactly what this would result in... The globalists don't care, and they aren't going to warn you about what's happening on the West Coast."

The irony was that if anyone could be accused of having ulterior motives, it was Jones. He had a direct financial stake in the fears of radioactive fallout, selling, by then, multiple products explicitly advertised as solutions for radiation exposure.

After checking out of the Half Moon Bay Lodge, we drove ten minutes to Surfers' Beach—the location of the viral YouTube video—where we were scheduled to appear on the live show. But Jones wouldn't be there to interview us like usual. His uncle had passed away and he was attending the funeral that morning, leaving Knight to host in his absence.

Jakari and I stood atop a bluff overlooking the ocean as we joined Knight on the air. Adan carried the Geiger counter down to the beach to test for radiation and found similar numbers to those previously reported—around 160 radioactive particles per minute—while Jakari emphasized the dangers of prolonged exposure. According to the Nuclear Regulatory Commission, a typical natural background radiation level was anywhere from 5 to 60 counts per minute. I felt uncomfortable standing in the middle of numbers five times higher than what was considered safe.

Back at the vehicle, as we packed our things, I received a call from Jones. He had been listening to our interview outside his uncle's funeral and was displeased with Jakari's "lackluster tone." He felt we'd downplayed the situation. "It's about resistance and awakening," he said. "The reason you're there is to do your own research and show what the local and national news refuse to show."

We had only just begun our trip, but at that point there was no evidence to suggest a grand cover-up of anything, though I didn't say this to Jones out of fear of seeming uncooperative.

"They're trying to cover up how serious this is, and we need to force the mainstream media to cover it," he said. "We don't need to be humble and act like we aren't an authority on this, like we aren't professionals. We *are* the professionals, and we need to acknowledge the hierarchy. We are the real, new, emerging media." Jones paused for a moment to catch his breath. "Sure, we aren't physicists, but we have physicists advising us. We need to start being more confident. We are breaking massive worldwide news, and we have to be aggressive. People are looking for leadership."

I had no clue what he meant by "physicists advising us." As far as I knew, there wasn't anyone guiding this trip other than Jones. I understood why he thought Jakari and Knight's interview was uninspired and boring...because it was. Neither of them had the explosive personality Jones had. Knight relied on British humor (mostly puns), and Jakari always seemed a bit nervous.

Jones demanded we go back on the show and be more authoritative. I was certain Jones wasn't asking us to embellish to the point of outright fabrication, but Jakari was uninterested in my opinions. Nevertheless, he agreed to reconnect with Knight on the show. During their second conversation he repeated the same things from the first go-round, defiant and unwilling to mimic Jones's bombastic fearmongering.

After the second interview concluded, and we didn't hear anything else from Jones, we left Half Moon Bay and began our drive north. We stopped at San Francisco Bay, underneath the Golden Gate Bridge, to file a report for the nightly news that evening, rehashing the readings from Surfers' Beach. Waves lapped the stony embankment as Adan climbed down with the Geiger counter and found normal levels of radiation. My eyes drifted up to the iconic vermilion steel, realizing I was standing in the exact spot from which James Stewart spotted Kim Novak in Alfred Hitchcock's film *Vertigo*.

Afterward, we drove north for three hours, taking Geiger counter readings on the beach every half hour. Unlike Half Moon Bay, the radiation readings we took the rest of the day were normal and I posted our reports on YouTube.

The following morning, I received a call from CJ, one of the radio producers.

"Uh, okay, so…" he stammered, sounding nervous. "Jones wanted me to call you guys…and tell you…" Between his pauses I could hear talking in the background, what sounded like Gucciardi, though I couldn't make out specifics. I put the call on speakerphone and motioned for everyone to quiet down.

"Jones is pretty upset and doesn't want you posting any more to the channel—" CJ said before being interrupted by Jones shouting in the distance.

"No one listens," Jones cried out. "It's like being in a battle with piles of dead bodies. Men, women, children. Dead. Everywhere! And I'm saying look. Look! We're next! And you people act like it's nothing!"

"What's his problem?" Jakari asked behind the wheel. I shrugged, overcome by defeat. I knew what was happening. I'd been in the presence of Jones and Gucciardi when someone hadn't done what Jones wanted, and the conversations were never kind. Gucciardi turned to rubber, bouncing all of Jones's aggravations back at him. The purpose was to stir Jones's rage, amplifying his disappointment onto others, ensuring it didn't redirect onto himself. It was a smart tactic, but it never resulted in a fair reckoning for the target, which in this instance was the three of us.

Jones grabbed the phone from CJ, sounding like he was struggling to breathe, every word sharp, piercing, followed by strained, intermittent gulps of air. "I'm trying"—gasp—"to figure out"—gasp—"how I've failed so miserably." He wheezed out a prolonged breath before continuing. "I'm so bad at this, I can't convey how fucked we are as a country, as a species. I mean, you guys understand that it's over, right? If we don't fix this now, humanity is done." Jones transitioned seamlessly from exasperation to condescension, followed by insisting we were "literally fighting psychopathic demon creatures."

Jakari interjected, explaining that we were reporting what we'd found, and despite Jones's claims, the numbers were much lower than anticipated. This didn't go over well. Jones's voice became muffled, and I heard a loud smashing sound through the phone. It was difficult to make out specifics, but he kept repeating, "I can't do this anymore," and "I'm done," until the fissures faded to silence.

"Guys..." CJ said, after Jones had left. "I've never seen him this angry. Please, anything you can do to help us out here."

"What do you expect from us?" Jakari asked, reiterating our predicament as the rest of us sat mute. I was stunned into silence by Jones's outburst, afraid that whatever I said would only make the situation worse.

"I know, I know," CJ said. "I'll tell him you're doing your best, but if you can try and get creative, anything to show you're making an effort, we'd all appreciate it." He sounded desperate, and we reluctantly assured him we'd try to figure something out.

We drove in silence, trying to forget the call that morning and carry on with our responsibilities. We pulled off at multiple beaches—Moonstone, Agate, Redwood Creek—but the radiation levels were all normal. On our drive, Jones called back, this time using his own phone.

"Look," he said to me, breathing heavily, "I know it's not your fault, and I'm not mad at you. But is Jakari mentally ill?"

I looked up at Jakari, sitting in the passenger seat while I was in the back, glad I didn't have the call on speakerphone. "I don't think so," I said, confused.

"I'm serious," Jones continued. "Why would he post videos saying there aren't high radiation levels? It's literally why you're there."

I could've told Jones that even though Jakari was on camera, I was the one posting the videos, and that I thought the plan was to keep the audience up to date with our findings, regardless of what they were. But I didn't want Jones to redirect his anger at me, so I kept my response brief.

"We've had a hard time finding anything above normal outside Surfers' Beach," I said.

"Then you don't fucking show it. Listen, listen, listen," he said repeatedly. This was one of his mantras, a word that he would stammer out as he considered what would follow, incapable of silence. "I want you to search the definition of 'reporter' on your phone. Do it now."

I typed "define reporter" into Google and told Jones when it loaded.

"I want you to read it out loud to Jakari," he said.

"I should just read it to him?" I asked, hesitating.

"Yes," Jones said.

I looked at Jakari, trying to convey with my expression that I was being forced to do this. "Jones wants me to read this to you," I said. "The definition of a reporter is: 'A person who reports, especially one employed to report news or conduct interviews for newspapers or broadcasts.'" I shook my head as Jakari looked angry and defeated.

"Good," Jones said over the phone. "Emphasize the words 'employed to report the news.' I'm paying you guys to report what's really going on, to show what the mainstream media refuses to report. Not to read digital numbers off a machine. That's something a six-year-old could do. People are dying all over Japan, it's a huge cover-up, and now they're trying to hide that it's happening here. These are the same people who used Agent Orange in Vietnam and lied about it. Do you understand?"

I said I understood, though I had no idea what Agent Orange had to do with radiation from Japan or how what Jakari was doing didn't match the definition of being a reporter.

As we crossed California's state line and neared Eugene, Oregon, we learned from Dew that Jones had gotten so angry during our initial conversation that he'd thrown a computer monitor across Gucciardi's office and stormed out of the studio, leaving the crew to rebroadcast a previous episode for the first thirty minutes of the show. (Going to "rebroadcast" was a fail-safe Jones relied on when equipment malfunctioned, or when he was in the throes of a tantrum.)

Jones no longer wanted us on the show unless we found increased radiation, and Dew instructed us to focus on nothing else but getting those results. The consensus back in Austin was that the numbers Jones wanted were real; we just weren't savvy enough to find them.

Our search became one of desperation. Instead of sticking to the coast as Jones first suggested, we got creative. If the beaches weren't filled with mutated dolphins and melting starfish, we would move inland and take a different approach. We stopped at every seafood market we could find to test Pacific-caught crab, sea urchins, and blue fin tuna. We loitered at piers and docks, bartering with fishermen to purchase crabs directly from their boats. I walked the beaches, praying to a God I didn't believe in that we would stumble upon neon sea life, washed ashore, festooned with debris from the Fukushima reactor. At night, my dreams were filled with the sounds of Geiger counters crackling and beeping, signifying what in any other circumstance would be a warning, but to us would be the sweet sound of relief.

I felt angry, defensive, anxious, and fearful, but more than anything, I felt confused. Something inside me was certain Jones wanted us to lie, to fabricate information to sell a product, to make money. But he never explicitly said this. In all our conversations with him, he never said the words "I want you to lie." Instead, Jones had tricked us into examining our abilities, doubting our convictions, and questioning our sanity. If there was a word we needed to define and read aloud at that moment, it wasn't "reporter." It was "gaslight."

When we arrived in Portland, after driving eight hundred miles with little to show for it, we were told Jones wanted us to cancel the last leg of our drive to Seattle. He wanted us to fly back to San Francisco to a military base that had been abandoned years earlier after a radioactive leak. This had nothing to do with Fukushima, but if we could at least get increased numbers on the Geiger counter, he would have something to work with.

The next day we flew from Portland back to San Francisco, rented another car, and drove out to the military base, arriving at an empty guard post and ignoring the NO TRESPASSING signs. We walked through abandoned warehouses with long-empty cages that looked to have, at some point, held animals. As I took video of the San Francisco skyline from a dilapidated pier, the others checked for radiation, swinging the Geiger counter in every direction, hoping to catch static.

I kept watch for security or police to appear and charge us with trespassing—at least if that happened, we could film the interaction and claim the reason they wanted us to leave was because someone, somewhere was trying to cover something up. But no one came, and after an hour we left with nothing but a lingering ghostly feeling and useless footage of an eerily empty military base.

That evening we drove back to Half Moon Bay to interview locals in town about the high radiation levels on Surfers' Beach. As we drove, Jakari plugged his phone into the car stereo. "When I was a kid, my dad used to play this song all the time," he said, scrolling through a playlist. Through the speakers I heard the ocean, followed by the richness of Otis Redding's voice.

> *Sittin' in the mornin' sun,*
> *I'll be sittin' when the evenin' comes.*

Jakari turned the radio up as the dark ocean rolled past the window, the coastline slipping by in the night. "(Sittin' On) The Dock of the Bay" filled the car, and for the first time since we'd landed in California, maybe even since I'd arrived in Austin, I felt completely at ease.

My throat swelled as I sank into a quiet sentimentality in the passenger seat. We were defeated. Morale was low. There was no plan other than to put one proverbial foot in front of the other. To run out the clock. None of our ideas had panned out, and according to Jones's reaction, we each, in our own way, were useless.

That evening, I called Lacey. I barely had time to speak with her while traveling, and I missed her, my dogs, and the comfort of home. Since I was an introvert, sharing hotel rooms and spending long hours cooped up in a vehicle with people I hardly knew was wearing me down.

"We've tried using this stupid fucking Geiger counter everywhere and there's no increased radiation," I said, pacing the hotel parking lot.

"Isn't that a good thing?" she asked.

"No! Jones thinks it's here and there's nothing we can do to convince him otherwise. In fact, the 'convincing him' part is what seems to be making him so angry."

"That does sound frustrating," she offered. "But if you can't find what he wants…then you can't find it. There's nothing you can do about it."

"You don't get it, he won't take 'no' for an answer," I said.

"Then what does he expect you to do?" she asked.

"Honestly, I don't know," I said.

Lacey started laughing. Since arriving in Austin, she had been looking for art teaching jobs, positions in galleries, anything to start her career after college, but nothing proved successful. She had always been resourceful, refusing to be financially dependent, so she took a nanny job, biding her time until something else came along. She was noticing the parallels in our jobs. "I spend my days taking care of a five- and eight-year-old—watching them throw tantrums when they don't get what they want, unable to rationally communicate their emotions, blaming others for their own mistakes. Your job doesn't seem that different."

Over the next few days we drove south, stopping to file hollow reports in San Luis Obispo, Avila Beach, and Playa Del Rey, arriving in San Diego, where we would end our trip. While Jakari continued to repeat the dangers of radiation exposure, focusing on the numbers at Surfers' Beach, he never lied about our findings or made it seem as if we'd discovered anything outside of Half Moon Bay to support Jones's narrative.

On the last day, a few hours before our scheduled flight, we stood on a pier overlooking the San Diego Bay for our final live appearance with Jones, when a fan approached us wearing an Infowars shirt with an image of an assault rifle above the words COME AND TAKE IT. He was nervous and excited to meet Jakari, so Jakari pulled him into frame, live on the air.

The man said he lived five miles away and rushed over when he heard us on the show. Jakari asked him what he thought about the increased radiation at Surfers' Beach in Half Moon Bay. "I wasn't surprised because I knew it was all coming here," the fan said, his voice shaky. "I'm just glad you guys went there because I don't have my own Geiger counter." Jakari told him that even though he likely had nothing to worry about in his area, he still needed to protect himself and asked how he planned to do that. "Well I'm obviously on that nascent iodine," he said. "I've got ten more bottles coming."

I heard Jones cackle in my ear. "We did not plan this," he said on the show. "People are going to say this fella is a conspiracy and we had him pop up out there."

It was hard to believe this person had appeared out of nowhere to do an impromptu ad for the iodine supplement. After all the hand wringing and childish tantrums, after Jakari refused to stretch and exaggerate our findings, Jones was getting the product placement he wanted all along.

In the following years, I would watch Jones luck out time and time again. No matter how much he pushed the line of decency, and often jumped over it with appalling force, things would somehow pan out for him.

"What's amazing is that's how big this show is," Jones said, turning coincidence into evidence of his popularity. "We are the new media. We are the real media."

When we arrived back at the office, Dew was waiting. His hands were clasped behind his back as we stood abreast like toy soldiers. I thought Jones would have been there to give us the verbal beating himself, but he had gone home for the day and left Dew holding the whip. "Next time, trust Jones when he tells you something," Dew said. He sounded exhausted, like he couldn't believe he had to convey something so obvious. "He's not making this stuff up out of thin air. He knows what he's talking about."

Much like our phone conversations with Jones during the trip, Jakari was the only one to speak up. "This doesn't feel right," he said. "It seems like Jones was just using this trip as an opportunity to sell iodine."

Dew's face turned gray; every muscle sharpened to a point. He looked at Jakari as if he'd challenged him to a fight by saying the subtext out loud. "I wouldn't float that theory to Jones," he said in a vaguely threatening way. "And I'll do you the favor of not speaking about this further." Dew told Jakari he should consider everything Jones had done for him—picking him as the winner of the reporter contest, hiring him when he had no prior experience. Dew insisted Jones wasn't motivated by money, that the only reason he was selling supplements in the first place was to grow the operation, build more studios, hire more reporters. "Wouldn't *you* like to make more money?" Dew asked with a smirk, attempting to break the tension.

We laughed nervously. For a reason I couldn't articulate, I felt a sense of shame as I nodded my head up and down.

"Well," Dew said, shifting his gaze from person to person, until he'd met each of our eyeline, "how do you think that happens?"

A few months earlier, that speech might've worked. But by that point, I'd noticed a change in Jones's behavior. He started to pay close attention to the clothes he wore and how he presented himself on and off his show. His bathroom had a small wardrobe closet that was now filled with brand-new tailored suits: striped navy, gray herringbone, black twill. The conversations he had in the War Room became pointed, severe, and more pretentious. He still came into the office angry about the news, but more often he was consumed by one thing: money.

He needed comprehensive audience metrics so he could acquire sponsors on top of the products he was already selling. He expected the crew to create advertising plans each week, so he knew what to promote to increase revenue. He pushed the video editors to start including ads at the end of every video they posted online to drive his audience to buy more products.

When someone forgot to do one of these things, he would storm into the War Room, slam the door behind him, and launch into a tirade, using a phrase I'd never heard him use before. "We're not selling penny stocks!" he'd shout. "We're not some small-time investment firm. We're legitimate. We're big!" It wasn't until he started using that metaphor—penny stocks—that I realized where all of this was coming from.

Before the California trip, Jones had seen *The Wolf of Wall Street*. He was obsessed with it, talking about it in the office constantly and returning to the theater to see it numerous times. The film was based on the life of Jordan Belfort, a stockbroker who engaged in corruption and fraud on Wall Street, exploiting unsuspecting investors with high-risk, low-value investments (penny stocks), leading to his eventual downfall. Somewhere in Jones's mind, he had recast himself as the benevolent version of Belfort—on a mission, yes, but also chasing the same scale, the same bravado.

Not too long ago, I was certain I wanted a role in the important work I believed Jones to be doing. I had uprooted my life to be a part of it, but I could no longer see the plot. Now I wondered if any of this was real, if what we were doing had any impact at all, or if we were just caught in an echo chamber in service of nothing but one man's desire for wealth and infamy.

8

BOW TIE

The California trip had left me lost in an all-consuming uncertainty, convinced that we were to blame for Jones's anger. I needed time to see things clearly, but time wasn't something we were afforded. Back in Austin, the death wheel continued to spin, leaving little room for introspection.

One morning, I arrived to find the hallway walls, office doors, and computer screens plastered with sheets of letter-size paper. Each page displayed the same image: a screenshot of David Knight at the news desk, a circle drawn around his right shoulder with the word "UNACCEPTABLE" scrawled beside it in red marker. The problem wasn't that Knight was dressed unprofessionally; it was that his suit jacket had bunched up, creating a distracting wrinkle in the fabric.

Dew summoned us to the conference room. While wearing closed-toed Velcro sandals with white socks, he announced we would have a wardrobe check before every report. Each reporter was given a thousand dollars to revamp their attire. Dew insisted it was crucial we understood this wasn't "amateur hour." That we were the *real* news, and it was time we started acting like it.

A man I had never seen before walked into the room. He was dressed in a button-down oxford tucked into chinos, looking more like the person who should be handing down sartorial guidelines. Once Dew had sufficiently conveyed Jones's disappointment, he turned to the stranger now seated next to him, gripping a yellow legal pad.

The man stood up and introduced himself as Buckley Hamman, a former creative director from Chicago who had recently moved to Austin, and Jones's cousin. In the early years of Jones's career, from 1996 to 1999, before Mike Hanson, Waco, or Bohemian Grove, Buckley worked as a camera operator for Jones. It was his father, Jones's uncle, who passed away while we were in California, prompting their reconnection and leading to Jones offering him a new role as the operations manager at Infowars.

According to Jones, Buckley's father, William Forrest Hamman, was a helicopter pilot in Vietnam and later worked in logistics for the US government, specifically in Central America during Iran-Contra. While on visits to the Hammans' during summers as a teenager, Jones's uncle regaled him with stories of the 1980s covert operation where the United States secretly sold arms to embargoed Iran in exchange for hostages, then funneled those profits to support the Contras, who were fighting the Sandinista government in Nicaragua. His uncle described a world of power and corruption, where both political parties were controlled, and even told Jones that he was involved in trafficking children out of Central America, framing it as part of a larger pattern of exploitation and conspiracy by government entities. As Jones told it, this was a pivotal moment in his upbringing that helped pave the way for his beliefs.

"I'll be in the office next to Gucciardi," Buckley said, tucking the legal pad under his arm, "so you guys come find me if there's anything I can do for you." He disappeared out the door like he had somewhere to be, leaving me with the impression that he might be the only person at Infowars—aside from Lydia—who had experience in a typical office setting and understood how to act professionally.

A few weeks later, Dew asked if I would stay late to help him set up cameras for an interview the following day. Preparation, especially a day in advance, was unheard of in that office, so I asked Dew who had prompted it. "Tucker Carlson," he said, rolling his eyes. I vaguely knew Carlson as the Waspy, bow tie wearer who occasionally flashed onto my television screen. He had previously hosted shows across the cable news landscape—CNN, PBS, MSNBC, and Fox News—though none had yet achieved the notoriety of *Tucker Carlson Tonight*, which would debut two years later. That show, echoing much of Jones's style, offered pedantic monologues tinged with conspiracy, masking bigotry and racism as populist sentiment. Carlson's tenure at Fox ended in 2023 with his abrupt firing and the cancellation of his show. But he didn't disappear. He doubled down, building an online media empire that carried the Infowars blueprint. Jones himself occasionally appeared as a guest, and together they fed extremist narratives deeper into the bloodstream of American discourse.

At the time, Carlson was the editor in chief of the *Daily Caller*, a conservative news site he cofounded in 2010. Even though I'd never paid much attention to Carlson's work, I was aware of the comments he'd made about Jones in the past. During the Iowa Caucuses in 2012, he was approached on the street by Adam Kokesh—the same "satanic" bearded guy who appeared on Jones's show my first day. Kokesh questioned Carlson about whether he believed 9/11 was an "inside job," which Carlson roundly denounced. When Kokesh brought up Jones, Carlson huffed: "I'll tell you what, I don't want any Alex Jones people in my house," he said, following that up with "Alex Jones freaks me out."

It seemed, a year later, Carlson had changed his mind. He was in Austin on a wild boar hunting trip and wanted to meet Jones in person. According to Dew, Carlson's secretary had sent an email asking if Jones wanted to have lunch. Instead, Jones invited him to the studio to film an interview and be a guest on his radio show.

Jones seemed anxious as he awaited Carlson's arrival. Sunlight filtered through the blinds, casting a hazy glow in the War Room as he paced, sighing, moving in concentric circles. Every few minutes he would change direction, like a caged animal searching for a way out. His eyes kept darting toward the metal cabinet where he kept his vodka hidden, approaching it with determination and hesitation, opening the door and standing there as if deciding whether to take a drink. At one point he even pulled out a white Dixie Cup but ultimately tossed it back into the cabinet and slammed the door shut.

As we waited, the seconds stretched into what felt like hours, amplifying the anticipation. Finally, the War Room door creaked open, revealing Carlson dressed in a slate blue fleece vest. He strode over, his face twisted into an unsettling grin as he smacked on gum and let out a loud, almost maniacal cackle for no apparent reason before shaking Jones's hand. They exchanged pleasantries, but Jones, especially in social situations, was incapable of hiding his emotions. He still held a grudge against Carlson and wanted to make sure he knew it. "I saw the video where you said I freaked you out," he blurted, not angrily but more as though his feelings were hurt.

Carlson's face fell, his jovial expression disappearing. He apologized, playing it off like he was just trying to avoid Kokesh. "This guy put a camera in my face and asked if 9/11 was an inside job. Then he brought you up and wouldn't back off—"

Jones interrupted him, seemingly to abate Carlson's discomfort. "He followed you around and so you made that comment about me, but, I mean, I thought it was entertaining."

"It was pretty funny," Carlson said, playing along.

"Well, it was a long time ago. But I've always admired the work you've done so I really appreciate you coming," Jones said, reaching out to shake his hand for a second time.

"Oh, are you kidding? I was having breakfast with a friend of mine in the media business, and he said you were a great guy, and I should meet you," Tucker said, not revealing the identity of said friend. "So here I am."

The two men were still visibly uncomfortable, though Jones tried to break the tension with a lighthearted jab at Carlson's former fashion choices, referring to him as "Mr. Bow Tie." Carlson didn't seem thrilled with the joke, and as we moved into the studio for their interview, I noticed Jones was sweating profusely. He fumbled his words, messing up the start of the interview, and we kept having to bring him paper towels to wipe his face.

As they settled in, Jones seemed to relax. He expressed his admiration for Carlson, calling him a pioneer in mainstream media who had successfully transitioned to alternative media, and asked if he believed the mainstream news ecosystem was dying.

"There's no question about it," Carlson replied, his tone firm. He recounted the moment he was abruptly fired from MSNBC, a turning point that compelled him to carve his own path online. He and Jones both lamented the decline of major outlets, with Carlson predicting that in a decade, the likes of *NBC Nightly News* and the *Washington Post* would be relics of the past.

The conversation turned to Matt Drudge, the man they both regarded as the original disruptor of the media landscape. "He was willing to give the finger to everyone who had power," Carlson said. "I remember going to a speech he gave at the National Press Club in '98, and he basically said 'You're all going away, you'll all be unemployed. You are obsolete, and I am the future.' People scoffed, and I kind of scoffed because the herd instinct takes over, but I was thinking he was probably right. And it turned out, he was."

For Jones, Drudge was a source of inspiration and a benchmark for success. His website, the Drudge Report, was the first to break the Monica Lewinsky scandal, and had altered the course of American politics. Jones saw Drudge as a kingmaker, capable of propelling fringe figures to the mainstream. His relationship to Drudge was a calculated effort of flattery and strategic alignment, knowing that a Drudge link could boost his numbers and legitimize his content to a broader audience. Jones often tailored his headlines with this in mind, crafting them not just for his own audience, but specifically for Drudge's eye, a kind of subliminal pitch to be plucked from obscurity and placed on the home page of one of the most trafficked news sites in the world.

Carlson laughed, his disbelief evident as he remarked how much he agreed with Jones. Taking advantage of the vulnerability, Jones pivoted the discussion toward 9/11, intent on persuading Carlson that the government had prior knowledge of the attacks, permitting them to unfold. Carlson pushed back firmly, asserting that no credible evidence suggested that anyone in power had allowed the tragedy to occur intentionally. He believed such notions only served to amplify people's fears, and there were already enough genuine concerns to address. Instead, he pointed to immigration policies as a more significant conspiracy, a collaboration between Democrats and Republicans to flood the labor market with low-wage workers, thereby suppressing American wages.

"That's documented," Jones said with certainty.

"Absolutely!" Carlson responded, his voice rising in enthusiasm. "That's a real conspiracy, right in the open." As Carlson launched into a barrage of accusations against both parties, Jones directed his ire toward the left, claiming that the Democratic Party exploited racial politics to engineer demographic shifts, facilitating immigration and extending social services to create a dependable voting base. With no substantiation, he also suggested that Democrats were encouraging illegal voting among immigrants.

Jones then redirected the conversation back to the entire reason he had agreed to meet with Carlson—to drag him even further into his rabbit hole. He pulled out an iPad and presented what he considered conclusive evidence of a government conspiracy behind 9/11. This included footage of 7 World Trade Center's collapse, accompanied by a BBC report that had announced its fall before it occurred. Jones believed this was a deliberate act of misdirection, trying to persuade Carlson that the attacks were a pretext for something more sinister. But Carlson's attention drifted to the woman reporting on-screen.

"Why would she be a correspondent?" Carlson wondered aloud, noting her modest appearance. "Only the British would put a woman like that on TV."

Jones nodded but didn't respond. Carlson sat there quiet, watching the screen as Jones kept looking over to gauge his reaction, but he didn't seem to be swayed, reluctant to fully plunge into the depths of Jones's beliefs when it came to false flags.

The reason 9/11 held such significance for Jones was because he owed his career to the tragedy. There were other highlights from his twenty years on air, but nothing compared to when he, two months before planes hit the World Trade Center, predicted the attacks live on his show. More than any other moment, this was used to give credibility to his beliefs, propping him up as a modern-day Nostradamus.

Even I was blown away when I first saw an edited YouTube video showing Jones calling out Osama bin Laden by name, mentioning the World Trade Center, encouraging his audience to contact the White House and let them know they would be held responsible if an attack occurred. The reality, I discovered years after I quit working for him, was that Jones had twisted the facts. He hadn't predicted anything. Bin Laden was already a known threat. The World Trade Center had already been attacked in 1993. And those words Jones spoke? They weren't even his. Bill Cooper, another conspiracy theorist talk show host, had made similar claims before him.

Jones echoed Cooper's sentiments, and then took credit for them, earning a reputation as the guy who saw it coming. Meanwhile, Cooper never had the chance to claim that title. In November 2001, as authorities arrived at his home to serve an arrest warrant for aggravated assault and tax evasion, Cooper reportedly shot one of the deputies and was killed in the ensuing standoff with the Apache County Sheriff's Department in Arizona.

When the interview wrapped, Carlson turned to Jones with a look of disbelief and excitement. "That was totally fun," he said. "I can't believe I agree with you on everything. What the hell's going on with me, man?" Carlson pulled his assistant aside, and there was an urgency in his voice. "Do you think I'm going crazy? Did you agree with most of that?"

Before his assistant could respond, Jones interjected, "You'll get some heat for it," he said, his tone shifting to one of solidarity. "But that's good. You want heat."

Carlson stepped into the radio studio to appear on the live show, where Jones had multiple assault rifles out on his desk. He was like a kid, putting his favorite toys out to impress a new friend.

"I love the Second Amendment," Carlson said.

"We just like to openly have guns out, to acclimate the socialists to liberty," Jones said, pointing a rifle at the camera, aiming it at the crew in the control room.

"I love that about Texas," Carlson replied.

Before he left the office, the two agreed they would shoot guns together the next time Carlson came to town. Little did they know, this was the beginning of something much larger, a convergence that would shape the very fabric of a post-truth era.

9

INHERITANCE

In the spring of 2014, a year after I started working for Jones, a news story broke about a cattle rancher in Nevada. Cliven Bundy, whose family began running cattle in the Virgin Valley in the early 1800s, was one of the last ranchers left in Clark County. For two decades the government had tried to phase out grazing in Bunkerville—the city where he owned a small farm—to address environmental issues and open it up for development. In 2013, Bundy lost a legal battle with the federal government after refusing to remove his stock from public land. As a form of protest, he stopped paying his grazing fees. This resulted in the United States Bureau of Land Management obtaining court orders directing Bundy to pay over a million dollars in fees and fines. When he continued to refuse compliance, the feds began rounding up his cattle.

"You hear about this story in Nevada?" Dew asked Jones one morning, pointing to an article he had pulled up on his computer. Armed militia groups and anti-government protesters were descending on Bundy Ranch as tensions with federal agents escalated.

"This is big," Jones said, as if he could see the future.

"I agree. Might be good to get someone out there." I could hear the squeak of Dew's chair and could see out of my periphery he was looking in my direction. "Josh..." he said when I failed to acknowledge him.

"What's up?" I said, trying to sound casual as if I hadn't been listening to their conversation.

"Nevada—" Dew said before Jones cut him off.

"These feds, the Bureau of Land Management, they're thugs. They're mercenaries. They have snipers, armored vehicles. They're literally trained that anybody who wears a cowboy hat and a work shirt is the enemy."

"I think Knight would be good for this," Dew said.

"Get Josh and Knight on a plane," Jones said. "We'll go with a skeleton crew on this one so they can rove with the crowd. My gut tells me this is probably going to end in bloodshed."

A sinking feeling, amplified by Jones's predictions of carnage, hit me and I mentioned that it sounded dangerous.

Jones stopped his manic pacing and looked over at me. "You don't want to go?"

Maybe it was his genial tone, or the fact that he'd asked me in the first place, but for some reason I answered honestly, admitting I preferred to sit this one out.

"This story will be everywhere," he erupted, stomping over to my side of the room. "No one in the media will cover it properly. Red-blooded Americans fighting the feds. They'll spin it like they're literally Al-Qaeda terrorists on the American frontier." He was incredulous, shocked that I didn't recognize the gravity of the situation, sickened that I didn't want to plant myself in the middle of it. He walked over to Dew, turning back to me once he'd reached the other end of the room. "Don't you want to be famous?" he asked.

His question caught me off guard. What did being famous have to do with anything? Before I could gather my thoughts, he began shouting, "Don't you want to be famous!?" He said it repeatedly, aggressively flailing his arms until I was too confused to think straight. Who said I wanted to be famous? That wasn't the reason I'd taken the job. If anyone craved fame, it was Jones, so why wasn't he going himself? Of course, I didn't say any of this out loud. The last thing I wanted was to provoke Jones when he was angry. So after he stormed out of the room, and without discussing it further, I agreed to go.

David Knight and I traveled to Nevada, landing in Las Vegas and driving an hour out to the town of Bunkerville. The flickering neon lights disappeared behind us as we entered the vast, arid desert.

Hovering in the sky, above the staging area, was a large hand-painted banner reading LIBERTY, FREEDOM, FOR GOD WE STAND. There were multiple recreational vehicles parked in a dusty turnoff by the highway and some demonstrators camped in tents. We milled around the area, shooting a quick interview with Ammon Bundy, Cliven's son, and spotting a few protesters in Infowars T-shirts before walking down the hill to Bundy's house. The door was open, and two militiamen stood out front, gripping assault rifles. A man wearing an American flag bandanna stepped out of the house.

"Glad you guys could make it out," he said, shaking Knight's hand and speaking like he knew us. He offered to act as an intermediary between us and Bundy, but Knight declined.

"He knows we're coming, but thanks for the offer."

The man ignored Knight. "Wait here and I'll check if Bundy is still available to speak with you. If so, I'll escort him out when he's ready."

The bandanna man turned back to the house, and Knight called Jones. "Pete Santilli is here, acting like he brokered this conversation with us." Jones said something to Knight that I couldn't hear and after a minute he hung up. "It's what I thought," Knight said, speaking softly so the militiamen couldn't hear us. "Santilli is trying to run the show here, likely because he's a fed."

Santilli had a radio show with a right-wing, conspiratorial bent, like Jones. For some reason, Jones believed Santilli was a covert agent collaborating with the FBI and advised us to keep our distance from him.

"Hey, guys," a voice behind us said. It was Santilli, standing in the doorway. "Let's do a quick pre-interview so I can make sure Bundy knows what you're planning to cover."

Knight politely said we wouldn't be doing that and walked off. I followed behind as Santilli disappeared back into the house. A few minutes later, Cliven Bundy stepped out. He was much shorter and older than I imagined. I got the sense that Bundy wasn't interested in any political movement, not yet at least. He seemed to have one thing in mind: his cattle. But Jones and other media outlets were looking to appropriate the family's fight against the federal government and twist it into something they could use.

The next morning, a few hundred protesters gathered at a stage where Bundy and his family would address the crowd, many of them armed with handguns holstered on their belts and rifles slung over their shoulders. Ranchers, militias, members of the Oath Keepers, and other anti-government extremists from across the country rallied in Bundy's defense. When Bundy arrived surrounded by militiamen, he claimed his people were ready to take the country back. The sheriff was standing onstage when Bundy made his demands. He told the sheriff to disarm the Park Service and deliver their weapons to him, bulldoze the ticket kiosks at the entrances to National Parks, and free his cattle from the Bureau of Land Management. To top it all off, he wanted his request met within an hour. It was clear that Bundy thought this was a classic Western and he was John Wayne.

The sheriff tried to reason with Bundy, but it didn't work. There was no convincing a man who believed he was ordained by God and frontier justice. With nothing left to say, the sheriff stepped down from the stage and disappeared. The crowd lingered, waiting to see what would happen next. As I stood behind the camera, feeling the anticipation of the moment, a deep sound like thunder echoed behind me. I turned to see dozens of cowboys on horseback cresting a hill, the leader proudly waving an American flag. The crowd roared.

Bundy seized the moment, instructing protesters and the horse-mounted wranglers to travel over to the preserve where the cattle were corralled and block off the highway. He wanted the livestock freed, allowed to graze on what he claimed was his land, and he asked his supporters to make this happen by force if necessary. Everyone dispersed to their vehicles. A feeling of dread came over me as I realized these people weren't just there to protest. They were looking for a showdown with the federal government.

This was exactly why Jones had sent us there, to capture the flashpoint, the spectacle. I turned to Knight, told him to wait, and sprinted off to retrieve the rental car.

We arrived just as the protesters barricaded the highway, stalling traffic for miles in both directions. Under the overpass was a large cattle gate, keeping Bundy's livestock from returning to the land they'd previously grazed on. On one side were cowboys on horseback and armed militia members; on the other side were armed state police, federal rangers, and snipers. Civilian protesters were also positioned on the overpass with rifles aimed at the officers below. "You're gonna have to arrest us all or shoot us all," a protester shouted. I readied myself, cautious of those around me, waiting for the crack of gunfire and scanning the area, deciding where I would take cover.

After a tense standoff, one of the federal agents turned away from the gate and rejoined the armed men gathered behind him. One by one, they lowered their rifles, signaling defeat. Ryan Bundy, another of Cliven's sons, jumped onto the cattle gate and shouted, "The West has now been won!" The crowd cheered. Ammon seized the moment, cutting down the sign that marked the area as restricted and holding it high for all to see. The federal government had backed down, no one was arrested or hurt, and it wasn't long before the cattle came ambling through the wash, back into the Bundy's possession.

That afternoon, Jones called, insisting I get a video out immediately. He mentioned the movie *Open Range*, starring Kevin Costner and Robert Duvall, drawing parallels between the film and the current situation, blurring the lines between fiction and reality. I recognized the similarities—cattlemen standing up to corrupt authority and fighting for their rights. But the way Jones talked, it was as if he believed we were actually living in the movie.

That night, I edited footage of the confrontation, uploading it to Jones's YouTube channel with the headline HISTORIC! FEDS FORCED TO SURRENDER TO AMERICAN CITIZENS. By the next morning, it had already garnered a million views.

Returning from the windswept deserts of Nevada, I felt a personal sense of accomplishment. Our willingness to take risks and get in the middle of the confrontation had paid off. The video I'd posted had surpassed a million views, prompting outlets like Vice News to ask for permission to use our footage. Jones, elated with the attention our video was getting, gave me a significant bonus check and sang my praises to the other crew members. My reluctance to visit Bundy Ranch had been reframed as bravery, and I began to acclimate to those unfamiliar feelings of pride, achievement, and self-esteem.

Still, thoughts of California—the lies, the manipulation—remained. I had shared everything that happened on the West Coast with Lacey, and she wouldn't let me forget it. Her skepticism surfaced when I recounted my days, complained about the inconvenience of travel, the stress of managing Jones's personality. But anytime she questioned his decency, or his veracity, I grew defensive, insisting that what happened in California—or even day-to-day in Austin—was far more complicated.

The family she worked for were respected lawyers in Austin: one a professor at the University of Texas, the other an intellectual property attorney for Apple. I wondered what they thought of me, of Jones, of the reason we moved to Texas.

"Have they said anything?" I asked one evening.

"What do you mean?" she said.

"Do they think I'm some crazy conspiracy theorist?"

"They don't really know what you do," she said.

"Why not?"

"I just haven't told them," she said.

"They weren't curious why you moved halfway across the country?" I asked.

"Yes." She sounded brusque and impatient. "I mentioned you got a job for a news company here."

I felt my anger rising. I desperately clung to the pride of being associated with Jones. When I noticed it slipping through my fingers, I tried to grab it quickly, afraid that if I didn't, I'd be forced into questioning the value of my work, something I wasn't ready to face.

"There's not some ulterior motive here," she said, "I just didn't go into specifics."

"It's one thing to work for some Channel 5 network affiliate, but I got a job with one of the biggest alternative news sites in the world," I said.

"Good god, okay!" Lacey shot back. "If it's that important, I'll tell them."

The truth was, the people she worked for had no clue who Alex Jones was. And Lacey didn't yet understand enough about my job to be embarrassed by it. I was picking a fight without realizing it. The confidence I felt at work didn't hold when I stepped into the conventional routines of home, and it didn't make sense. Everyday life stood in sharp contrast to the disparate urgency I'd felt with Jones, where he led us to believe that the world itself might crumble if we faltered, that the fate of humanity hinged on our ability to bend reality to his will.

I don't remember when I first heard about Michael Brown's death, or the specific circumstances that led to my standing between riot police and protesters in Ferguson, Missouri. Five months had passed since Bundy Ranch, though in a strange reversal of the time warp, it felt like only five days. One minute, we were back from Nevada, and the next, I was standing in a dark street, watching the red dot from a police officer's rifle dance on the chest of a Black man holding his arms to the sky.

Two days earlier, protesters had burned down the QuikTrip where Brown was last seen alive, furious over his unjust killing. Jones had sent me with Jakari and Joe Biggs—a retired United States Army staff sergeant whom Jones had hired as a reporter shortly after we'd returned from Bundy Ranch—when the city of Missouri imposed a curfew, fearing more unrest.

Jones made documentaries on America's police state. It was a fundamental part of his platform. He railed against the militarization of police, the heavy-handed tactics used against protesters, framing the events in Ferguson as a reflection of rising tensions between citizens and law enforcement. Though he always avoided the larger systemic issue of race.

We parked outside a liquor store that was closed for the night and walked toward the crowd gathered by the burned-down gas station. The street was blocked off. We stepped through a crowd of protesters until we reached two mine-resistant ambush-protected (MRAP) vehicles and a row of officers wearing thick black helmets, holding riot shields.

Jakari and Biggs began asking the protesters to recount what had happened that evening as I filmed. It was clear, at least among the three of us, whose side we were on. Other reporters hovered along the edges of the crowd, gas masks dangling at their sides. We mocked their goggles, helmets, and vests with the letters P.R.E.S.S. in glistening white. Their gear was protective, but it also signaled to the police that they were covering the protest and not a part of it. We, on the other hand, *were* a part of it (at least that's what I'd convinced myself). Standing alongside the protesters, we scowled at police and their pathetic display of power.

A loudspeaker blared from atop one of the tanks. "You are unlawfully assembled, and you will be subject to arrest." There were a few more warnings from the police to disperse, all ignored by the crowd.

And then the explosions began.

Tiny crystals of light ricocheted in the air, followed by loud blasts. Everyone around me began to run. *Bang! Bang! Pop!* Jakari darted to the right. Biggs vanished through a cloud of smoke to the left. In the chaos, I ran back down West Florrisant Avenue, toward our parked car. Flash-bangs lit up the surrounding area. Through the fog, I saw a protester pick up a billowing smoke bomb and hurl it back at the police, leaving a vapor trail like a shooting star.

"I've been shot!" I heard Biggs shout in the distance. I spun around and saw the police advancing in my direction. Biggs had accidentally run toward them, and they'd shot him. My eyes began to burn like they'd been doused in gasoline and lit on fire. My throat closed. It felt like someone was grabbing hold of my guts and wrenching them with all their might. As the air turned red, I realized the canisters being fired at us weren't smoke bombs; they were tear gas.

I doubled over and threw up on the sidewalk. Stumbling toward a car, I begged a pair of onlookers for water. A woman handed me a cup of watered-down Coke, which I splashed onto my face, grumbling my appreciation as best I could. Maybe the press vests and gas masks weren't so cowardly after all, I thought, wiping vomit from my mouth.

In a clearing of smoke, I spotted Jakari on the sidewalk across the street, shouting at a protester attempting to set a pile of trash on fire. "Bro. Bro. Stop! What are you doing?" Jakari said as a second protester ran over and kicked the fire out. I tried to get his attention, but my throat was still swollen shut from the chemicals in the air and I couldn't speak above a whisper. Just as I began to move in his direction, he launched himself over a chain-link fence into someone's backyard.

It wasn't until I looked behind me that I realized why Jakari had taken off—the line of police were now running at full speed in our direction. Even if I made it across the street in time, there was no way I would've been able to climb the fence, so I ran down a cross street, into another neighborhood.

The houses were all built close together with fences in between and I had nowhere to hide, afraid to cross through anyone's property. (I didn't know the norms in Missouri, but where I grew up there was a good chance you'd be shot sneaking through someone's yard, especially with all the chaos happening close by.) The neighborhood was a respite until the red cloud drifted over the homes and I felt the burning in my throat and eyes return.

I spotted a car with its lights on, parked in the middle of the road. Inside was a woman, late twenties, scrolling through her phone. I approached slowly, trying not to alarm her. She rolled the window down. There was a notepad in her lap and a camera next to it. "Sorry to bother you, but I ran into this neighborhood to get away from the cops," I said, trying to speak through what felt like a bad case of strep throat. "I'm with the media." She unlocked the door and I fell into the passenger seat, thanking her between fiery coughs.

Her name was Alice Speri, a journalist working for Vice News. Before she had a chance to ask what media outlet I was affiliated with, she received a call from her producer. As they spoke, I sat in the passenger seat wiping the fluids from my face. She held the phone to her ear, but it was quiet enough that I could hear the man's voice instructing her to safely find a way out of the area and report back when she did. He asked if she was alone, and she said that another reporter had gotten in her car. "Who are you with?" she said, and I told her. "He's with, uh, Infowars," she repeated to her producer, the name sounding like a punch line.

"Get away from him," her producer said, his voice low and severe. "He could be dangerous." She glanced over at me, and I turned toward the window, trying to pretend I hadn't heard him. I wanted to remind him that they'd had no issue being associated with us when they called to ask for our footage from Bundy Ranch, but I kept quiet.

"I think it's fine," Alice said, laughing it off. They spoke for another minute before hanging up. "Sorry about that," she said, assuming I'd heard her producer's warning. "Don't worry, I won't kick you out."

We eventually made it out of the neighborhood, and she dropped me off with Biggs and Jakari a few blocks away. Biggs lifted his shirt to show me the softball-size welt on his stomach, the outer ring inflamed and already turning purple. "I got shot," he said with a grin. He and Jakari were elated to have been in the melee, still riding high from the adrenaline of the incident. But I was shaky and despondent, trying to think of an excuse to fly back to Austin that night.

The next day we searched for gas masks, eye protection, anything to prepare for another night. But all we could find were painter's masks and safety goggles from Home Depot. That morning I'd woken up with swollen eyes and a sore throat, but Biggs—who was shot with a rubber bullet at point-blank range—had it much worse. His wound bulged twice as big as the night before, the color now deep purple like an eggplant. He wore his injury like a badge of honor.

We stopped for pizza in downtown Saint Louis, near our hotel. As we ate, Biggs talked about his time in the service as an Army staff sergeant, and his deployment to Iraq and Afghanistan. Potentially dangerous trips like the one in Ferguson were one of the reasons he accepted the job offer from Jones. It was an opportunity to relive his glory days.

"This is the first time I've felt that rush of combat since leaving the military," Biggs said, overjoyed.

"You miss it?" I asked.

"Oh yeah, those guys were my family... and then it's just over." He stared down into his beer before taking a long drink. "I mean, don't get me wrong, there are parts I don't miss. I killed someone my very first day in Iraq. I knew at some point it would happen but had no idea it would be in the first twenty-four hours."

I pushed my plate away, no longer interested in food.

"I was eighteen years old," Biggs continued. "We were doing what's called a left seat, right seat ride. I'm driving and the guy next to me says, 'I'm a week away from going home, I got a wife and two kids, so listen to what I say. If I tell you to speed up or slow down, then do it. If you don't, I'll punch you in the face.'"

Jakari and I sat there silently. The restaurant was empty other than the three of us.

"We're getting ready to drive through this town called Ashraf," Biggs said, "and he tells me they've been known to stop you on the road while these fuckers stationed in the hills ambush you with RPGs. I'm thinking, easy enough, I just won't stop. Well, we're driving through this town and my heart is pounding; I'm just hoping nothing happens because I'm not fucking ready for this yet. Next thing I know, this guy steps in front of our vehicle and stops. I put the brakes on instinctively, and before I know it, I catch a right hook to the face. I slam on the gas, and... I can still remember the feeling of that guy's body under the wheels."

I was listening closely, but it took a second before I realized what he'd said. A body, under the wheels. "Jesus Christ."

"Was he a civilian?" Jakari asked.

"I don't know," Biggs said quickly, as if he didn't want to discuss that aspect of the story. "Three or four days I didn't talk to anybody. I was pissed off at that guy for making me do it, but I just had to tell myself that if I had stopped, then we'd be writing letters to mothers about how their sons were dead because I didn't do what I was supposed to do. I just learned to deal with it. That's what you have to do in the military, as sick and messed up as it is, you have to rationalize it. You have to bite the bullet, suck it up, and move on."

I didn't know what to say. Biggs wasn't the sort of person who welcomed condolences, but even if he was, I wasn't sure who to even offer them to—the man who Biggs had killed, who possibly had a family and could have walked in front of the tank for a million reasons other than to cause him or the soldier in the passenger seat harm, or Biggs, who believed this man was simply a casualty of war. Jakari sat there shaking his head, staring up at the ceiling. "I don't think I could do that," he said.

"You might think that," Biggs said, shifting in his chair, "but sometimes you don't really have a choice."

The following day, as we waited for nightfall to see how the cops reacted to protesters refusing curfew again, it felt more like a celebration than an uprising. The people of Ferguson, and the Black community at large in America, had lived as the prime targets of police brutality and systemic oppression for their entire lives. The elation in the air seemed to come from standing up to the constant onslaught and the attention they were bringing to the country after ignoring and therefore contributing to their plight for so long. Cars loaded down with passengers whipped and spun out through the streets, signaling a refusal to comply with anyone's rules but their own.

I thought back to the beaming faces of the cowboys at Bundy Ranch, triumphant after their standoff with federal agents. At the time, I saw a kind of symmetry between that moment and the protests in Ferguson, as if both were exemplary of people standing up to power. It took me longer than I'd like to admit to understand how fundamentally different those victories were. One was rooted in entitlement disguised as revolution, and the other in survival born of oppression. And the fact that I'd once placed them on the same plane revealed more about my own blind spots and privilege than about the events themselves.

Earlier that morning we returned to the destroyed QuikTrip to appear on Jones's show. Having witnessed the police attack the night before, he asked me to join him on air and recount my experience. Frazzled but eager to align with Jones, I parroted his narrative, launching into a vehement condemnation of the Missouri police and their abuse of power. Through Jones's lens of the "police state," this wasn't about civil rights. It was about control. During his clash with Dallas police on the anniversary of JFK's assassination, he had evoked Martin Luther King Jr., drawing comparisons between the struggles of Black Americans and his own run-ins with authority, as if both were equally oppressive.

It wasn't until Jakari attempted to interview the legendary comedian Dick Gregory that I realized we weren't entirely on the side of the protesters. Gregory had been a guest on Jones's show three times, most recently four months earlier. When we spotted him, Jakari approached and asked if he would be willing to speak with us. Gregory looked him up and down, spotting the Infowars flag on the microphone, and reluctantly agreed.

"Sir, what do you think about paramilitary forces being used against American citizens?" Jakari said.

"No!" Gregory said, staring up at Jakari in anger. "Being used on *Black* citizens!" The way he said "Black" sounded like he was spitting at us, fed up with Jones criticizing the militarization of police but refusing to acknowledge race.

The crowd nearby began to stir as a figure moved through them, heading in our direction. As the people parted, we saw that it was Jesse Jackson, leading a march. We followed behind as he led us down the street to the location where Michael Brown had been killed. It was at the end of a neighborhood in a cul-de-sac; children were standing on the sidewalk as families congregated on their porches and front doors, watching over a hundred people march to the spot where they had, six days earlier, heard the gunshots and seen the red and blue lights flashing through their windows, creating a dreadful show on their bedroom walls while a man lost his life on the street outside.

After the march, we returned to the QuikTrip, where dozens of cops had arrived, clinging to the sides of military tanks in full riot gear, carrying semi-automatic rifles, ready for another night of chaos. After watching the Bureau of Land Management back down against armed demonstrators at Bundy Ranch, I thought the police would be more lenient on the following night of Ferguson, especially with so much media attention and the arrival of high-profile figures. But there was one major difference between the people at Bundy Ranch and those in Ferguson.

The police moved swiftly, like bullies on a rampage. Bursts of light exploded in the sky; the air filled with smoldering fumes. I heard gunshots in the distance, unsure which side they were coming from. By the time the smoke cleared, Missouri had declared a state of emergency and the National Guard were being deployed to assist the police. When I heard there would be military on the streets, I decided I had to go.

Three months later, the grand jury was set to announce the verdict for Darren Wilson—the officer who fatally shot unarmed teenager

Michael Brown. I was still jumpy from the last time I'd been there and asked Dew if there was any way I could get out of it. In most cases this would've caused an explosive response from Jones, but Carlos was intrigued and volunteered to go in my place before word got back to him.

On the night of the verdict, Jones scheduled a live broadcast with Jakari and Biggs on the ground. The grand jury chose not to indict Wilson, and the peaceful protests from earlier in the day turned violent. At least a dozen buildings and several police cars were set on fire, officers were pelted with rocks and batteries, and reports of gunfire forced some Saint Louis–bound flights to be diverted. Jakari and Biggs reported amid the backlash as I sat on the other end of production, helping the crew in the control room. It was there I noticed Jones's narrative begin to shift. When we were originally in Ferguson, he claimed that the office had received emails from racist people saying that Infowars shouldn't side with Black protesters.

"It's like Katrina when they confiscated guns," Jones said, responding to the supposed callers. "They used the poor people as an excuse for martial law, then went into the high-and-dry areas, five-million-dollar houses, took all the guns, and handcuffed rich people. So all of you racist white people who are sending us this racist crap...you're idiots! They're going to come into your house and take you to a FEMA camp and rape your wives. Do you understand, you stupid racist dumbasses?!"

For Jones, everything was binary, black and white; every person, event, and moment of cultural significance was pushed into one of two categories: good or bad. The protesters were "good" the first go-round, but by the second trip to Ferguson, as demonstrators rioted after the officer was acquitted, Jones turned on them. He used the destruction as an informational cudgel to discount everything the protests stood for, accusing Black people of only wanting to loot and burn down businesses when their voices weren't heard, not acknowledging it was one of the only recourses they had left. At the Bundy standoff, as the cowboys pointed their guns at police, took back the cattle, and destroyed the NO TRESPASSING sign, Jones saw this as a triumph.

Rioting was the foundation of Jones's belief system. When it came to tar and feathering British tax collectors in the 1700s, or American colonialists boarding three ships in the Boston Harbor and destroying property in defiance against the Tea Act, he was fully on board. But his narrative was shifting, casting the protesters in Ferguson, and the burgeoning Black Lives Matter movement, as the enemy. Jones's perspective, our perspective, had a clear bias, one that was, without a doubt, black and white.

10

MADMAN

I knew something was wrong when I heard him breathing heavily, more so than usual, moving quickly down the hallway toward my desk.

As I stared out the office window, bracing for Jones's arrival, the first vehicle appeared in the parking lot. Whoever was behind the wheel drove fast, erratic, like they were in a hurry to arrive somewhere they hadn't been invited. Close behind was an SUV, followed by a van wrapped in an American flag decal. For a moment I forgot Jones was approaching until I heard his voice behind me. "We're under attack." His tone had a burr of excitement that didn't match the words. Seeing the American flag on the van outside, I assumed they were fans of Jones's show who had somehow discovered the location of his office. Even though I tried to hide it, Jones was perceptive enough in that moment to notice my skepticism.

"See for yourself," he said, pointing out the window.

As I turned back to face the parking lot, a group of men in military fatigues jumped out of one of the vehicles and approached the office door. A few tried to peek inside as others banged with closed fists on the blacked-out glass. From the side of the building more people appeared, including a bald man wearing a red-and-yellow Italian soccer jersey. He had a megaphone strapped to his shoulder. As this scene played outside, Jones rummaged through the metal cabinet behind me, pulling out one of his usual white Dixie Cups and filling it with vodka.

"I know you're in there, Alex," the man outside said into the megaphone. "I just want to talk to you. Come on out so we can have a conversation."

Jones whispered for me and Dew to step away from the door. At first, I didn't recognize the man outside, but as I peered closer from around the corner, I realized it was Pete Santilli, the meddler who had been embedded with Cliven Bundy in Nevada. Santilli was at the helm of a caravan heading to the Southern border, a calculated move designed to fan the flames of anxiety over migrants crossing into America. Frustrated by Jones's silence and lack of support, he stood outside, his voice ringing out with urgency. "All right," he said, his words echoing through the parking lot. "I just saw someone in there, so I know you can hear me. Send Alex out. I just want to talk."

We heard a commotion coming from the other side of the building and darted past the door, moving swiftly down the hallway. By this time, many of the Infowars employees had congregated in the warehouse to see what was going on. Through the tinted glass of our loading bay door for delivery trucks, I saw more people in the back alley. We were surrounded. A metallic noise in the far corner of the room, what sounded like heavy metal scraping on hinges, caught my attention. The door of Jones's gun safe was open.

Cliff, an old high school friend of Jones's, was visiting the office that day, and I watched as he and Dalton removed two Barrett M82 sniper rifles from the safe. They lowered the bipod stands on each rifle and began loading the high-capacity magazines with .50 caliber rounds they pulled from heavy-gauge steel ammunition boxes. Jones paced back and forth like a pseudo war general. He claimed to have spotted one of the men outside carrying a gun. Dalton and Cliff propped the rifles on a long table in the warehouse and aimed them through the window at the strangers' heads. "If any of them break through the glass," Jones said, gulping down the rest of his drink, "shoot them."

This wasn't the first time I feared someone might be gunned down at work.

A week earlier, I sat in the back of Dalton's truck, surrounded by firearms as we made our way to a private ranch owned by Cliff.

We hit the road early that morning, the sun creeping over sand-colored pastures dotted with grazing cattle, heading to the same place where we'd taken John McAfee a year earlier. Upon arrival, Cliff walked me through basic range safety and showed me how to load and shoot some of the guns. I had little experience with firearms despite growing up in a small Southern town immersed in that culture. My father had a handgun for protection, but I had never shown much interest. Just then, I spotted Jones's white Ford Raptor cresting a steep ravine in the distance. He stepped out of his truck and stumbled toward us.

"You fellas ready to blow some shit up?" Jones asked, placing his hand on my shoulder. I could smell liquor on his breath.

His objective for the day was to make a click-bait video of explosions and women wielding guns. Since McAdoo was the lone on-air woman at Infowars, he forced her to join us. She didn't have much experience with firearms and her discomfort was palpable. Cliff tried to show her the ropes, but Jones grew impatient. "It's not rocket science, Lee Ann. Just grab hold of the thing and pull the trigger." He nudged me, chuckling like a teenage boy.

This, as far as I could tell, was how Jones acted around women—relying on sexual innuendo and treating them like objects for amusement. To be fair, he didn't treat the average man much better, but at least there was a modicum of respect. McAdoo fired an AR-15 at bowling pins we'd set up a few yards away. Despite her lack of experience, she was a good shot, missing the target only a few times.

It was hot outside and I huddled underneath a small tent with Dalton, Cliff, and Dew, loading spent magazines. McAdoo stood over by the cooler, and Jones kicked dust a few feet away, wielding an AR-15.

We were chatting, pressing bullets into the spring-loaded magazines, when suddenly there was a loud shattering sound. Instinctively, we dropped low, peering around to see what had happened. A patch of dirt exploded into the air between me and McAdoo, and it took a moment for my mind to catch up with the reality of what had just happened.

Jones had fired the gun at us.

The gunshot rang out, echoing through the open fields surrounding us. "Whoops," Jones said, pulling back the charging handle to check the gun's chamber. We had taken the magazines out of the guns, but Jones had failed to check if a bullet was chambered and didn't have the safety on—two of the most basic safety precautions Cliff had taught me, and tried to teach McAdoo before Jones grew impatient and interrupted him.

There was a moment of silence as we all took in what had happened. "Fuck," Dalton mouthed, glancing over at a wide-eyed Cliff.

McAdoo broke the silence. "What the hell was that?" she shouted.

"Will someone tell her it was a joke?" Jones said. He sounded bored.

"It's not funny," McAdoo said.

"Well, I apologize," Jones replied, rolling his eyes. "But if I wanted to kill someone, I could." His voice grew quiet. "It's not like I haven't done it before…"

We all looked at one another, confused.

"I'm kidding," he interjected with a sly grin.

In the face of McAdoo's righteous indignation, Jones didn't respond with anger but insisted he'd fired the gun in our direction on purpose, still trying to brush it off as a joke, like that somehow made it better. As she stood in shock, the others finally spoke up, running like mythical lemmings off a cliff to his defense. It was humiliating to watch them, aware of how insane Jones's actions were, treat McAdoo like she was unhinged and humorless. Although I cringed, I remained silent; not just among the cowards, but very much a part of them.

As far as I could tell, Jones had no real friends in his life who weren't beholden to him financially, and no relationships where the power dynamic wasn't in his favor. When he made mistakes, there was always someone there, if not many, to enable him.

Almost as quickly as the bullet was fired, the moment vanished. McAdoo calmed down, and no one brought it up again. We resumed loading magazines, cracked open a few more beers, filled an old television with Tannerite, and blew it up.

In the office a week later, Jones continued pacing back and forth in the warehouse, pretending to be in a war movie while Buckley was in the hallway, calling the police. Dalton and Cliff kept the rifles aimed outside, but no one approached the windows again. Before long, two officers arrived in the parking lot and spoke to Santilli. Santilli shouted at the building, asserting the police had deemed him and his crowd peaceful and lawful, emphasizing that they were not armed. "They came here to save you from someone with an iPad and a bullhorn," he said, mocking Jones.

We were all gathered on the other side of the windows, Jones acting like he knew all along they weren't armed, laughing, ignoring the fact that only minutes earlier there were sniper rifles trained on the people outside, people who shared many of the same conspiratorial beliefs as he did.

"You're a conspiracy theorist!" Santilli shouted into the megaphone. "You know who I am. I'm the guy you've been telling everyone is an FBI informant behind my back. I'm not an FBI informant, I'm a public informant. And you're a shill! Your dad is a dentist who did specialty work for the CIA. What's up with that? Alex, I came here to approach you and shake your hand, but you're too much of a pussy to come to the door."

The fact that neither of the shock jock conspiracy theorists recognized the irony of calling one another conspiracy theorists was not lost on me.

I walked back to my desk in a daze as everyone resumed their work. With each extreme encounter, we all grew more desensitized to the ridiculousness, compartmentalizing just how close we'd come to disaster. If Santilli had arrived just a few hours earlier or later and run into Jones in the parking lot, there's no telling what would have happened.

The weight of danger had become a familiar presence, and it was only compounded a few weeks later when another threat revealed itself. Austin's chief of police, Art Acevado, told Jones that his team had become aware of a man posting comments online speculating about the location of the Infowars offices and threatening to drive from out of state to kill Jones and his employees. Acevado said they had been keeping tabs on this unknown man and discovered, through his posts, that he'd figured out our address, rented a car, and was making his way to Austin. They stopped him somewhere along the outskirts of town, driving with a trunk full of firearms.

He urged Jones to take this man seriously, warning this wasn't the first threat, but Jones waved his caution away like an inconvenience. Yet as soon as Acevado left, Jones's poise evaporated and was replaced by a feverish energy. He moved into the War Room with Dew and me. "We're all in danger," he said, his voice urgent. "This isn't a game and we all better get deadly serious." Being a part of Infowars was not just a temporary sacrifice, but an irrevocable black mark on all of us, and according to Jones, working alongside him would forever stain our résumés and limit our prospects. "That's why we're all fighting to change the world," he said. "Otherwise, we won't be able to live in it." Dew looked reinvigorated by this pep talk. But I was horrified, my stomach in knots. It finally dawned on me: This wasn't just a job; it was a trap.

11

THE CROSSING

In 2014, Jones became fixated on the Southern border. All he had to do was say the buzzwords—illegal aliens, border crisis, invasion—and his listeners reacted. They got scared, angry, and started to pay closer attention to him, tuning into his show more frequently, and spending more money at his online store.

But this fixation wasn't just about attention or money. It ran much deeper than that. Jones was consumed by the idea of manifest destiny; he believed America was his birthright and he didn't want outsiders to redefine it. At his core, Jones identified with being an American, a Texan, a white man living in a country ruled by those who looked like him, and he believed he was entitled to everything America had to offer. He didn't want outsiders, those born into their own deserved fates, to spoil it. For people like him, America had to look and feel a certain way, and he saw it as his responsibility to maintain that.

Though I would have denied it at the time, I, too, had the same callous, self-serving ignorance deep down inside me. I had always insisted I was free of the prejudices that permeated my surroundings, believing I was an exception, an enlightened product of my environment. It was easier to think I was different from the people I'd grown up around, that I had somehow absorbed the culture without inheriting its biases. But that wasn't true. I benefited from the same systems, adopted the same assumptions, and stayed quiet when they served me. Jones had his justifications—border panic, election conspiracies, American exceptionalism. Mine were simpler: self-preservation, ambition, and the quiet comfort of going along. While there were differences, it didn't matter all that much when the outcome was the same.

If I had known where this was going, the irrevocable harm caused by our actions, I would've quit right then and there. That's what I tell myself anyway.

It began at Lackland Air Force Base in San Antonio. Multiple mainstream media outlets had reported an influx of unaccompanied children coming through the Southern border. Many of their families had sent them as a last-ditch effort of protection from violence in their home countries, hoping that since they were alone, they would have a higher chance of being approved for asylum and protection in America. The reactionary right-wing news outlets reported this was a cleverly constructed lie to pull on America's heartstrings. They believed those coming across were adults with criminal records.

Biggs used his Army ID to get us onto the base, and it didn't take long before we found where they were being held. The area was surrounded by chain-link fencing obscured with black tarps. We found a hole in one of the tarps and I was able to stick my camera through it to get video inside. As it turned out, there were only children there, hundreds of them. There was no way for Jones to spin this into his preconceived narrative, so instead he used our footage to craft a new story that the federal government was treating illegal immigrants better than veterans.

On the show, Jones likened current immigration policies to feeding pigeons, suggesting that such actions would only attract more of the same. The government's refusal to deport "felons, rapists, and murderers" was a deliberate strategy to dismantle border security, framing it, of course, as a false flag operation aimed at weakening the nation's defenses in service of a globalist agenda.

It was an effective mix of paranoia and conviction, designed to provoke outrage and rally support for his cause, and it was all a lie.

This rhetoric, like much of Jones's worldview, was rooted in the John Birch Society beliefs his father had instilled in him. In their publications, the JBS labeled the civil rights movement a communist conspiracy. The same charge was leveled at efforts to end apartheid in South Africa and white minority rule in Rhodesia. Any demand for racial equality by non-white individuals was cast as part of this so-called communist plot. While Jones swapped "communist" for "globalist," the ideological framework remained the same, allowing him to oppose immigration and racial equality movements without overtly expressing racist sentiments.

Over the next ten months I would travel to the border several times, each trip based on false or exaggerated reports, escalating into more absurd attempts to instill fear in the millions who viewed our content online.

Judicial Watch, a conservative activist group, claimed to have information from high-level law enforcement that Islamic terrorist groups were in Juarez, Mexico, planning to cross the border into El Paso, Texas.

Once in the United States, the report specified that ISIS members would spread throughout the country, setting off car bombs in the days leading up to the thirteenth anniversary of the 9/11 attacks. Homeland Security and the FBI publicly denounced the report, saying there was no truth to the warnings, but for Jones, the government downplaying the threat was reason enough to take it seriously. A week after Judicial Watch released their report, the Army announced they would be ramping up security at the base. Even though a Fort Bliss spokesperson said the new measures had nothing to do with terrorist threats, Jones and Biggs both believed this was a lie. Biggs had previously been stationed in El Paso and still had friends at Fort Bliss. One of those friends was a driver of a top Army general and had told Biggs he overheard the general on a phone call saying the security measures were due to the ISIS threat. Jones asked Biggs if his friend would confirm this on the record, but Biggs said he wouldn't.

Believing the border was wide open, Jones sent Biggs and me to El Paso. It was my first time in West Texas, and when we stepped out of the airport, the air was sweltering and dense; it felt like my face was covered in a wet towel with a hair dryer, turned to the hottest setting, blowing directly into my mouth.

Since California, Jones made it a point to give us directives before a trip, but he had been preoccupied as of late. He was in the middle of a contentious divorce, splitting his time relishing his newfound freedom and raging over the dissolution of his family.

We spent the day driving aimlessly through town. Biggs was treating this as a trip down memory lane. "I used to date a girl who lived there. That's my old gym. We used to get fucked up at that bar every weekend. Over there is where I nearly beat someone to death."

I stopped him after the last one. Up until then, his remember-when's had lulled me into an almost catatonic stupor. Though Biggs and I had traveled together a handful of times, and worked closely in Austin, he and I didn't have much in common. On trips we would listen to terrible '90s rock in the car and Biggs would try to make me laugh by randomly inserting the word "fuck" into songs. "'Black hole sun, won't you come, and *fuckin'* wash away the rain?'" "'Here they come to snuff the Rooster, *fuck* yeah!'" It was the closest we got to any sort of camaraderie. I didn't care for his brand of prideful masculinity, but this last reminiscence piqued my interest. We were stopped at a busy intersection, waiting for the light to turn, surrounded by fast-food restaurants and strip malls. "You almost beat someone to death here?" I asked.

"This guy swerved into my lane while I was sitting here, like we are now, and I lay on my horn. He flips me off, so I jump out of my truck, smash through the driver's side window, and drag him out through broken glass onto the pavement. I whaled on him until I noticed the light change and just got back in my truck and left him bleeding on the ground."

Biggs recounted this story like it was just another bit of information. When I asked if anything ever came of it, he made a vague comment about having a warrant out for his arrest and that he shouldn't even be back in El Paso. But Biggs often seemed shy and reserved. He had a sadness behind his eyes, a desperation to belong. I wasn't sure I believed his story.

His phone rang and I heard Dew's voice. He said Jones wanted to know our plans and what reports he could expect to see uploaded. Dew reminded us that if we didn't come up with a plan soon, Jones would be the one making the next call, and he wouldn't be happy. "Get creative," he said.

I don't know if it was his tone or his patronizing directive, but I snapped. "What the fuck does he want?" I shouted at the phone. "What are we supposed to do, dress Biggs up as a member of ISIS and have him walk across the border?"

It was silent for a few seconds, then Dew said he would call us right back. We were on our way to the hotel when the phone rang again.

"I spoke to Jones and he loved your idea," Dew said with excitement.

"What idea?" I asked.

"*Your* idea," Dew said. "We're getting everything together now and we'll overnight the costume and ISIS flag to your hotel. We're renting the costume from a shop downtown, and I found a stencil for the flag that should work well."

"You've got to be kidding," I said. "It was a joke!"

But it was too late.

That evening, Dew texted an image of himself wearing the outfit he was shipping to us. He had on a black headscarf, part of the material covering his lower face, and a black ankle-length robe called a *thawb*, meaning "garment" in Arabic. In his right hand was a replica of an ISIS flag, and in his left, a garish prop sword—a scimitar with a curved blade, straight out of Disney's *Aladdin*. Underneath all of this, to our utter shock, was the severed head of a white man, mid-scream. Dew had rented the *thawb* and headscarf from a costume shop in downtown Austin, Lucy in Disguise, and while there, he'd spotted the sword and rubber head and figured why not.

Biggs called Dew as soon as he saw the photo. "What do you expect us to do with that?"

"The head is a nice touch, right?" Dew sounded proud, telling us that he did the stenciling on the ISIS flag himself. I had to admit, looking at the flag in the picture, he'd done a good job. Biggs started laughing, and even though I felt that familiar icy fist of anxiety tightening its grip on my insides, I began to laugh too. The joke I'd made had turned into a reality, and it wasn't even an original thought.

Weeks earlier Jones had a guest on his show who performed a similar stunt. James O'Keefe was a self-proclaimed "guerrilla journalist" who'd founded Project Veritas, an organization who primarily went undercover to secretly record liberal groups and politicians, releasing misleadingly edited videos to discredit those groups. A month before our trip to El Paso, O'Keefe had dressed as long-dead terrorist Osama bin Laden and supposedly walked across the Rio Grande in West Texas to illustrate the lack of security along the US-Mexico border. He put on a silly-looking mask and a camouflage jacket and used a dramatic tagline ("Do you feel safe?") before making his walk. I reminded Dew that we were stealing someone else's idea, but they had already discussed it. Jones didn't want it to look like an outright theft, so Dew suggested we ramp up the absurdity.

"Josh, you film from the US side of the border," Dew instructed me over the phone. "Biggs will start in Mexico, simulating a beheading with the sword, and cross over holding the severed head and ISIS flag."

Biggs and I shared the same dumfounded expression. "No way," I said. "No fucking way. That's insane... we're going to get arrested."

"No," Biggs interjected, "we're going to get shot."

Dew downplayed our concerns, reminding us that Biggs had already walked across the border without a problem. But there *was* a problem. There were sections of the border that were open, especially in the steep mountains between Texas and Mexico, though it wasn't as easy to get through as we reported. I had recorded a video of Biggs climbing through an X-shaped vehicle barrier into Mexico to show how "wide open" the border was. What we failed to mention was that we had strategically waited for a border patrol agent who had been monitoring the area all day to drive out of sight so we could shoot the video.

"The border is wide open!" Dew said, fed up with our persistent negotiating. "Drive outside of town where there's no border patrol, and you'll be fine."

The box arrived at our hotel the following morning. The flag was attached to a baguette-sized metal pole and looked exactly like the ones I'd seen in beheading videos Jones had made me edit into a report where he claimed the US government had created ISIS. The rubber head, on the other hand, looked like something out of John Carpenter's

The Thing—impressive on-screen but ridiculous in person. Each individual component would have been easily mocked, but combined, especially at a remote border crossing, we were asking for trouble. Begging for it.

At the bottom of the box, Dew had included a bucket filled with miniature plastic skulls. Around that time, the ice bucket challenge was going viral, drawing much-needed awareness to the horrific and heartbreaking effects of ALS. Dew asked us to film a parody video, after we'd crossed the border, where Biggs would wear the outfit and dump a bucket of red Kool-Aid (to mimic fake blood) and tiny skulls in place of ice over his head to draw some of the viral attention to Infowars. "If there's a hell," I said as we piled everything back into the box, "we're going there."

The day before, during an ad break, Jones asked me to come on the show and talk about my experience of being at the border. This was something he did anytime we were desperate for content, and I hated it. In Ferguson and Bundy Ranch, he had brought me out from behind the camera, but all I could do was mumble about my surroundings or parrot his perspective, too afraid to say the wrong thing live on air.

Not only did I lack the skills to be a reporter, but I saw the hat trick they had to perform to meet Jones's unrealistic expectations. In the beginning I was passionate about the message I believed Jones was spreading—encouraging people to think outside the box and challenge the status quo—but I'd seen how the sausage was made and no longer knew how I felt about the stories we told, the ideology we propped up.

Before working there, it was easier to believe Jones's rhetoric, to allow his jumbled ideas and constantly shifting subjects to wash over me without much thought. There was a secretive group pulling the strings; everything was connected, and even though I couldn't make sense of how it all tied together, Jones could, and I trusted him. I let him do the thinking for me. When I shared stories from the job with Lacey, there was no mistaking the worry in her eyes. It wasn't just fear, but a quiet desperation. "You can't keep doing this," she said, and a part of me agreed. But walking away at that moment, cutting myself off from everything I'd worked for, was a risk I couldn't yet take.

Now my faith in Jones had turned into fear, and that was the element driving me forward. During our discussion on air, I regurgitated Jones's hysteria about the border, but toward the end I went blank. I had used up my limited ability to vamp, and ended up saying something I shouldn't have.

"Just wait," I said. "Once we do what we're planning to do tomorrow, there will be no doubt the border is wide open, and the dangers are real." I didn't even believe the words coming out of my mouth. The stunt, were we to pull it off, was performative, strategic, and in no way indicative of anything but our own desperate need for attention.

"You mentioned it on the show yesterday," Dew said now. "Jones is expecting it. So, unless you've got another idea..." Coming up with a viral idea, one that would demand attention and make Jones forget the plan, wasn't easy, so we believed we had no other choice but to follow through.

We drove to a concrete monolith marking the divide between the United States and Mexico. It had a plaque establishing the creation of the border line, but the reason we went there was that it was the only place we knew nearby that didn't have a towering fence blocking the passage between the two countries. When we arrived, there were three border patrol vehicles in sight. We continued past at least five more sections of the border, in and out of town, but there were agents at each location. Every time we turned down a dirt road or gravel path, we'd spot a white SUV with a border patrol decal, pretend to be lost, and head back the way we came. We were running out of options and daylight. If we didn't hurry up, we'd be forced to make a call to Jones that felt worse than being arrested.

In our desperation, as we inched farther away from the city, a solution appeared like a mirage outside the passenger window. I spotted, through a thin opening in a dense line of trees, a shallow stream. If I'd been looking in any other direction for even a second, we would've missed it. Biggs pulled down a dirt path just wide enough to fit our vehicle and drove until the tall grass opened to the water. "This could work," he said.

There was still a chance we'd be spotted from the road, but it was unlikely. We weren't on the border but the surroundings were the same, and we even had water to walk through as if it were a shallow section of the Rio Grande.

Across the water, what we were calling Mexico, Biggs hacked away at the sand with the plastic sword, pretending to sever a man's head. Once the thread had been sufficiently hewn, Biggs gripped the hair in one hand, hoisted the ISIS flag in the other, and began walking in my direction. He staggered through the sludge until he reached my side of the water, what we were calling America. He tossed the head toward the camera.

"Thank you, Obama, for leaving your Southern borders open so ISIS can terrorize America. We claim this land for Sharia Law," he said, improvising a horrible Middle Eastern accent, still holding the flag aloft.

A car passed by the narrow slit in the brush, and I shouted for Biggs to duck down. We waited, frozen, as the rattling engine dissipated. Once all was quiet, we ran through the mud, stuffed everything in the back hatch, and got out of there. Neither of us was proud of what we'd done, but the slimy creep of shame was nothing compared to the overwhelming relief of having completed the task. I spent the evening editing—cutting in clips of the concrete plaque we had stopped at earlier to make it look like we were at the border, meticulously scanning the background of the final location to make sure our lie wasn't obvious to anyone familiar with the area. I added in ominous music to make the final product even more vulgar and posted the video to YouTube with the headline SHOCKING! ISIS JIHADI CROSSES U.S. BORDER WITH SEVERED HEAD.

"I want to be very clear concerning this stunt we pulled down on the Texas-Mexico border," Jones said the next day before premiering the video on his show. "It's being done to draw attention to the fact the border is wide open. We're showing that even someone dressed like an ISIS member with a severed head and three-foot sword can walk right across into the United States."

Over the next few days, the stunt became one of the top ten most watched videos on the Alex Jones YouTube Channel, which, at the time, had grown to nearly a million subscribers and a total of five hundred million views. Jones pushed the video on his live show, lauding it as evidence of the porous border and the dangers of lenient immigration laws. "See the video on Infowars.com," Jones said on the air. "Please send it out on Facebook, Twitter, get it out to your friends and family. If the mainstream media picks this up, if alternative media picks this up, it could really draw some attention to what's happening and stop a false flag or a real attack."

Jones never found out we'd lied. Though, given the numbers, I doubt he would've cared. I told myself it was part of the job, that I'd minimized risk while still getting the result he wanted. What I didn't acknowledge was that I'd become complicit in a new way. I'd given up on my supposed veneration of the truth.

12

MEN IN BEIGE

Over the following months, I traveled almost exclusively with Biggs. Jones had been so pleased with our work in El Paso that we'd become the dynamic duo he relied on for generating content in the field. He expanded my title to field producer and made travel an official part of my job responsibilities.

Because Jones believed ISIS could gain access to the country through our open borders, we traveled to Manhattan on the thirteenth anniversary of the September 11th attacks in what Jones anticipated would be another tragedy. But nothing happened.

The next month, we followed two Ebola infections of nurses in Dallas that Jones was determined to use to stoke fears by insisting this was the catalyst for an all-out pandemic. We led his audience to believe there was a major cover-up underway, and helped push Jones's theory that this was the beginning of the end for humanity. Back at the office,

Buckley and Dew recorded a parody of the song "My Sharona," replacing the lyrics with "My Ebola," and made a music video where they ran around the office in clown outfits claiming the government was spreading Ebola on purpose.

For good measure, after the nurses had recovered from Ebola, and no other US cases were discovered, Jones sent us to the border town of McAllen, Texas, to claim people infected with Ebola were likely coming over the border. There was zero evidence of this, but it was such low-hanging fruit in right-wing media that Jones couldn't resist. The Southern border was the salt of conspiracy theories—it could be paired with any topic, at any time, to add an extra layer of xenophobic fear.

As the ISIS fervor escalated, Biggs and I returned to El Paso. Judicial Watch had released another report, this time from an anonymous Mexican army field officer and federal police inspector, claiming to have evidence of a functioning ISIS base across the border in Anapra, a neighborhood in Juarez. Neither of us had recognized the implications of our actions, and by the time we landed in El Paso for the second time after more than half a year, we had become seasoned bullshit artists, void of conscience.

The echo chamber was relentless, pulling me back into a spiral of doubt—wondering if, beneath the layers of exaggeration and fearmongering, there might be something genuine at play. When I first encountered Jones and his ideas, I felt ashamed for not previously seeing the truth of the world as he portrayed it. If I'd failed to recognize something presented as so blatantly obvious, how could I ever trust myself again?

With no visuals to capture on the ground in El Paso, Biggs contacted a pilot he knew from his military days who offered to take us into the sky along the edge of the border. It wasn't a plan per se, but it had the trappings of serious journalism, and for Jones that was enough.

When we arrived at the airport, we had to help the pilot push his single-engine Cessna out of the hangar. While we were struggling to move it forward, I noticed, through the window, only two seats in the front of the plane with nothing in the back. Once the wheels hit the tarmac, the pilot—who was quiet and didn't seem to care about the details of our flight—carried over a lightweight aluminum chair with torn upholstery and threw it in the back.

"What's this?" I asked.

"Your seat," he said, unfastening the door—what amounted to the entire side of the plane—and placing it in the hangar.

"Uh, I think I'd like to keep the door on."

"It'll be better for the camera," the pilot said, walking back over with a thin piece of fabric. "Don't worry, we'll fasten you into the hull. That chair's just for comfort; it won't keep you from falling out." He handed me a harness to strap over my chest, hooked the strip of fabric to a small piece of metal inside the cabin, and connected them with a carabiner.

Up in the air, without leaning out the edge of the plane, all I could see were the distant mountains. I made sure my harness was secure, even though the material looked like it could fray at any moment, then I dragged the detached chair toward the edge of the plane, scraping its metal legs along the cabin floor. As I leaned over, I pointed my camera down at the ground and hit record. The wind howled through the plane, causing it to shake violently as the engine roared. I couldn't hear anything being said in the cockpit without extra headphones.

I wasn't sure what we were even looking for—a building with an ISIS flag flying outside it?

Afterward Biggs and I sat in our hotel room, perusing the footage we'd gotten during the flight. I had attached four GoPro cameras to the bottom of the plane—two on the wings, and two at the nose and tail. Combined with my camera, we had plenty of footage to look through; the only problem was finding anything useful.

"Maybe that's some sort of compound," Biggs said, pointing to an aerial view of what looked like a concrete slab.

"I don't know," I said reluctantly. "Not sure if anyone would buy that."

We continued scrolling through the footage, scanning each frame for meaning like a moronic Rorschach test.

"That could be a coyote or a lookout," Biggs said, spotting a truck parked at a dead end in the mountains. Next to the truck was a row of columns casting human-size shadows on the street.

"Look at this over here." Biggs dragged his finger along the computer's track pad and stopped the video above what looked like a small church with a steeple. Next to it was another concrete slab that looked to have burn marks on it. "This could be some sort of altar for ritual sacrifice... of humans."

"An altar?" I asked. "That looks like a basketball court. The church I went to growing up had something similar." If we wanted to avoid a call from Jones the next morning screaming about the money he'd spent to send us there, and our incompetence, then we'd have to at least try and turn this nothing flyover into something.

I cut together the aerial shots that weren't just vegetation and soil, and Biggs recorded a voice-over. He repeated the same things we had joked about earlier, crafting a narrative around arbitrary shadows and structures. I layered ominous music underneath and edited together a dramatic intro using footage of the plane taking off from different angles. The video we posted online—titled AERIAL FOOTAGE: REPORTERS INVESTIGATE ISIS BASES IN MEXICO—was nothing but conjecture.

The call that came the following morning wasn't from Jones but Dew, and he was elated. He praised the work, expressing that it was exactly what they were looking for. Jones was impressed, Dew said, noting how we had taken a dead end and transformed it into a compelling report.

Biggs gained notoriety among Jones's followers, using his military service to lend credence to his viewpoint. As he made a name for himself through his bold stunts, he grew more confident and daring. In El Paso, he reached out to an old military friend to drive him into Anapra. His plan was to ride around and search for the supposed ISIS base, though this plan baffled me. It's not like he would stumble upon a giant sign reading ISIS BASE HERE. Yet Biggs remained undeterred. We had managed to spin our aerial report into a hollow victory, and now he intended to replicate that on the ground.

This kind of superficial reporting was precisely what Jones wanted, but I refused to join in this time. "There's no way I'm driving into Anapra," I said, exasperated. "It's one thing for us to pull a stupid stunt here but I'm not fucking around in Mexico. We don't know the area! We don't know what the cartel situation is there."

Biggs dismissed my concerns and suggested he would ride with his military friend, Diego, into Anapra while I stayed back in El Paso, a precautionary measure in case something went wrong. I pointed out that Jones would expect me to accompany him. "The whole point is to video this and post it online," I said.

"I already thought of that," Biggs said. "I'm going to attach GoPro cameras inside the car and shoot what I can on an iPhone from the passenger seat. I'll tell Jones we need a contact on the American side of the border. Don't worry, I got you. You won't have to go over."

Biggs kept his word. On the live show the following day, Jones asked when the two of us were crossing into Mexico, and Biggs told him, for security measures, I would stay behind in case something went wrong. "If we both go over there and something happens, then we're pretty much screwed," Biggs said.

"This is how it always happens in the movies," Jones said with a smile. "The people split up. We probably should've sent three people down there, or four."

"Yeah, well, the more of us that look like me in the same vehicle, the more suspicious that vehicle's going to look," Biggs said.

On the air, Jones acted like he was concerned for Biggs's safety. "I want to talk to you immediately, as soon as you get out of there, to know you're okay. Because I'm going to be standing around the telephone and won't be able to get anything else done until we know that." But behind the scenes, he encouraged Biggs to go into Mexico and said he was excited about the attention the report would bring, no matter the outcome.

After our segment of the show was over, we made our way to Diego's house. Diego had family who lived in Mexico and was familiar with Juarez and Anapra, though that was where his expertise ended. Since his military days, he had become a real estate agent in El Paso. When we arrived at his home, he was outside using a water hose to create mud in a patch of dirt beside the driveway. Dressed in a baggy flannel shirt, a dirty baseball cap, and paint-splattered jeans, he seemed intent on a task. He scooped up a handful of mud and carried it over to a beat-up Toyota Tacoma, smearing it over the license plate.

"What the hell are you doing?" Biggs asked, stepping out of the car.

Diego said that obscuring the Texas tag was essential for their trip to Anapra. The cartel's presence loomed large there, with paid lookouts stationed on corners to report suspicious activity. An American truck, with American plates, and a white man in the passenger seat who looked like law enforcement, would raise too many red flags.

Diego reached inside his truck and tossed a baseball cap to Biggs. "Put that on," he said, motioning to the cap on his own head. "We'll look like a couple of *jornaleros*, but we'll be fine." I helped connect the GoPro cameras inside the truck, and then they left, heading south for the Bridge of the Americas, the main crossing into Mexico.

As they drove over the Rio Grande and crossed through the port of entry, I hiked along the western base of Mount Cristo Rey. It was eerily quiet, and no other vehicles were parked in the turnoff at the trail's head. I had a sinking feeling something bad would happen, though this wasn't out of the ordinary. I walked southwest toward the border, capturing footage of cacti, a cargo train, and jagged drainage ditches dug into the side of the mountain, until I reached a rusted fence and the town of Anapra beyond it. The only bright colors came from clothes scattered in the dirt and crumbling structures pockmarked throughout the rutted terrain.

While in the middle of capturing footage of the area, I heard footsteps close by. All I could think was that I would go missing on that mountain and my disappearance would become fodder for Jones's narrative.

The footsteps grew closer until I spotted movement along the path below. It was a border patrol agent waving me down. This time, I was relieved to see the border patrol and walked toward him. As I got closer, I made sure the camera's microphone was turned on and recording. The agent introduced himself and asked what I was doing out there. I told him I worked for an online news outlet called Free Speech Systems—the name we used when we wanted to maintain anonymity. I mentioned the Judicial Watch article and asked if he'd heard about it. He said he had, though nothing officially. As far as he knew, no one in the border patrol took the report seriously. There was nothing on their end indicating the sources or claims were real. What was real, however, were the cartel dangers.

"I patrol this area regularly," he said, "and at night you can hear gunfire over in Anapra. Not an occasional shot, but consistent gunfire. Every night." He pointed to a post where the border fence abutted the mountain. "There's a hole in the fence right there where the cartel traffics guns and drugs. We've caught them a few times, but there's too many of them and too few of us to make much of a dent."

The border patrol agent told me I could do as I pleased, it was public land after all, but he suggested, come nightfall, I not linger in the area alone. I told him I was on my way out and thanked him for his kindness.

I didn't know the first thing about the problems at the border, about the individuals and organizations who tirelessly tried to make a difference. I had no clue why people chose to cross over illegally, what circumstances led them to that decision, how far they had traveled, or what it cost them to leave everything behind in hopes of living in a country that I just happened to be lucky enough to have been born in. But the longer I spent in Jones's world, the more it dawned on me how speculative and unserious the ideas were, how little any of us knew about the things we so passionately advocated or condemned.

Biggs called once he had crossed back over into El Paso. He'd been gone so long, I began to wonder if something had happened, but most of their time had been spent stalled in traffic at the border crossing. When we met back up at the hotel, both Biggs and Diego buzzed with adrenaline.

"That shit was fucking crazy," Biggs said.

"He was definitely a lookout," Diego added.

"Pretty sure he had a pistol concealed in his waistband."

"He had a gun on him, no doubt about it."

I couldn't have gotten a word in if I tried, so I sat on the edge of the bed in Biggs's hotel room, listening. Biggs had left his DO NOT DISTURB sign on the door handle that morning and housekeeping didn't clean his room. I spotted blood smeared across the bedsheets and pillows—a sight I had encountered once before in Arizona. Biggs had been involved in combat operations and hostile encounters overseas, earning two Purple Hearts, the second after a traumatic brain injury that led to his medical discharge from the Army. He had sustained internal wounds, with shrapnel still lodged in his stomach, causing him to cough blood on occasion. Jones didn't provide health insurance, which left Biggs struggling to get proper care through the VA.

I zoned out, staring at the stains on the white hotel sheets, until I snapped back to reality and realized Biggs and Diego were still deep in conversation.

"And that place…" Diego said, breathless.

"That fucking place…" Biggs sounded nostalgic for something that had just happened. Like if he could, he would've stayed in Anapra just for the thrill. "Josh, you gotta see this. We were driving through that shithole of a town and accidentally found a mosque"—he paused for effect—"surrounded by barbed wire."

"How do you know it was a mosque?" I asked.

"Because it had a fucking minaret," he said, referring to the tall slender tower where the call to prayer was announced. "Same architecture I saw in Afghanistan. I recognized it immediately."

"Okay, well, so what?" I said. "Maybe it was just a mosque."

"Surrounded by barbed wire?" Biggs said, annoyed. "Give me a break…"

I suggested the presence of barbed wire might have been an indication of the cartel threat, and Diego reiterated that Anapra was indeed a dangerous area, where people lived in extreme poverty under the control of the cartels. Even from my vantage point on the mountain, I could see the reality of life there, the scarcity, the ramshackle homes and tarps covering exposed roofs. But Biggs wasn't hearing it.

I imported all the footage and scanned through it. Biggs pointed out the moment that struck him as relevant, the people standing on corners he deemed cartel lookouts. It all seemed relatively normal. When they made it to the mosque, I agreed the barbed wire was odd, but it didn't seem out of place. The area was run-down, and if we were guessing—which was exactly what we were doing—it was more likely an old mosque the cartel had turned into a processing facility for drugs or weapons. But what did *we* know? There was no proof this supposed mosque had anything to do with ISIS.

"Pause right here," Biggs said, pointing out a young kid riding past on a bicycle. While they circled the building, the kid rode by a few times. "This could've been another lookout. He was probably told to keep an eye on us from someone inside the mosque."

I laughed. "Based on what? It's just a kid. There's nothing indicating he's a 'lookout.'"

Biggs reminded me that during his four tours in Iraq and Afghanistan, part of his job was to spot children Al-Qaeda would use as decoys or lookouts. Some of these children were armed with explosives or weapons, and Biggs was responsible for using his judgment to weed them out. (I assumed "weeding them out" meant killing them, but I didn't ask for clarification.) "Maybe I know what I'm talking about with this," Biggs said. And he had a point.

While Biggs was overseas, I was in film school, learning about scriptwriting, cinematography, lighting, and preproduction budgets. While he was getting shot at or trying to avoid land mines, I was interning and working on film sets. I was out of my depth, had no idea what I was talking about, and Biggs had already called Jones on the ride back from Mexico and told him he'd gotten footage of the ISIS base in Anapra. With clever editing, and a biased narrative, stationary shadows would move, insignificant structures would be imbued with meaning, and once again we would have to turn an improbable nothing into a persuasive and compelling something.

As I sat in my hotel room that night editing the video, I relinquished all editorial input. I hadn't been in the car. I didn't see anything firsthand, so if Biggs believed he had discovered a secret ISIS base in Mexico, then that's what I would show.

If one was inclined to trust the Judicial Watch reports claiming there were ISIS bases across the border, then they might very well think

Biggs had discovered one. But if the viewer was skeptical, curious, or at least capable of seeing through the ideological bent of our claims, the report would prove nothing more than the existence of Muslims in Mexico.

The day after we posted the video, Biggs received a call from an unknown number. We were in the middle of checking out of the hotel, so he ignored it. Our flight back to Austin was scheduled later that day, and we planned to get lunch in town before making our way to the airport.

On the drive to the restaurant, Biggs got another call from the same unknown number. This time he answered. He sat there silent. I couldn't hear what the person on the other end of the line was saying, but if Biggs's stone-cold face and proper affectation were any indication, it wasn't good.

He pulled off the road into the mostly empty parking lot of a movie theater. Biggs wasn't speaking much, and it was difficult to glean any information from the few words he used. After several minutes, Biggs said he would check his schedule and call them back.

He tossed his phone in the cup holder. "That was the FBI."

"Right..." I said, thinking it was a joke.

Biggs said the counterterrorism agent stationed in El Paso had seen our video and wanted to speak with us in person.

"What exactly did he say?" I asked, panic setting in.

"He said he was with the FBI and watched our videos and wanted to know if we'd be willing to meet in person."

"For what purpose?"

"Fuck if I know. The guy asked our availability, and I told him I'd call back."

My head was spinning. I said the FBI knew we'd lied, and we were about to face the consequences. I wasn't sure what the repercussions would be, but I predicted the worst. Releasing a video claiming there was a terrorist base without any evidence should be illegal—inciting panic, disorderly conduct, disturbing the peace at minimum.

"Fuck you, I didn't lie," Biggs said. "I think that's an ISIS base."

I rolled my eyes. "That report doesn't exist in a vacuum. We have plenty of other stupid shit they could come after us for. Maybe they saw the stunt we pulled last time we were here. You consider that?"

Asking Biggs to ponder the obvious prompted me to do the same. I set aside my frantic selfishness and considered what we'd done. It was just dawning on me, far too late, that I'd edited and posted a video showing an identifiable religious gathering place in a dangerous area, leading people to believe it was a hideout for terrorists.

It wasn't until I quit working for Jones that I recognized the danger we put millions of marginalized people in by spreading racist, xenophobic fear porn. Growing up, I had fought with family and friends about their blatant Islamophobia post 9/11, had self-righteously commended myself for being more evolved than the bigots surrounding me, and here I was doing something far worse. What happened if the wrong person saw that video and was able to locate the mosque in Anapra? What if they decided to take actions against what we made them believe was a dire threat? The responsibility would fall on all of us. The responsibility would fall on me.

Biggs called Jones to let him know what happened. "It's a trap!" Jones said, providing his standard alarmist interpretation. "They're trying to lure you somewhere so they can set you up." The only reason the FBI contacted us was because Biggs had stumbled onto something they were trying to hide. "That's a frickin' ISIS base!" Jones said, celebrating what he believed was incontrovertible evidence. "We got their asses!" At first, he wanted us to shoot a report detailing the call, but then he decided that would draw too much attention and the FBI could use it as an excuse to arrest or "disappear" us. No, we needed to get out of there. The FBI likely knew about our scheduled flights, so our best bet was to take the rental car and drive the eight hours back to Austin. Don't wait, don't call the rental agency because the FBI would be in touch with them. Just leave, immediately.

Then again, maybe we *should* meet them. Jones suggested this with a sudden shift in his demeanor, realizing it was an opportunity to generate an elusive story. The idea of recording the encounter took shape. Texas operated under one-party consent laws, meaning only one person needed to agree for the conversation to be legally recorded. All it would take was to open the voice memo app on my phone, hit record, and slip it into my pocket before we spoke to them. Afterward, we could post the conversation online, a bold declaration of defiance to show the FBI what happened when they tried to intimidate us. Jones had made up his mind again, and this was the plan.

Biggs called the agent back and scheduled a meeting for later that day at the airport. As Jones requested, we shot a video outside the airport about our pending FBI interview. We told ourselves this was for our protection if the meeting went awry, but it was clear what we were doing—hyping the FBI call, preparing to publicize our confrontation for attention.

Inside we passed through security, found our terminal, and posted ourselves in a food court near our gate. Planes and baggage trolleys passed by the angled glass wall that curved up and over our table. The agent called Biggs, asking for our specific location in the terminal. (If we had any doubt about his credentials, they were eased when we learned he was able to bypass security and meet us outside our gate.) I pulled our work iPhone out and started recording. Carefully I slid it into the breast pocket of my jacket, making sure the microphone was facing up so the audio wouldn't be muffled.

Two men in their forties approached us. I expected Mulder and Scully—FBI agents dressed in dark suits—but these guys looked more like Johnny Utah in *Point Break*, wind beaten and road worn. They were both wearing earth tones, I guess in case they had to blend into their West Texas surroundings. The agent's partner was quiet and seemed to be there only as an observer.

We took a seat across from the two agents, who both removed their worn-in baseball caps and placed them on the table. "If you guys don't mind, I'd like to have a candid conversation, and want to make sure, before we begin, no one is recording," the first agent said.

Biggs assured him we weren't, but I kept quiet. The other agent glanced down at my chest, right where the phone was. He sat there without saying a word and I felt like all three of them could see the sweat dripping down my face. I reached for the phone and stopped the recording. "Sorry about that," I said, tossing the phone into my carry-on bag. Biggs nudged me under the table, but I ignored it. He wanted to play spies, but I was too nervous. All I cared about was discovering why the FBI asked to meet with us and then, as quickly as possible, getting the hell out of there.

"No problem," the first agent said. "I know you guys are journalists, but if we could keep this from becoming the story, we'd appreciate it." He spoke to us in a way that legitimized our presence, like we were professionals and not two idiots traipsing through their town like we owned it.

I was beginning to fully recognize how much my perspective had changed over that past year. I'd gone from being deadly serious about Jones and his ideology to being a cynic. This had become madness, whereas a few months earlier it was a mission.

The FBI agent said he and the rest of their outpost had been tracking our reporting and were impressed with our work. Jurisdiction laws kept the FBI from investigating on the ground in Mexico, so they had been gathering information through us. Biggs straightened his posture and placed his forearms on the table, clasping his hands together. "Anything we can do to help," he said, trying to sound official.

"We're looking for any information about what you saw over there. The exact location of the building in your video, the surroundings, anything you feel would be pertinent." He directed his attention to me. "Were you there too?"

I shook my head, too stunned to talk.

"No," Biggs said, "it was me and a guy I know from the area—we were in the military together."

The agent asked for his name as the other one pulled out a notepad and wrote it down. Our conversation didn't last long, and other than giving my full name and contact information, I didn't say much. Biggs shared the details of what he'd witnessed across the border, attempting to use his military credentials as validation for his opinions on the mosque. The agents listened intently, jotting down notes, and making Biggs feel—as was evident by his authoritative tone and stature—like an honorary G-man.

I, on the other hand, felt sick. Biggs didn't know what he was talking about, I was convinced of it, but they were acting as though the information was reliable. It's possible they were indulging his posturing to gather information, but it didn't feel that way. (Of course, if they were good at their job, it wouldn't.)

All that time I'd assumed we were existing in a vacuum, screaming into the void, yet there I was sitting across from two FBI agents who said they'd been keeping track of our work and gathering information from it. In retrospect, they should have been gathering information *on* us, not *from* us. And maybe they were. But as we boarded our plane, and Biggs walked a little taller through the aisle, I was left with a feeling of confusion, verging on dissociation, wondering what had just happened.

I returned home, shaken, and told Lacey about the meeting. She couldn't understand my involvement with stories about immigration and the border. To her, that wasn't me. If anything, it was closer to what our conservative families believed. I struggled to express just how controlling Jones was, the way he twisted facts and instilled fear, casting a long shadow over the entire office. She'd met him at an Infowars Christmas party and found him more boring and irritating than maniacal. But the more of his rhetoric she heard, the more concerned she grew with my working there.

"You need to get out of this job," she said. "I know you're worried about what comes next, but it'll be fine, we'll figure it out."

I told her I couldn't quit. She didn't make enough money to support us while I looked for another job, and I couldn't fathom spending the little time I had off from work searching for one. Even though I knew it wasn't fair, it was easier to act like money was the main problem, or her contribution wasn't enough, or that I was too exhausted from working all the time to take responsibility for my own inaction. The truth was, I wanted to leave, but I was too afraid. I was certain that after two years working for Jones, I would never be able to get another job—banished into poverty as penance for my transgressions, and rightly so.

13

WHY DO THE HEATHEN RAGE?

As far as I could tell, Buckley had been hired to run interference for Jones and his growing instability. Up to that point, he had done reasonably well. Jones wasn't easy to manage, but Buckley worked hard to anticipate potential problems and mitigate fallout when things went wrong. After meetings, he apologized to those Jones had demeaned or berated. Often, he pulled me aside to offer encouragement, expressing gratitude for my hard work. He also handled warehouse issues, like supply chain disruptions, and organized the team during crises, like the almost weekly ensuing panic when Jones misplaced his car keys.

I'd hear a commotion in the distance, followed by Buckley bursting through our doorway. "Have you guys seen Jones's keys?" he'd ask, scanning every surface.

"Have we checked the conference room?"

"What about his bathroom?"

"The kitchen?"

"Maybe they're in the studio?"

"Did someone move them, goddammit!?"

Inevitably Jones would appear, reaching his breaking point. "Fuck it all!" he would shout, descending into his signature self-pity. "The country is over. We're so screwed. Everyone is distracted with screens and sports and fucking television shows, and our brains have completely shut down. I can't do it anymore. I can't live like this!"

Just when his grievances peaked into a full meltdown, someone would rush in, breathless, holding his keys, and the pressure would instantly, unceremoniously, dissipate.

Since his arrival a year earlier, Buckley had worked to legitimize Infowars. Jones had his on-air persona, which was the company's lifeblood. That couldn't be touched. But Buckley was responsible for the business side, managing daily tasks and behind-the-scenes operations. He made genuine attempts to structure the company according to conventional business standards, but Jones's self-destructive tendencies only intensified, making it impossible to keep the chaos at bay.

It started, like most abusive relationships, with words.

Jones expected the radio crew to scour news stories every morning and print all the relevant headlines—covering mainstream outlets and the usual cast of reliably unreliable bullshit peddlers like Zero Hedge and WorldNetDaily. If it supported his talking points, he wanted a physical copy on his desk.

The same applied to health-related news that could serve as a marketing angle for his products. Cancer rates rising? Print it. A dubious study warning about GMO foods? Print it. A lawsuit over a municipality's water quality? Print it. The content of the articles and the validity of the headlines were irrelevant; if any bold words backed his claims, he needed them front and center. Often, he formed opinions—and even entire narratives—based solely on headlines, rarely bothering to read the articles themselves.

This meant thousands of pages were printed each week. After every show, someone from the radio crew would gather the articles and put them in a manila envelope for Jones to reference later. Occasionally, they would be sent to my desk if I was filming and editing a video related to a topic he covered on the show. The envelopes were labeled with titles that made Jones laugh, like SUCCULENT PLUMP or JUICY GIBLET. The stacks often lingered for days before being tossed in the trash, but sometimes I'd forget about them, and they would remain untouched for weeks.

One day, I remember Jones coming up behind me and spotting one of the envelopes marked SUCCULENT PLUMP in bold black marker.

"Say 'succulent plump,'" he said, using a childish tone that rose at the end of each syllable. "Come on... say it..."

I laughed but didn't repeat the phrase. Following his orders had become routine, but this felt too submissive even for me. He kept insisting until I caved, fearing that if I didn't, his playful demeanor might shift to anger. "Succulent plump," I said, the words feeling strange as they left my mouth, like chewing sour candy.

Jones grabbed my shoulders, satisfied. He had started this game after I'd been there a year, and while I was flattered that he felt comfortable enough to be playful, it soon turned demanding. He'd ask in a teasing tone, but if we didn't comply, his voice would drop to a low, gruff demand: "Say it? Say it. Say it!" He'd often lean in close, hovering until we repeated the phrase, then continue his conversation or walk away, pleased with his influence.

This repetition game was just the beginning. After a period of verbal dominance, Jones turned to physical intimidation.

This new iteration of the game was limited to a select few and took place behind closed doors.

One day, Gucciardi was in my office discussing a marketing idea for a new supplement when Jones suddenly demanded he be punched. Gucciardi refused, but Jones pressed on. "Don't be such a wimp," he taunted. "What're you scared of?" After a few more refusals, Jones managed to wear him down. Gucciardi lightly tapped his knuckles against Jones's arm. This scenario played out repeatedly with Gucciardi, Dalton, Buckley, and Dew, as Jones went down the line, demanding each of them hit him, never relenting until they all complied.

But the worst incident happened late one night during a grueling 48-hour marathon broadcast. Jones sporadically held what he called "moneybombs" to raise funds through audience donations. These marathons varied in length, sometimes lasting 24 hours and other times stretching to 72.

Around midnight on the second day of the moneybomb, Jones stumbled into the War Room with his usual entourage: Gucciardi, Dalton, and Buckley. Dew, Tillman, and I were at our desks when they arrived, completing Jones's inner circle. The strong scent of alcohol permeated the air as they staggered in. Jones, ruddy faced and reeling worse than the others, went straight to the cabinet where he kept his stash and poured a white Dixie Cup full of Grey Goose Vodka.

Spirits were high. Just moments earlier, he had announced on his show that we had hit our million-dollar goal, with hours still left to go. Although not all the funds came from donations—the total included product sales during the 48-hour broadcast—Jones considered it a victory and was clearly in a celebratory mood. The group had come to discuss with Dew how to get the reporters to start pushing the products in their reports, and as they gathered around his desk, I noticed Jones's eyes glaze over. He grabbed Gucciardi's arm and pulled him in close, his voice a conspiratorial whisper.

"Hit me," Jones said, slurring his words. Gucciardi waved him away, continuing his conversation with Dew, but Jones stepped right into their line of sight, no longer whispering. "Come on, dammit. Hit me!"

Knowing there was no getting out of it, Gucciardi reluctantly tapped his fist against Jones's arm, which seemed to satisfy him. He darted around the room, his breaths strained and chaotic, staring wide-eyed at objects as if they might spring to life at any moment. Tillman and I exchanged glances, both bewildered as we watched Jones stumble through the space.

Suddenly, Jones snapped out of his trance and made a beeline for Dalton. "Hit me," he said, downing the last of his drink and setting the cup on Tillman's desk. Dalton hesitated for a moment. Unlike Gucciardi, Dalton didn't seem all that opposed to the idea and gave in.

"Harder!" Jones shouted. Dalton hit him again. "I didn't even feel that," Jones said, swimming in his gargled words. But it had escalated too far, and Dalton backed off. Up to that point, Jones sounded jovial, but his tone had shifted. "I'm serious," he said, sounding surprisingly sober, pointing to his arm. "Hit me right here, as hard as you can."

Dalton put his hands up in surrender, but Jones stepped closer, pulling up the sleeve on his black polo and slapping his hairy biceps. The shirt was so tight, the fibers popped as he stretched it up his arm. Dalton looked around the room, signaling for help. We all watched with nervous grins, waiting for his response. After a few tense seconds, he yielded, rearing back and striking Jones's arm.

"Again," Jones said.

Dalton hit him again.

"Again!" Jones repeated, clenching his arm tighter to absorb the blow.

Dalton hit him again.

And again.

And again.

The last time was hard enough to knock Jones backward as he roared with laughter and massaged his arm, now a bright pink. Jones motioned for Dalton to come closer. "My turn," he seethed.

"That wasn't the deal," Dalton said. It was clear Jones didn't care what Dalton had or had not agreed to. There was blood in the water, and Dalton braced for impact as Jones reared back and threw a wild punch. His depth perception must have been off, because instead of making full contact, he grazed his arm.

"Shit," Dalton said, rubbing his arm. "You nearly ripped my skin off."

"That didn't count." Jones sounded whiny, like a child complaining he'd missed his turn at bat. "I get one more."

Dalton agreed, on the condition he got to reciprocate, which only seemed to delight Jones more. On the next try he made direct contact, and the two of them continued trading punches, each time hitting harder, louder, until Jones was howling and snorting like a wild animal. He crossed to the other side of the room. A listener had sent in a vintage Soviet military banner with Joseph Stalin's face on it, and someone had hung it on Jones's liquor cabinet. Jones began punching Stalin's face on the flag, denting in the sheet metal doors. "Fuck you, you commie bastard! You anti-American filth!" Jones's chest heaved as he knocked the hinges loose. He breathed fiercely, spit flying from his mouth as he shouted, teeth so tight it appeared they might shatter.

In his ecstatic metamorphosis, he spun back toward Dalton and hit him hard on the arm. This time the sound was different. Wet. At first, I thought it was just a mix of sweat, hair, meat, and gristle, but when Dalton lifted his shirt, wincing in pain, I realized the reason behind the new sound. It was blood.

Upon impact, his already fiery skin had burst open, releasing a crimson trickle down his arm. Jones wailed and pounded his chest, stumbling around the room like a mad gorilla. Dalton laughed it off as he kept checking his arm, using his hand to wipe the blood away as it pumped to the surface. This was the first time I witnessed a burst of physical violence between Jones and a coworker, but it wasn't the last. A few weeks later, Jones cracked Tillman's ribs as they traded punches at a bar in downtown Austin.

Once a week, employees would go out for "crew nights," an opportunity for everyone to come together, complain about Jones, and drown their sorrows. I avoided these outings—I had enough of my coworkers during the day—and wasn't there when Jones and Tillman went at it. But the following morning, holding his side and moving delicately, Tillman moaned about running into Jones at a bar the previous evening. "He was so drunk, he didn't even recognize us at first," Tillman said. "He pushed and pushed until I agreed to punch him. Then the stupid son of a bitch gut punched me." He and Jones wrestled until they broke a table and got kicked out of the bar. "He's lucky I didn't break his neck," Tillman said.

When Jones got to the office, Tillman changed his tune. He went from being assertive to wounded, reluctantly mentioning the pain he was in and how he thought he'd broken one or more of his ribs. "Suck it up," Jones said, laughing it off. "Quit acting like a baby."

Tillman was around ten years older than Jones, a scrappy fighter who'd spent time in prison. Physically, he wasn't someone to scoff at. But in Jones's presence, he was submissive like the rest of us. Jones held the power, always, surrounding himself with people beholden to him so he could remain domineering and controlling. Because of this, he could turn full-grown adults—some with successful, battle-scarred careers in the military or rough-hewn, troubled pasts—into bootlicking sycophants, willing to take a beating.

Only once did Jones sidle up and ask me to hit him. It was during a weekday, and like everyone else, I refused until he wore me down. The whole time, I pictured what his return punch might do—me folding up like a cartoon accordion. Doing my best Jake LaMotta impression, I threw my weight into the punch. His biceps felt like a brick wall, and for a split second I thought I'd broken my hand. But Jones didn't flinch. In fact, he didn't even seem to notice. He patted me on the shoulder with a look of pity and walked away. If Jones could transform these other muscular men into squeaking gerbils, I never stood a chance.

That morning Jones brought his three children and their family dog into the office. Before the show, and after refusing to apologize for potentially breaking Tillman's ribs, Jones chased the dog around the War Room. It was an English bulldog named Captain, and they were tongue wagging and snorting like they both had a deviated septum. The dog was having a blast, zooming around desks, dodging chairs and cabinets as Jones chased him down the hallway.

As the fun and games moved to the other side of the building, Buckley walked into the War Room. "That dog has no idea," he said, watching over his shoulder as they disappeared around the corner. "One day Jones is going to eat him."

I laughed, knowing precisely what he meant. Captain had no idea that one day, when he least expected it, he would be wholly consumed by Jones's temper. We all would.

Years later, Jones would recount on his radio show that during Easter dinner at his home, he spotted Captain perched on a table, licking a coconut cake his mother had made. In a panic, Jones yelled for him to get down. The sudden shout startled Captain, causing him to fall off the table and break his neck, leaving him lifeless on the dining room floor.

The abuse Jones inflicted with his fists was one thing, but more often than not, all he needed to push someone over the edge was his voice.

In the spring of 2015, Jones organized a protest at a local Planned Parenthood. He had signs printed with black-and-white photos of Klan members above the words PLANNED PARENTHOOD IS THE KKK.

It was a last-minute demonstration and around thirty Infowars fans showed up. I was there with Jones, Dew, and Jakari, live streaming audio and video to Jones's show. A group of young counterprotesters were also in attendance. They were part of the Red Guard, a Marxist-Leninist-Maoist collective of community organizers. During the protest, they stood in front of the KKK Planned Parenthood signs and tried covering them with black fabric.

"You're out here trying to block people's signs with your shroud of death to make sure no one thinks about what's happening to those kids inside," Jones said.

The counterprotesters ignored him.

"Whatever college professor sent these guys out here, they told them not to talk because they're dumber than a box of rocks," Jones said into the microphone.

"I have nothing to say to you, Alex Jones," said one of the guys with the Red Guard.

"That's because you're a trendy," Jones said.

"You are garbage," he replied.

"I'm garbage?" Jones asked, his voice growing louder. "I know you're trying to shut down free speech but I'm glad you came out here because you will save thousands of children now, bare minimum, as this goes viral. No weapon formed against us will prosper, demon. Thank you so much for what you've done."

Moments later, the counterprotesters formed a line and tried to knock Jones down. He grabbed one of them by the collar and his supporters rushed in to pull them apart. A man wearing a 9/11 WAS AN INSIDE JOB T-shirt began screaming: "They are throwing babies in the dumpsters behind this building. We need to stop them!" The crowd was out of control, but I kept the camera on Jones as he continued to whip everyone into a frenzy.

"These people are literally the scum of the planet," Jones shouted. "Is this the best the devil can offer, these weaklings that are here like Renfield, protecting Dracula's castle?" His words were a calculated attempt to provoke and unhinge. And they worked. One of the opposing demonstrators grabbed his microphone, ripped the cord out of the camera I was holding, and ran away, disconnecting us from the live show. Jones thrived in the chaos. He was a provocateur who relished dragging people to their emotional breaking point, then turning their reactions into spectacle.

Later that afternoon, Lacey heard about the Planned Parenthood stunt from a local radio station on her drive home from work. "Please tell me you had nothing to do with that," she said, repulsed.

"It's not like I organized it, but I had to be there with Jones," I said.

"What the hell is the matter with you?" she asked.

Lacey had begun working as a teacher at Austin's oldest community art school, and, through her friendships and experiences, was firmly developing her own passions. What began as a broad interest in women's rights, racial injustice, gun violence prevention, and climate policy soon turned into something more granular. While I was content to critique things in the abstract, she was drawn to the architecture of solutions—how policy worked, or didn't, at the ground level. In her free time, she hosted fundraisers for Planned Parenthood and volunteered in down-ballot races for local candidates who supported greater access to health care, criminal justice reform, and raising the city's minimum wage.

Meanwhile, I spent my days at a media company built on conspiracy theories and misinformation—peddling narratives that often undermined the very causes she fought for. It was as if our move to Austin had created a fork in the road and we'd diverged from each other into different worlds.

Lacey tried to encourage me to look deeper at what I was a part of, to see how Jones's words were reactionary and dangerous. She'd spend hours breaking down the lies propping up his ideology, showing how his rhetoric was its own kind of violence. And she was right. But after days spent dodging his outbursts and watching coworkers be humiliated just so he could vent his personal frustrations, I was too exhausted to untangle my own beliefs or build a framework that made sense. I just wanted to go home and shut my brain off.

It was during this time that Jones completed his new studio, transforming the appearance of his show. He even started applying makeup before going on air. The reason for revamping his aesthetic was simple: Jones wanted to reach a broader audience. He understood that younger people didn't care about the trappings of conventional media, but if he wanted to attract older viewers, and appear more credible, he needed all the help he could get.

I hadn't anticipated this change shifting my perception of his world, but in some ways it did. Until then my experiences had revealed the lack of journalistic integrity at Infowars, yet when I stood in that sleek new studio, surrounded by the wall of screens, the custom news desk, and the expansive control room, the show appeared more legitimate, or at least more stable. For a moment, the lies, the manipulation, the abuse, were all easier to overlook. And it didn't hurt that I was being rewarded for my actions: Jones showered me with praise, often applauding my efforts, and by that point, he had even doubled my salary.

14

THE WORLD BENEATH HER

The luster of the new studio faded quickly, and my conversations with coworkers turned to exit strategies. We pondered how much longer we could endure the chaos, what opportunities would be available to us after the stain of working there, and struggled with the nagging fear that this might be the most interesting chapter of our lives. As I look back, it's striking how our private discussions contrasted with our public personas. The way we interacted with one another was so different from how we behaved around Jones or in front of the camera. To the audience, we were passionate about the information, committed to the ideological fight, but behind the scenes, there was a blossoming air of misery.

Jones must have sensed our discontent because he began scheduling more meetings. What was initially reserved for trip planning transformed into roundtable discussions where he attempted to boost morale by soliciting feedback. We all knew better than to trust the promise of open dialogue or an acceptance of ideas that might conflict with Jones's method of functioning—a sort of sweaty, mad dash stream of consciousness where he was the conductor and we were the orchestra, waiting for his hand to rise and burst forward with direction. We could have ideas, sure, and if Jones liked them, he would grant us permission to move forward. If they were failures—meaning they didn't generate views—it reflected poorly on us, but if they were successful, he would pass the idea off as his own.

By the end of 2015, Jones noticed I was overwhelmed and told me to post a job listing on Craigslist in search of "another Josh," someone who could go on trips, run cameras, edit videos, and play the obsequious subordinate.

Dew scheduled interviews at a sports bar near the office. To weed out some of the more incendiary applicants, the Craigslist post didn't mention Jones or Infowars. There was still an expectation they knew Jones and believed in his rhetoric, but Dew wanted it to be secondary. The first requirement was their willingness to be consumed by their work. During the interviews, instead of inquiring about their skills and abilities, Dew focused more on their personal lives.

"Are you married? Are you in a relationship? Do you have children? A dog? Any responsibilities that would keep you from being available day or night?"

After Dew scared off our first interviewee, I expressed my concern over the legality of his questions. He reminded me that unless I wanted to continue going on every trip and getting calls to film Jones late at night, we had to make sure the new hire would be available.

A precedent had been set, agreed upon by people like Dew, requiring us to be more than just employees at Infowars. We had to be followers, zealots, true believers in the church of Alex Jones. It felt like we were in a cult seeking a new member, someone willing to sacrifice their identity for the cause.

It took only four interviews before we found the perfect victim. Francis was tall and lanky with plaster skin and a goofy, crooked smile. At nineteen, single, and a high school dropout, he was easily malleable. The job listing hadn't mentioned Jones or the company, but Francis turned out to be a listener, already privy to the ideas and partial to the politics. He was green, eager, and his inexperience made him easy to take advantage of. For the same job, I started with a salary of $40,000, but Jones believed that, at his age, Francis would be desperate enough to take much less. He was right. Jones offered him $20,000 per year, and Francis accepted without hesitation.

Not long after he started, Jones summoned me, Dew, Biggs, and Francis into the conference room. The reason for the gathering was Jones's latest idea: He wanted us to travel to Muslim majority communities to investigate what he referred to as "The American Caliphate." To Jones, the implications were dire. These communities posed a threat to American culture. It was a predictable progression from his Southern border beliefs. Initially he claimed his only problem was *illegal* immigration, but then it turned into any "outsider" coming into the country, and eventually anyone who didn't look, act, or believe as he did.

"We'll come up with a name," Jones said, sitting at the head of the conference room table. "Like, 'The Islamistans in America.' Something like that." He seemed to know we weren't going to find anything of note because he kept telling us to be elusive in order to create more attention. "We don't want to give out all the information, for security reasons," he said.

During the meeting Jones reminded us that the State Department was funding "radical Jihad Training Centers." He wanted us to use the El Paso trip that Biggs and I had taken as evidence to justify our unrelated "investigations" of these communities. This was how Jones crafted his narratives. He used an exaggerated version of the past—one he had convinced himself was true—to validate his assessment of the future. Biggs had "confirmed" an ISIS training facility in Mexico—he didn't—and the FBI then "briefed" him on the threat—they didn't—so now we had "proof" there were terror cells in America—we didn't.

What Jones really wanted was videos of Muslim neighborhoods that he could put ominous music over and claim they were taking over America. "Show the places that don't sell alcohol," Jones said, "the minarets in Deerfield, or whatever it is with the 'Halalala' call to prayer." He mocked the Muslim prayer with a crass impression. "Stuff like that is the gold I need."

He also wanted us to confront Muslims in their communities. "Don't be scared, this is America," he said. "These people are in public. If someone comes up and says, 'Don't film me halalabalala,' just say, 'America, America, we're in America.' Stuff like that is cinematic."

"Tell them to speak English," Dew said.

"Durka durka Muhammad Jihad," Jones replied, trying to get a laugh. "If they don't want to be filmed, ask them if they decry what happened in Paris." He was referring to the coordinated terrorist attacks that took place a month earlier. Three suicide bombers struck outside a football game after failing to gain entry to the stadium; another group of attackers fired on crowded cafés and restaurants, and a third group carried out a mass shooting at a concert. Jones wanted average Muslims who had no connection to the attacks to decry them. He insisted the responsibility of individuals fell on the group, unless it came to his own group: white people. If a white person committed a crime or perpetrated a mass shooting, they were a crazy lone wolf, or even more convenient, the whole situation was a false flag.

To maintain some semblance of ethics, Jones included his perfunctory but meaningless caveat for us to also interview "nice Muslims." Asserting that we weren't trying to "spin these stories."

Jones wanted this to be an ongoing investigation. He didn't want us to terrorize these communities only once; he wanted us to plan multiple trips to keep the focus on them indefinitely. "And I'm telling you," he said, sitting forward, "you guys hit some home runs, you won't be getting three-thousand-dollar bonuses. You guys hit home runs, you'll get"—he paused, careful not to give a specific number—"bigger ones. Because this shit is working. When everybody does the stuff I want, it hits on all cylinders. We doubled the sales last week from last year. I'm definitely going into the black at a nice juicy level now. It's very good."

The first location we arrived at was a sleepy, fog-covered hamlet in Upstate New York. Islamberg was founded in the 1980s by mostly African American followers of a Pakistani cleric named Mubarak Ali Shah Gilani, who encouraged devotees of his conservative brand of Sufi Islam to establish small settlements across the rural United States. Gilani had faced suspicions regarding his ties to Jamaat ul-Fuqra, an organization briefly labeled a terrorist group by the State Department in the 1990s, though he denied any connection. The residents of Islamberg had no history of violence; in fact, some had publicly denounced the Islamic State in a Reuters interview earlier that year, asserting that those involved were not true Muslims.

In April 2015, Robert Doggart, a former congressional candidate from Tennessee, allegedly planned to travel to Islamberg to burn down multiple buildings, including a mosque and a school. Doggart told a confidential source working with the FBI, "I don't want to have to kill children, but there's always collateral damage." He was eventually arrested following a federal investigation and sentenced to nearly twenty years in prison.

We were set to arrive at Islamberg only days after the FBI issued an alert to law enforcement to be on the lookout for a man named Jon Ritzheimer. He was the leader of an anti-Islamist movement in

Arizona and had posted a threatening video to the community two weeks earlier. In the video, he brandished a handgun saying, "We're fucking ready for them! Bring it on, you Muslim fucks! You want to come fuck around in our country? We're ready for you." He added, "I'm urging all Americans across the US everywhere in public, start carrying a slung rifle with you, everywhere. Don't be a victim in your own country. Fuck you, Obama."

As we drove into the hills, the dark and damp forest closed in around us. "This is some *Friday the 13th* shit," Biggs said, gripping the steering wheel. I rolled down the window and held out my camera, capturing the fleeting images of trees rushing past. Every so often, I caught glimpses of a lake appearing through the thick foliage like a makeshift flipbook. Among the dense oak and spruce trees, I noticed scattered NO TRESPASSING signs until suddenly, the thick forest gave way to bright sunlight.

"There it is," I said, pointing to a gravel road leading to a gated entrance. At the turnoff, in full view, was a sign that read ISLAMBERG in bold white letters. At the bottom of the sign, in smaller letters, it read WELCOME FRIENDS.

Biggs had hopped out of the car to take a photo of the sign when he noticed something in the distance. He rushed back, his face tense with concern. "There are two men watching us," he said, shutting the door and pulling into the gravel drive. We oscillated down the potholed road, slipping in and out of the narrow gashes in the dirt until we reached a rusted cattle gate. Biggs clipped on the hidden camera and approached the two men while we stayed in the vehicle. As he spoke with them, a truck pulled up and two other men stepped out.

"They all look chill," Francis said, his eyes scanning the four figures surrounding Biggs. My mind, however, was plagued with thoughts of Jones's looming reaction—what he would praise, what he would criticize. This fear-induced response had been ingrained in me over time, resulting in me putting Jones's needs above all else, regardless of the circumstances.

They continued speaking for another minute before one of them handed Biggs something and he made his way back to our car. "That's their newspaper," Biggs said, passing it over to me.

"They won't let us in?" I asked, both relieved and disappointed.

"Nope, it has to go through a whole channel. They have to look up my name."

"Well, if they actually researched us, we wouldn't get in anyway," Francis added with a shrug. He was right. Biggs had told them we were there to debunk the claims that Islamberg was a terrorist training camp. He asked for permission to enter their property and gather footage, assuring them we would use it to "put the rumors to rest." But a quick search of his credentials would reveal our true intentions. Our approach was not in good faith, and it would be foolish for them to trust us.

We left Islamberg and headed to the nearby town of Deposit to interview their police department. Inside, we were greeted by the chief of police—a middle-aged man with a rugged New York accent, reminiscent of the rural Southerners I grew up around. Biggs told him we were journalists from Texas investigating "Muslim camps," and asked his opinion on Islamberg. The chief stood behind a wooden desk wearing a faded uniform, his face weathered, lines etched deep around his eyes and mustached mouth.

"I have a fairly large percentage of my population here in the village that's part of the Muslim community," he said, nodding toward the hills in the distance, "so it's not a big deal. They're all good citizens. They're very quiet."

Biggs raised an eyebrow. "We read reports that say they're armed and guard the place."

"They shoot," the chief said, dismissing his comment. "It's America."

He told us the community of Islamberg had a scout program for children in the summer where they taught them how to handle firearms—what he referred to as "The Fresh Air Fund," a nonprofit that provided summer camps for low-income communities. The rumors of gunshots being heard on the property likely originated from this scout program. There was an irony to these concerns, given that the same people who were suspicious of Black Muslims teaching children to shoot were in full support of firearms education among white Christians, throwing a fit anytime gun control measures were mentioned after a mass shooting.

As we prepared to leave the police department, a woman from the county clerk's office bustled in and handed us a slip of paper with the mayor of Deposit's number written on it. Back in the car, Biggs dialed the number and spoke with the mayor. He described the individuals in Islamberg as great people, expressing nothing but positive sentiments. He mentioned how they had invited him to Christmas parties and dinner in their homes, emphasizing their kindness and commitment to being part of the community. His sincerity painted a picture of a tight-knit and welcoming group, one that clearly made an impression on him.

We never released the phone call with the mayor or even mentioned it on air. Instead, we used an edited clip of the chief of police claiming Islamberg was secretive, omitting all the positive comments he had made.

Cell service in Deposit was unreliable so we drove twenty minutes back to Hancock, where we'd stayed the night before. We were set to appear during the third hour of Jones's show. He had a special guest lined up for the first hour, and he wanted to leave plenty of time in case the conversation ran long. That guest was Donald Trump.

Just months before, Jones had approached the upcoming presidential election with the same familiar rhetoric, decrying both sides for their venality and deceit. When Trump descended an escalator in Manhattan to announce his candidacy, we all shared a collective laugh. Even Jones was unenthused, calling Trump a mobster, claiming corruption ran through his veins. He maintained that the left-right paradigm was a false choice, a performance dichotomy to elicit tribalism in the populace. The only way his conspiratorial world made sense was if those in charge were chosen and controlled by the elite.

But Jones's attitude changed once Trump agreed to engage with him directly. As Trump's rhetoric increasingly echoed Jones's own worldview—painting the political system as corrupt and rigged—the chance to bring him on the show became too important to pass up.

After we'd left Austin, we learned that Trump would be a guest, and Biggs was jealous. "Jones doesn't even like Trump," Biggs said, sulking in the passenger seat.

I remembered a story Anthony Bourdain once shared where he talked about how greedy and destructive Trump was to the communities where he had real estate, specifically with the casino he built and ultimately abandoned in Atlantic City. Bourdain said the people who knew Trump the best, the New Yorkers who had a front row seat to his schemes, despised him, hated his guts, saw him for what he truly was: a joke.

It was the same as the narrative we encountered in Islamberg. Those viewing the community from afar, and spreading unfounded rumors online, had no firsthand experience with the people who lived there. Their opinions were meaningless. But the citizens of Deposit, the elected officials who interacted with the residents of Islamberg, they were the voices we should've given credence to, the people we should have trusted.

We hadn't listened to Trump and Jones's interview that morning, but according to the headlines on Infowars, the conversation had gone well. As Biggs scrolled through the news, another headline caught his eye: a mass shooting had occurred in San Bernardino, California. The details were still coming out, so we weren't sure of the specifics. Biggs mentioned that police were searching for someone with a "Muslim-sounding" name, but that meant little without further context.

Later that evening, I heard a knock at my door. Peering through the peephole, I saw Biggs, phone pressed to his ear. When I stepped into the hallway, he put the call on speakerphone. An officer identified himself as being with New York's Joint Terrorism Task Force. He explained that the residents of Islamberg had reached out after our visit, and he was calling to verify our connection with "Free Speech Systems," the name Biggs had given to the men in Islamberg.

Biggs provided the office number, and the officer assured him that if everything checked out, he would inform the residents we weren't a threat.

But the truth was, we *were* a threat. We didn't have guns, but we were armed with cameras and a clear agenda. If they let us in, we would find something to twist into a sensational story. Even if they were kind and welcoming, we would warp their hospitality to suit our narrative. Fear was the name of the game, and nothing would stand in the way of the highly profitable business Jones had created.

After Biggs ended his call, the same officer contacted me—on my personal phone—to confirm my presence in New York. It was a brief conversation, and when I hung up, Biggs returned to his room. Moments later there was another knock at my door and it was Biggs, again, only this time with a look of shame as he lowered his head and stared at the ground. Jones wanted us to shoot a report about the calls we received from the police.

"How does he know?" I asked.

"I told him," Biggs said. The excuse he gave was that Jones "needed to know," but I knew the real reason Biggs had told him. Like the rest of us, Biggs was desperate for Jones's approval. We might have secretly loathed him, denouncing him behind his back, but we had been conditioned to crave his validation, no matter how fleeting.

I don't think any of us understood why we felt this way. Sure, he was our boss and had financial power over us, but it went deeper than that. It was a struggle against our fear of failure—more precisely, the fear of being *labeled* a failure. In Jones's world, where he was the arbiter of truth, being deemed worthless became an undeniable fact.

I understood the desperation, but that didn't mean I wasn't furious with Biggs for breaking one of our cardinal rules: Never contact Jones unless necessary.

Jones insisted we file a report claiming the police had threatened us to keep quiet about Islamberg. He wanted me to go on camera and assert that the officer knew about my presence because "they" were spying on my phone and tracking my location.

"What the hell are we going to do?" Biggs said.

"Why didn't you tell him the calls weren't threats?" I asked.

"Are you kidding?" he said. "He had his mind made up the moment I mentioned it."

"Yeah, well, what did you expect." A statement rather than a question. It was easier to blame Biggs for reaching out than to consider Jones's rationale. Jones was a tyrant, a lost cause, but I believed Biggs should have known better.

For some reason this was a line neither of us wanted to cross (though dressing like an ISIS member and lying about walking across the border was no problem). With gritted teeth, Biggs filed his report. Meanwhile, I stood firm in my refusal to be paraded on camera like a trained animal. As luck would have it, Jones seemed satisfied with Biggs's report and never mentioned the one I didn't submit. Part of me felt relieved, while another part wondered if I would ever have the courage to confront Jones face-to-face.

The following day we left New York and headed to Michigan. It was clear no one would be getting back to us about visiting Islamberg, and by that point, we'd already posted enough problematic reports that any return would have been unwelcome. We ignored certain facts, fabricated others, and took situations out of context to fit our narrative, posting headlines like:

DRONE INVESTIGATES ISLAMIC TRAINING CENTER
SHARIAH LAW ZONES CONFIRMED IN AMERICA
INFOWARS REPORTERS STALKED BY TERRORISM TASK FORCE
REPORT: OBAMA'S TERROR CELLS IN THE US
THE RUMORS ARE TRUE: SHARIAH LAW IS HERE!

During the live show, I noticed a shift in Biggs's demeanor; he seemed angrier, though I couldn't quite place why.

"They can track us, journalists looking for the truth, and call Josh even though no one ever mentioned his name in association with this trip, but they can't stop this terrorist attack in California?" he said, more indignant than he'd been in previous reports. He believed that the shooting was a false flag orchestrated by the American government, and by the end of the interview, Jones instructed us to book a flight to San Bernardino.

I knew when the details emerged, it wouldn't matter if the attack took place on the other side of the country or if the people in Islamberg had no connection to the perpetrators in San Bernardino. Certain people were going to draw imaginary lines, and we were helping them do it.

The attack in San Bernardino had taken place at a Department of Public Health training event and Christmas party in a rented banquet room of a government building. The perpetrators were a married couple—one American born of Pakistani descent; the other a Pakistan born green card holder—radicalized over the internet and expressing a commitment to Jihadism and martyrdom. Using semi-automatic pistols and rifles, they killed fourteen people and seriously injured twenty-two others. This incident marked the deadliest terrorist attack since 9/11 and the worst mass shooting since the Sandy Hook tragedy.

Jones's response followed a similar pattern to Sandy Hook. If people called in to his show or commented on his videos, insinuating he was covering something up—like not immediately labeling a mass shooting a false flag—he would switch course, beholden to those who bought his products and helped prop up his worldview. Beyond the financial aspect, I believe Jones felt a deep sense of obligation to his audience; when the mainstream dismissed him, they were the ones cheering him on.

Looking back at that time, this was the moment a light switched on. A very dim, almost imperceptible light that would continue to grow in me over time.

It was early morning when we boarded our flight back to Austin. I took a window seat at the rear of the plane. An older woman wearing a hijab sat next to me with a young girl. The girl was giddy with excitement, bouncing in the middle seat, holding a clear plastic bag of pretzels. The woman leaned over and asked if I would let the girl sit by the window. "This is her first time on a plane," she explained with a smile. I agreed and moved my bag from under the seat.

As we flew toward Austin, I couldn't help but think of the children who lived in Islamberg. How afraid their families must have felt when their communities were threatened, and strangers appeared asking questions. How we chose to look past these people as individuals, and impose unfair, racist suspicions on them on top of what they were already forced to deal with. And for what, clickbait headlines, more views on social media?

As I sat on the aisle, the plane lifting into the pale blue sky, I glanced over at the little girl staring out the window in wonder, her face glowing from the light reflecting off the clouds. She was amazed, joyful, innocent, carefree, and completely unaware of the world beneath her.

15

EVERYTHING THAT RISES MUST CONVERGE

By then I no longer knew who I was, what I wanted, or what I hoped to find by remaining in Jones's world. I was caught in a liminal space, focused only on the moments that passed by, each one moving so urgently, so insistently, it felt impossible to hold on to them long enough to understand what was happening. Jones, on the other hand, seemed certain of himself, navigating each instance with clear intent. He was busy crafting a precise future, gathering a disparate group of thought leaders, from wildly different perspectives, into his realm of untruth.

In August 2015, Jones invited former grand wizard of the Ku Klux Klan David Duke on his show. A listener had called in and asked Jones why he hadn't embraced Duke, whom the caller described as one of the "most eloquent voices of reason out there today." Jones's rationale for condemning Duke in the past was ignoble, boiling down to a petty personal grudge—Duke had called Jones out for not being antisemitic enough, urging Jones to take a stronger stance against what he referred to as "Jewish control" over media and politics.

Many of Jones's beliefs were rooted in antisemitism, though he acted oblivious to this fact. (Hard to believe, considering the John Birch Society was widely criticized by historians and civil rights groups for echoing antisemitic tropes and tolerating figures with antisemitic views.) Jones's favored terms like "globalist" or "New World Order" were widely recognized by far-right extremists—many of whom Jones associated with—as coded language for Jewish people.

I had grown up in a small town where Jewish people were an abstract concept. The first time I even heard the term "antisemitism" was when *The Passion of the Christ* hit theaters and everyone in my church was up in arms because the media had accused Mel Gibson of it. If I hadn't gleaned the deep-rooted antisemitism in Jones's worldview, I had to assume I wasn't alone. And when someone called him antisemitic, or in the case of Duke, not antisemitic enough, it riled him into a defensive fervor.

Jones walked a fine line using dog whistle language when discussing topics like the border, Muslims, and discrimination, but then acted like he didn't use race or religion as a tool. Occasionally, he decried racism, saying the "global technocrats" used race to divide and conquer, distracting the masses from the true fight for liberty and freedom. But then, in the same breath, he'd rant about how Black people committed more crimes and Muslims posed an existential threat.

Jones also created false equivalencies between advocacy groups like the National Association for Advancement of Colored People (NAACP) and UnidosUS (formerly the National Council of La Raza), accusing them of being "just like the Ku Klux Klan"—a dangerous distortion that allowed his followers to dismiss real struggles for equality.

And it was this same willful perversion of facts that led Jones to invite Duke for a "debate" on his show.

As they spoke, Jones tried to distance himself from Duke's overt bigotry, but as it turned out, the two had similar viewpoints with interchangeable bogeymen. To Duke, the culprits were Jewish people, and to Jones, they were globalists. When the interview ended, Jones attempted to justify his actions, claiming, "I'm simply here, really trying to have sophisticated thought."

The day we returned from San Bernardino, before I could even process the whirlwind of the previous week, Jones had lined up another controversial interview with a vocal antisemite: the leader of the Nation of Islam, Louis Farrakhan.

All these men—each with his own unique brand of extremism—clashed with the image of Jones that I had once held as a truth teller, an image that had been deteriorating since I started working for him three years earlier. What I hadn't yet realized was that there was no definitive Alex Jones. He was a chameleon, always shifting to suit his surroundings, especially if he saw an opportunity to draw more attention to himself.

In early January 2016, Jones, Dew, and I were scheduled to fly to Phoenix for an interview with Farrakhan at the Nation of Islam headquarters. A few days earlier, on New Year's Eve, we gathered for a preliminary meeting in the conference room. Dew suggested Jones ask Farrakhan about radical Islam and how we, as a nation, could protect ourselves from it. But before anyone could respond, Jones blurted out a non sequitur. "Aren't the Smurfs all about drugs or something?" he asked.

Buckley chimed in without hesitation, a clear display of his lifetime spent with Jones. To the non-initiated, Jones's comment might throw them for a loop, but for Buckley, it was just another Thursday. "They must be," he said casually. "They eat mushrooms or something."

"They sing songs," Dew added, playing along. "They don't wear shirts."

"These things gossip," Jones said, referencing Jonah Hill's character in *The Wolf of Wall Street*—a movie he was still very much obsessed with. In the scene, Hill, Leonardo DiCaprio, and two others were discussing the terms of hiring little people to function as lawn darts. I understood the reference, though I had no idea how it fit into the conversation. In fact, I didn't understand what we were talking about at all.

"All right," Buckley said, trying to get back on track with another proposed question. "What do you think of the fate of Islam in the near future and in the long term?"

"Actually, *that's* the next question," Jones said with a sarcastic seriousness. "Where are all the Smurf women?"

Buckley again indulged him, pretending to scribble the question down with exaggerated focus. "Where...are...all...the...Smurf...women," he said, punctuating each word with dramatic flourish.

Jones grinned. "This could be a fun interview." Buckley tried again to regain control, but it didn't work. "Actually, this is the next question..." Jones interrupted. "Honorable Minister Louis Farrakhan, do the Smurfs gangbang the—what's the girl's name?"

"Smurfette," Dew and Buckley said in unison.

"Honorable Minister Louis Farrakhan, do the male Smurfs gangbang Smurfette?" Jones had a big grin on his face. "Is that a good one?"

Dew cackled. "That's the number one question. That's how you start the interview off."

Jones then did an exaggerated, effeminate impression of Farrakhan's hypothetical response. "I thought this interview would be more serious."

"Hey, I'm not into Scientology, you're into Scientology," Dew said, referencing Farrakhan's rumored involvement with the church.

"I was about to say...I'm talking about thetans and volcanoes." Jones spun around, the chair squeaking under his weight. "Now, Steve Quayle says it's fourteen-foot giants that rape you." Jones was referring to a regular guest on his show who claimed ancient extraterrestrials ran the government. "I'm kidding! I can't handle this shit anymore...Is it the lizards? Is it the gay reptoids? Or is it the fucking Smurfs?"

Suddenly, his tone shifted. His eyes fixed on my phone sitting on the table. "Is this all being recorded?"

We'd been instructed to document meetings, but apparently, Jones had forgotten.

"Yes," Buckley said, his tone direct.

Jones froze, his expression changing from playful to cautious. Attempting to lighten the mood, he claimed he was just practicing his Howard Stern impression, but the nervousness was evident as he took a deep breath and leaned back in his chair. He wanted to be taken seriously, to be seen as a thought leader, despite all evidence to the contrary. With genuine apprehension he said, "Can you imagine this getting released later?"

We arrived at a resort and spa in the neighboring city of Tempe, Arizona, greeted by the soothing rush of water in the lobby. The atmosphere was indulgent—smooth stone floors, towering ceilings, a lavish waterfall—and yet the rooms didn't have minibars. Once we got settled in, Jones called Dew and asked us to find him alcohol.

Ten minutes later, in the pitch-black of the desert night, we stumbled upon a liquor store and loaded up: vodka, whiskey, a case of club soda, and a twenty-four pack of beer—the last item for ourselves. Dew looked at the selection and wondered if it would be enough. We were staying in Arizona for only three nights, and the first was coming to an end. "It'll be enough," I said, struggling with the heavy cardboard box they had given us for the haul. "At least I think so."

The following day we arrived at the Nation of Islam's headquarters, a sprawling property surrounded by iron gates in a quiet suburban neighborhood. Security was tight and we stood with guards for what felt like an eternity, awkward and unsure, until Farrakhan himself appeared. He wore a tan three-piece suit and approached Jones with a wide grin.

After the two men exchanged pleasantries, we were led to a secluded room at the far end of a courtyard. Inside, two chairs faced each other, flanked by cameras along the walls and a control room overlooking the setup where they would record their own version of the interview. Jones wasn't exactly the most trustworthy guest, and I understood their caution. But Farrakhan was welcoming and complimentary, expressing how much he had learned from Infowars and praising the "wonderful things" Jones had achieved.

As the interview began, Farrakhan equated the disproportionate killing of Black men by police to the revolutionaries of 1776. He endorsed Trump's proposed Muslim ban and aligned with Jones in condemning Planned Parenthood and abortion access. But what struck Jones most was their shared belief that the media had turned them into villains. Proof, in both their minds, that they were outsiders, speaking truth to power.

After the interview we were invited to dinner at Farrakhan's home. The atmosphere was tense and ceremonious as we sat in a waiting room with central members of the Nation of Islam. Jones tried to make small talk—playing the amenable Texas guest—but Farrakhan's loyalists sat in silence, awaiting their leader's arrival. It was as if we were intruding on some unspoken ritual. The room itself felt like a time capsule from the 1970s, with everything adorned in white and gold. Finally, a door opened and a young man welcomed us into the dining area, where Farrakhan was already seated at the head of a long table. There was no mistaking the formality—crisp white tablecloths, fine porcelain dinnerware, ornate valances, and long, floor-length drapes framed the windows. I felt out of place with my unkempt beard and long hair pulled into a loose bun.

As we settled in, women and children entered, taking their places at two smaller round tables in the back while Farrakhan's wife sat beside him. The food itself was forgettable, but the conversation wasn't. Farrakhan, like Jones, darted from one topic to the next with an ease that made the dinner feel more like an extended, bizarre lecture. He mentioned Kanye West and Kim Kardashian's recent visit, complained about the media's treatment of him, and then, without skipping a beat, praised Donald Trump before segueing into his plans to strengthen ties with the Church of Scientology, lauding its leader, David Miscavige, as a good man.

Dew and Jones stifled their commentary, all three of us glancing at one another, trying not to laugh.

In the end, the evening was as uneventful as it was uncomfortable—a dinner with two controversial figures who will go down in history as some of humanity's least admirable representatives, surrounded by their loyal minions who likely won't be remembered at all.

The next morning, at Jones's insistence, Dew and I joined him in the hotel hot tub before we packed up and made our way to the airport. All the alcohol bottles we bought our first night were now empty, and we left Phoenix with another interview behind us. Connecting with Farrakhan was never Jones's goal; instead, he was intent on pulling himself into diverse and often controversial circles, each encounter serving as a stepping stone to reach new audiences. With every problematic figure he engaged, he was expanding his influence, piece by piece, and building a network that stretched beyond his previous reach.

It wasn't long before Jones set his sights on another infamous personality, this time seizing an opportunity for a financial collaboration. The connection came through Mike Norris, son of actor and right-wing activist Chuck Norris, and Gary Heavin, the billionaire founder of the women's gym Curves. Norris was directing the movie *Amerigeddon*, with Heavin producing—one of those Christian patriot propaganda pictures with dialogue so bad and a plot so thin, it made Michael Bay look like Andrei Tarkovsky. They invited Jones to play the role of a US senator.

He accepted the part and began inviting Heavin onto his show to discuss current events from a Christian nationalist perspective. This was a notable shift, as Jones had largely avoided such topics when I first started listening to him, though the underlying themes had always been present.

Heavin, a devout evangelical, frequently appeared on Jim Bakker's show as well. Bakker, a televangelist famous for his marriage to Tammy Faye Bakker, had a storied past in Christian broadcasting. I remembered Tammy Faye's vibrant makeup and extravagant hair from the shows my parents watched when I was growing up. Bakker had faced serious legal troubles in 1989, accused of sexual misconduct and found guilty of defrauding his viewers of over a hundred million dollars. He was sentenced to forty-five years in federal prison but was released after just five. Following his divorce and prison stint, Bakker returned to what he did best, using religion to grift his supporters. He began selling survival gear and storable foods while building a religious compound in Branson, Missouri, offering overpriced apartments and emergency bunkers to his devoted audience.

Encouraged by Heavin, Jones recognized the potential for profit and was eager to team up with Bakker, either by interviewing him to establish a public connection—like he had done with Farrakhan—or through a more direct business arrangement involving the sale of Bakker's survival food. Heavin was scheduled to speak at Bakker's compound, and Jones wanted Francis and me to accompany him. We were sent under the auspices of filming Heavin's speech, but the real objective was to get a feel for Bakker and his operation and report back to Jones.

We arrived at an airfield outside of Austin and boarded one of Gary Heavin's private jets, expecting a pilot to fly us to Missouri. To my surprise, Heavin himself was at the controls, and it was just the three of us on board. I had never flown on a private jet before. At first, I was enamored with the extravagance. When we boarded, Heavin offered us a cigar from a humidor, saying he owned a small company in Cuba that exclusively hand-rolled his private stash. "Only women roll these cigars," he said, raising his eyebrows as we each took one. Firearms were out in the open, and as we ascended, I chewed on a cigar while Francis examined a pistol, turning it over in his hand.

On the way, we picked up Steve Quayle, who believed giant aliens lived underground and ran the government. Quayle was a conspiratorial radio host even stranger than Jones, and he was scheduled to appear on Bakker's show that same weekend.

We touched down at a small municipal airport in Missouri after dark, greeted by multiple black SUVs waiting for us on the runway. Given Heavin's wealth and Bakker's apparent obsession with money, I assumed there were financial ties between the two. If I had to guess, Heavin made major donations to Bakker, and Bakker provided him with a platform to spread his doomsday gospel and promote his projects like the upcoming movie.

Bakker's "Christian retreat," nestled in the southwest corner of the Ozark Mountains, sprawled across 700 acres. From the outside, the stucco building looked like an aging hotel or a neglected apartment complex, but inside, it transformed into a prepper Disneyland. The interior featured vibrant facades that mimicked a quaint main street, complete with a general store offering an array of knickknacks and souvenirs—tabletop nativity scenes, religious-branded body lotion, wooden blocks inscribed with THROUGH GOD ALL THINGS ARE POSSIBLE, and cookie jars etched with HE FILLS MY LIFE WITH GOOD THINGS! They even sold menorahs and shofars, attempting to reclaim the sacred objects of Jewish worship.

As we wandered deeper, we stumbled upon a towering fifteen-foot marble statue of Jesus, arms outstretched as if beckoning us to gather at his feet. Beside this colossal figure stood a beauty salon and the Grace Street Cinema, where you could get your hair done and then settle in to watch *The Passion of the Christ*, which appeared to be playing indefinitely. Across the room was the production stage for Jim Bakker's show.

After a live taping of his program, guests had the option to visit the Fireside Café, offering a daily buffet filled with the same fare found in Bakker's infamous survival foods, including his "Fiesta Buckets," marketed as "Mexican food that real live Mexicans approved of." The ceilings soared three stories high, with balconies overlooking the room below. These weren't just decorative features; the apartments were real, and available for sale. Bakker's devoted followers could not only visit this strange kingdom of grift but also make it their home, watching his show from the comfort of their own private opera boxes.

The next morning, we made our way to a separate building: a vast warehouse jammed with survival gear, storable foods, water filters, and supplements. Shelves overflowed with books and DVDs, covering everything from demonic possession to 9/11 conspiracies. As I moved through the aisles, I couldn't help but scoff at the absurdity of it all. Beneath the veneer of Christianity, the scheme—similar to Jones's business model—was obvious: Create an atmosphere of perpetual dread by twisting current events to fit an ideology, then conveniently offer a solution to the very problems you've fabricated or amplified, all for profit.

Later that day, as I watched a live taping of Bakker's show, the similarities only intensified. Heavin and Quayle joined him as guests, and their conversation spiraled into wild accusations that Hillary Clinton was a demon from hell, and Trump was America's last hope. It felt like a more conservative, less entertaining version of Jones's show.

"Josh!"

I stopped, looking around for the unrecognizable voice that called my name. Seeing no one, I continued walking, assuming they were speaking to someone else—after all, it was a common name, especially among religious zealots.

"Josh Owens!"

I spun around, startled, and saw two men staring at me from across the room. Their bearded faces were unfamiliar, but as I drew closer, I noticed their Infowars T-shirts.

"We spotted you earlier but didn't want to bother you."

"Yeah," the other added, "we figured you were busy."

They spoke to me as though we were old acquaintances. It took a moment before I realized they recognized me from Jones's show. I rarely appeared on camera, but they picked me out of a crowd. Recently, I had even cut my long hair and beard, making it easier to blend in, yet there I was, standing out. One of the men asked if Jones was teaming up with Bakker, curious about my presence there. I mumbled something about promoting Heavin's film, offering a strained "nice to meet you" before retreating backstage.

I had convinced myself, despite Jones's insistence to the contrary, that I was still anonymous, still capable of existing in the real world. Work, of course, would be different—slathered in the occupational gunge of Alex Jones—but I liked being able to pretend I was someone else in my day-to-day life. And though I would never choose to spend my time with Jim Bakker or anyone who associated with him, being recognized left me feeling unclean, ashamed, as if I were wearing the world's largest dunce cap.

It was hypocritical to judge these people, to pretend I wasn't, by my own once-enthusiastic choice, squarely in their camp. I was reaching a crossroads, where the void of self-awareness was becoming visible in the contrast of my surroundings.

That afternoon we filmed Heavin's speech; it was a dire warning about America's future, conveniently tied to a promotional push for his upcoming movie. When the cameras stopped rolling, the hours stretched ahead. It was rare being on a trip without Jones or a story to embellish, and perhaps it was the absence of both that made the stillness unbearable. I began to wonder if one of the reasons I'd allowed myself to get so lost, so caught up in Jones's world, was because it was easier than looking inward. At Bakker's compound, when the chaos wasn't right in front of me, all I wanted was a distraction, anything to outrun the creeping introspection and the oppressive dullness of that place.

"I'm beginning to see why *we're* here and Jones isn't," Francis said as we walked the grounds.

"Could you imagine..." I said. "The food sucks and there's no alcohol for miles around."

The only vice at our disposal was Francis's nicotine vape, so we made our way back to the apartment and passed it back and forth, watching television ads for holy water and mail-order prayers until we finally collapsed from boredom.

Early the next morning, Bakker invited us to breakfast in his private dining room before we left. Heavin and Quayle were already there, along with a visiting pastor from Florida and his wife. Bakker walked in wearing a linen suit and a baby blue baseball cap embroidered with a white cross. Up close his makeup was thick, his skin cracked and leathery. We were served bacon and overcooked scrambled eggs, which, if I had to guess, came from one of Bakker's survival buckets, as he commented on their "delicious taste" and "impressive shelf stability," like he was trying to sell the product while we ate.

The conversation turned to politics, specifically the upcoming presidential election. Trump was the favorite of the room, though there wasn't a full-throated endorsement from anyone. Instead, the focus was more on the alternative candidate's gender.

"I'm sorry, but I just can't see how that would work," the visiting pastor said in a Southern accent. He was in his mid-forties, his wife slightly younger.

"Give the nuclear codes to someone who can't control their emotions once a month?" Quayle said, scraping his plate clean, presenting his comment like a bad joke at an open mic.

"We can't have a woman president," Bakker declared, giving everyone a look that said, *It's just not how things are done*, and then saying, out loud, "It's just not how things are done." He laid his fork down with dramatic precision. "Tell me this. Did Jesus have any female disciples? Did any females sign the Declaration of Independence?"

"They're called the founding fathers, not the founding mothers," Quayle said, trying out another punch line.

"Can't argue with that," the pastor said.

"You really can't," his wife said, without a trace of irony.

I finished my tasteless eggs and sat in silence, waiting for the witless chatter to end. It had been a long two days and I felt exponentially dumber than when we'd arrived.

The flight back to Texas was faster since we weren't detouring to drop Quayle off in Colorado. Instead, he was heading to Heavin's ranch in the Hill Country, right next to George W. Bush's property, and the two were scheduled to appear on Jones's show. During the return trip, Heavin treated us to a tour of his expansive estate, stopping at several hangars to showcase his collection of vintage cars and airplanes. It felt like a billionaire's toy chest, only instead of miniature models, we were surrounded by the real thing.

Back at his home, his wife made lasagna and invited Francis and me to eat while Quayle retired to the guest house. After dinner we sat on their back porch, overlooking the Texas hills. Heavin lit a cigar and, leaning against the wrought-iron railing, asked me where I saw myself in five years. I looked up at him, my face blank with confusion.

"Five years," he repeated, the question hanging in the air. "What's your plan? What do you want to do with your life?"

He seemed genuinely curious, but I couldn't figure out why. Heavin didn't know me, and I didn't know him. I considered that maybe this was just how billionaires communicated, in lofty terms with grand, sweeping questions, as if every word had a deeper meaning.

I was a camera operator and editor for Alex Jones—one of the least serious people in news media—being asked by one of the wealthiest people in the world about my life's purpose. The truth was, I didn't have an answer. The only certainty was that I no longer wanted to work for Jones. Around the office, some coworkers had started calling him the "Energy Vampire" behind his back. He would drain and drain until there was nothing left to give. And at the time, deep down, I finally felt empty.

"I have no idea what I want to do with my life," I admitted to Heavin, leaning back in my chair, watching the sun vanish below the horizon, wishing I were somewhere else.

16

VIRGIL AT THE GATES

When Jones decided to back Trump, he went all in. Part of his motivation stemmed from his burgeoning relationship with Roger Stone, Trump's former campaign manager and longtime confidant. Stone was a notorious political operative who had started his career in the 1970s, where he became infamous for "trafficking in the black arts" during Richard Nixon's presidential campaign. He was rumored to be involved in spying and orchestrating "dirty tricks" to undermine opponents, earning a reputation that followed him into Ronald Reagan's campaign, where he solidified his status as a political slimeball. Through Roy Cohn, the notorious American lawyer, Stone met Donald Trump. He seemed to pop up in nearly every major political scandal, like the Forrest Gump of corruption.

Given Stone's dubious past, he was the kind of figure Jones should have opposed. Yet Stone wooed him with flattery and a willingness to appear on his show, even securing a high-profile Trump interview that boosted Jones's credibility. Their relationship quickly evolved, forming a bond that blurred the lines between admiration and manipulation. It was clear Jones was playing a much larger game behind the scenes, but the full scope of his strategy hadn't yet come into focus.

After Jones's relationship with Stone blossomed, and Trump appeared on his show stroking his ego, my job changed. Jones wanted us to be at every Trump rally, mostly because there were regular clashes between supporters and protesters outside, and these videos were gaining attention online. "Hate watching" was hardly new, but it reached a fever pitch during the 2016 election. All I had to do was point the camera in any direction, and the footage was tailored for social media.

One of the most chaotic rallies took place in Orange County, California, where Dew and I navigated through throngs of supporters and protesters. By the end of the night, we had captured blood-soaked faces and smoldering police cars, returning to Austin with hundreds of thousands of views and a heightened incentive to cover more Trump rallies. We also attended a few of Hillary Clinton's events, but the atmosphere was subdued. While her supporters were passionate, they couldn't hold a candle to the circus surrounding Trump.

Then, in Saint Louis, I stumbled upon an altercation outside a Trump rally that would become the most-viewed video I shot during my time at Infowars. A young man in a plaid shirt, sporting a trimmed beard and gelled hair, was locked in a heated exchange with a group of protesters. Their back-and-forth resembled a chaotic, less-structured high school debate, filled with aggression and posturing.

"It's 2016, not 1916. The good old white days are over."

"I'm 'racist,' but that's not racist?"

"You've never experienced oppression in your entire fucking life."

"You don't know me."

"You're a fucking white male!"

As their argument fizzled, the guy in plaid stepped toward me. "Josh Owens, right?" I was thrown off guard, looking up from the screen where I'd been focused for the past fifteen minutes. "We met at Ferguson," he said. I vaguely recalled his face—one that I thought somewhat resembled a young Brad Pitt—remembering a brief interaction in the aftermath of flash-bangs and menacing riot police two years earlier. He knew I worked for Infowars and mentioned his availability if Jones ever needed another reporter on the ground. I took his number and said I would pass it along.

As the crowds dispersed, I left the event. What was unfolding outside was far more captivating than Trump's speech inside, even though his speeches were spectacles in their own right. It was curious to watch the media latch on to his most incendiary comments, playing them ad nauseum on their shows, when on the ground the real draw wasn't Trump himself, but the frenzy and rhetoric he provoked.

Before heading back to my hotel, I uploaded the video to Jones's YouTube channel. By nightfall, it had already surpassed a million views, and the numbers kept climbing in the days and weeks that followed. The two young men arguing against Trump became memes, emblematic of the right's claim that progressives were too incoherent to debate. Their points, they implied, were so absurd, they couldn't be reasoned with. The main players in the shouting match were reduced to caricatures, each knighted by online trolls with their own nicknames: "Carl the Cuck," a jab at the young man's parochial looks, and "Aids Skrillex," a crude dig at the other's gaunt frame and vague resemblance to the DJ. The instigator, who would later move to Austin and become one of my coworkers, was christened "Owen Shroyer the Cuck Destroyer."

The relentless ass kissing and groveling directed at Trump had reached a critical juncture, a moment so defining, it could make or break Jones's crusade to shape the election in his candidate's favor. Everything hinged on one pivotal event: the Republican National Convention.

Jones had never attended the RNC because, in part, he hadn't been all that interested in the outcome. In his estimation, anyone who could even get close to becoming the party's nominee was an automatic shill for the establishment.

But now that he was stumping hard for Trump and had put his reputation, however fraught, on the line, he had a desire to make his presence known in Cleveland at the RNC. He saw it as an opportunity to cement himself in the growing Make America Great Again (MAGA) movement by showing up and drawing as much attention as he could muster in the span of three days.

Jones wanted a concerted takeover of the city of Cleveland. We rented multiple Airbnb's throughout the city, one directly across from the convention center where Jones could broadcast his daily show, and three others outside the cordoned-off convention hub.

Raymond had driven the RV and parked it across the Cuyahoga River, which ran through the city, setting up a satellite so Jones could pirate a radio station like he did at the JFK anniversary in Dallas. But this time, he was determined to take over the skies too, weather be damned. He had a giant banner made, reading HILLARY FOR PRISON 2016, and hired two pilots to fly it over downtown. On the ground, mobile billboard trucks with giant LED screens would play an ad of Jones endorsing Donald Trump and denigrating Hillary Clinton. Everything was designed for maximum chaos; Jones wanted to make sure the whole city knew he was there.

The first event we attended was dubbed the "America First" rally. Jones was slated to speak alongside Roger Stone, and when we arrived, I couldn't shake the feeling that we had stumbled into the freak show of the circus. We were miles from the convention center and, given the audience, clearly not a part of the official proceedings. Many of the attendees wore HILLARY FOR PRISON Infowars T-shirts, and some carried holstered handguns on their hips.

It was impossible not to notice how much things had changed since the JFK rally three years earlier. Jones's celebrity had reached another level. In Dallas he had fervent supporters but there was a mom-and-pop feel to those who came out. At the RNC, Jones was no longer just a radio host; he was a rock star. He'd even hired armed security for the long weekend, a far cry from the scrappy operations we had once run. When he took the stage, the crowd erupted in applause like he was their new messiah.

"If you think the awakening we've seen so far is big," Jones shouted into a microphone, "this planet and the globalists haven't seen anything yet!"

After he and Stone regaled the audience with their histrionics, the two weaved through the mass of eager fans clamoring for a moment with their heroes.

"Alex Jones, can I get a picture?"

"Stone, you're the man!"

As they disappeared inside Stone's tour bus, I walked up the hill, away from the crowd, to pack up the camera equipment and get out of there. As I reached the top, my phone rang. It was Jones asking me to come back to the bus and bring a camera.

The crowd lingered outside, waiting for Jones or Stone to emerge. A young man dressed in a skintight suit opened the door and inquired rather snobbishly as to why I was there. "Let him in!" Jones shouted.

Inside the bus, Jones and Stone were seated on a bench along the right side, while a film crew occupied the left. They were filming a documentary for Netflix. The atmosphere was strangely professional—almost absurdly so, considering the spectacle outside. Jones waved me over and directed me to sit in a swivel chair across from them. I sensed, by his eyes narrowing and collapsing down toward the camera, that he wanted me to start filming. The lens wasn't a wide angle, so I had to press myself against the side of the bus to get Jones and Stone in the shot.

There was a short man seated to the right of Jones, slouched down, pulling at the sleeve of his hoodie. At first, I didn't pay him much attention, assuming he was with the other film crew. But as I focused in on his face, a brief surge of familiarity swept over me. He wore round glasses, was an evident introvert, and gave off a different vibe from the bombastic personalities surrounding him. It wasn't the first time I'd seen him next to Jones, I was sure of it, though I envisioned them much younger, in a café or something, surrounded by giant trees. And then it hit me. The stranger in the bus was the writer Jon Ronson.

The last time he and Jones had crossed paths was sixteen years earlier, at Bohemian Grove in California. In many ways, that trip to Bohemian Grove launched both of their careers, though in opposite directions. Jones rode the wave of conspiracy culture, peddling fear and paranoia, while Ronson used his skepticism and journalistic integrity to pierce the dark heart of that very culture, calling out its absurdities with precision and humor. But there they were, seated across from one another in the cramped confines of a tour bus.

It didn't dawn on me until later how surreal it was to be present for their first meeting since that fateful summer. Bohemian Grove had been my window into Jones's world, but I hadn't known Ronson followed up with his own work to demystify the entire spectacle. I wondered—what if I had been exposed to Ronson's perspective first? What if I had encountered his rational approach, his calm deconstruction of Jones's grandiose theatrics? Would I have been drawn into the allure of conspiracy, or would I have seen through the smoke and mirrors? Perhaps my life would've taken a different path.

After their conversation, Ronson paused at the door of the bus, asking Jones if they could reconnect before the convention ended. Jones hesitated for a moment, then suggested that Ronson give his number to me instead, claiming I would be easier to reach. Ronson looked a bit disappointed to be passed off but handed me his number before stepping outside. Once he'd left, Jones remarked that Ronson was writing something about him again, adding with sarcasm that it would, of course, be fair. Despite his initial reluctance, Jones felt a kinship with Ronson and changed his mind, instructing me to send Ronson his personal number and see if I could gauge what he wanted from Jones.

Later that day, I texted Ronson.

> Hey Jon, this is Alex's cameraman Josh Owens. Alex's number is +1 (XXX) XXX—XXXX. Feel free to text or call me anytime if you can't get in touch with Alex.

He responded immediately.

> Hey Josh! Thanks so much. Have you guys got plans for interesting things over the next day or so? I'd love to shadow if so! Jon.

Twenty minutes later I got back to him.

> Other than chasing down UFOS and the infamous Chupacabra we are just kind of winging it. Ha. Alex is doing the radio show downtown near the convention center, but if things start getting crazy or Jones has any grand ideas I'll be sure to let you know!

The following afternoon, Stone contacted Jones and invited him to the convention center. The reason was vague, but Jones hinted at the possibility of meeting Trump in person for the first time. As we waited in the lobby for security to pull the vehicles around, Stone called Jones and told him the meeting had been postponed for some reason. Jones seemed upset, rejected, angry at himself for caring about meeting Trump in the first place. "Fucking bullshit," Jones muttered under his breath.

While we regrouped, Biggs burst into the lobby. "Did you guys hear?" he asked, trying to catch his breath. "The commies are protesting nearby. A bunch of fucking Antifa douchebags are threatening people."

This was the first time I'd heard of "Antifa," later learning it stood for "anti-fascist." Antifa was a decentralized political movement opposing the far right and white supremacy. They often donned black clothing, masks, and helmets during protests, engaging in confrontational tactics that sometimes escalated into violence.

"We're going," Jones said.

Biggs confirmed they were at Public Square—a historic park in the center of downtown Cleveland, just a short drive away. As we exited the lobby onto the street, Buckley tried to dissuade Jones from going, adding fuel to his already fragile mood.

"Don't fuck with me right now," Jones shouted, raising his fists and slamming them into empty space like an infant. "I'm fucking serious, man. You keep acting like you're the one running shit around here and I'm sick of it."

Dew stepped between them. "Me and Josh can go over first to scout it out."

Jones bristled, his eyes ablaze with fury. "The next person who questions me is getting fired. No one listens and I'm fucking done. I'm done!"

"We're not questioning—" Dew started to say before Jones interrupted.

"That's it!" he said, pushing through them. "I'm going to beat the fuck out of these commie pieces of shit. Everyone in the car, right now!"

Jones had a reputation for launching into raucous, often graphic rants on his show, reveling in the details of physical violence. These tirades were theatrical, using grotesque, almost pornographic imagery to shock his audience, and they seemed to come from a deep place of insecurity. These scenarios sometimes served as metaphors, and other times used what seemed like real memories, even implying that he'd once beaten someone to death.

Jones could be intimidating in his anger, even if the stories felt like a childish way of conveying his seeming obsession with revenge. But standing on the streets of Cleveland, this felt different. It was the first time I'd heard Jones threaten physical violence before a protest, and I wondered if it was a reflex to Buckley's and Dew's comments, or if this time, the threat was real.

The driver dropped us off at Public Square, leaving Jones with only two of his three guards. A hundred or so people were gathered in the park, red communist flags waving in the air. As we approached, the press descended—thrusting microphones into Jones's face, asking why he was there and what he planned to do. With the speed at which he moved, and his silence toward the media, I got a bad feeling.

His main guard, Quentin—or Q—stayed close as Jones forced his way through the protesters. At some point, a stranger handed Jones a megaphone, which he held aloft. "We are here to take this country back and we won't be intimidated by you punks," Jones said, his words echoing through the loudspeaker. The deeper he pushed himself into the crowd, the harder it was to stay near him.

"Fuck Alex Jones!" one protester shouted.

"Fascist bastard!" said another.

Along the perimeter, militiamen stood watch, wearing bulletproof vests with assault rifles draped across their chests. Beside us, a protester wearing a Guy Fawkes mask held a sign that read, AMERICA WAS NEVER GREAT.

"What you've got is big giant megabanks funding a bunch of communists and cop killers and other organizations that want to start martial law in this country and derail our elections," Jones said in the megaphone. "Ladies and gentlemen, we are here to tell George Soros and Barack Obama and Hillary Clinton and the rest of the globalists, 'You're not going to start a civil war in this country!'"

A handful of people cheered. But then, after a brief silence, the activists holding communist flags started chanting, "Nazi scum, off our streets!"

Jones, proving his previous comments weren't bluster, barreled into them headfirst. He swung his fists, trying to hit as many as he could. One protester grabbed Jones from behind while Q leapt forward, prying his grip loose. Buckley and Biggs jumped between them, pushing against the crowd.

"Nazi scum, off our streets! Nazi scum, off our streets!"

The chief of police emerged from the sea of cameras. "They started it," Jones pled, looking up at the chief in desperation. "They attacked me first." It was a clear lie, given the whole reason he'd gone there—to "beat the fuck" out of what he referred to as "commie pieces of shit." Around a dozen police forced the crowd back as two officers locked arms with Jones and dragged him away. I followed, thinking he might be arrested for assault, but then realized what was happening. The police weren't detaining him; they were escorting him to safety.

"Move back!" the officers barked, heaving Jones toward our vehicle. Before we pulled away, a cop stuck his head inside and told Jones he was a big fan. "I listen to your show all the time."

"Appreciate it, brother," Jones said, dripping with sweat, struggling to breathe.

The officer slammed the door and addressed the driver. "Now get him out of here."

As we pulled away, Jones exhaled, still shaken but with a grin spreading on his face. "That was crazy, huh? Those guys came at me, and I had no other choice. You all saw that, right? That guy leaned down and sucker punched me."

"Yeah, I saw it," Buckley said, his words flat. But Jones's momentum was already building; he needed to construct the story before any of us had time to think.

"He did it so none of the cameras there would catch it, and all the media could act like I attacked them," Jones said, still out of breath. "I guarantee the headlines will say, ALEX JONES BRUTALLY ATTACKS PEACEFUL PROTESTERS. Oh, they're so loving and gentle with their Mao tattoos and Stalin T-shirts. Might as well say, ALEX JONES BRUTALLY ATTACKS THE SWEETIE PIE COMMUNISTS."

Jones had worked up an appetite, and Buckley found an Italian place on the outskirts of town. We piled into the restaurant, where Jones ordered Bolognese and sat at the table googling himself. As we ate, I got another message from Ronson.

> WTF just happened? Did someone take a swing at Alex?

That morning, he'd inquired about our plans for the day and asked whether Jones had coined the slogan "Hillary for Prison." I told him he had, though later Jones confessed he'd stolen it from a bumper sticker he'd seen six months earlier. Ronson said he wanted to shadow us, claiming he was working on a story about how Jones had "grown in importance since the nineties." I'd planned to mention it to Jones, if the mood was right, but with the chaos of the day, it had slipped my mind. Even after three years I still felt nervous bringing something to Jones's attention, unsure how he would react. Would it trigger an explosion, or fizzle into nothing?

"Ronson reached out," I said, hoping the current lull was as good a time as any.

"What does he want?" Buckley said, annoyed.

"He's writing another book," Jones said, putting his phone down on the table. In the bus, he seemed happy to see Ronson, a blast from the past. But as with most things, Jones's feelings shifted depending on the urgency of the moment. He'd become increasingly paranoid of others' motives, especially if the connection didn't benefit him directly. In some ways, this was a smart move on his part, but I sensed Ronson wasn't interested in attacking Jones or writing an unfair story. "Ehhh," Jones groaned. "Let me think about it. Don't give him our location yet."

The following day, a flag burning was scheduled outside the entrance to the RNC. Gregory Lee Johnson, the man behind the protest, had been arrested in 1989 for burning a flag at a similar event, leading to the landmark *Texas v. Johnson* Supreme Court case that established flag burning as free speech protected by the First Amendment. Despite the controversy, Jones had no interest in countering the demonstration. Biggs, on the other hand, was determined to stop it.

"Look," Jones said. "I think it's cowardly to burn the flag, but he has a right to do it."

Biggs's face reddened with anger. As a veteran, Biggs had become a voice for a subset of Jones's audience that he struggled to connect with, given his lack of military experience. Biggs had also developed a certain entitlement after all the attention he'd gotten on our travels.

"Don't get mad at me," Jones said, using his placating baby voice, the one he reverted to anytime he had a contentious conversation with an employee and wasn't in a hostile mood.

"I'm not mad," Biggs said, though the strain in his voice suggested otherwise. "This matters to a lot of your fans. I'm going down there."

Jones hesitated for a moment, then relented. "Fine. Go, but don't start anything. And don't forget to film it."

Once Biggs was gone, Jones shoved himself away from the table. "I'm telling you," he said to no one in particular, "Biggs is a hothead, and he better watch out. I'm not going to put up with that shit." The irony of Jones, who had physically assaulted a group of protesters the day before, acting perplexed by Biggs's bravado, must have stunned all of us into silence because no one said anything. "Go down there and make sure that idiot doesn't hurt anyone," Jones said to me.

Out on the street, a crowd had gathered, but Biggs was nowhere to be seen. Then, deep in the throng of people, I saw a flame flicker and ignite. Screams erupted, followed by what looked like the early formations of a mosh pit in the middle of the street. Police officers swarmed the area and began pulling people away from the smoldering flag. Some were on foot, others on horseback or bicycles. In the chaos I was pushed into the security fence surrounding the conference center. Fortunately, a guard spotted the press credentials hanging from my neck and ushered me inside.

Months before the convention, we'd each submitted a state ID for background checks by the Secret Service for press passes. Jones had always claimed we were on a government watch list, that the feds saw us as a domestic terrorist organization and that we'd never be allowed to participate in official proceedings. I was certain at least one of us would be denied entry, but after a few weeks we received notice that we'd all been approved. Once again, Jones's dire predictions crumbled.

In that moment though, I was grateful to be an insider, watching the madness unfold on the other side of the fence. People were screaming, being hauled away in handcuffs. To my right, I noticed a familiar face staring out at the crowd—it was Ronson. Our eyes met, and we moved toward each other, neither of us mentioning I'd ignored his earlier text.

Since we couldn't leave the area through the closest exit, we made our way over to a courtyard dubbed Freedom Plaza and ordered a beer. Everything was washed in red, white, and blue; vendors sold cheeseburgers, pierogies, and kielbasas with sweet peppers. A country band played on a stage while a handful of Waspy-looking individuals swung their hips off rhythm. Ronson speculated about what had happened moments earlier, but I didn't tell him my suspicion—that the chaos was likely instigated by someone I worked with.

I later learned Biggs *had* been involved in the scuffle before grabbing the fiery flag and burning himself. Gregory Lee Johnson was arrested, but Biggs somehow avoided the police, instead having to take a trip to the emergency room. He told Jones he planned to sue Johnson to cover his medical bills, an idea Jones quashed instantly. "Absolutely not," he said to an incredulous Biggs. I think Jones was jealous it hadn't happened to him and wanted to avoid drawing more attention to it.

Biggs moved on from his short-lived crusade, but Johnson filed a federal First Amendment retaliation lawsuit over his unconstitutional arrest. The chief of police, Calvin Williams, the same man who had watched Jones assault protesters the day before and had his officers, who claimed to be fans of Jones's show, escort us to safety, had Johnson arrested. Three years later, Johnson won his lawsuit when the City of Cleveland agreed to pay him a settlement of $225,000.

As I strolled the convention grounds with Ronson, his calm presence was a relief. I'd convinced myself that Jones's intensity was the key to his success, but seeing how Ronson—an accomplished and successful writer—carried himself, I realized that destructive behavior wasn't a prerequisite.

A day later I found myself in the same place, only this time Jones was beside me and the anxiety had returned. We met up with Roger Stone, who led us to "media row," where 160 news outlets were stationed for the week. The Republican National Committee had put up drywall, installed lighting, air conditioning, and even laid carpet on the second floor of a garage, turning what had been reserved for parking only a few days earlier into a makeshift newsroom.

Jones was in high demand, giving interviews with radio stations and news outlets, networking with people like Ann Coulter, who he previously despised but was now warming to, united by their mutual affection for Trump. The atmosphere felt corporate, hobnobbing with industry types, a world where Jones never quite fit in. He was a shit-stirrer, thriving on attention, but in a setting where decorum reigned, he had to choose whether he wanted to be accepted in those circles or stick to his personal brand of chaos.

Most of the Infowars crew were in the media area, following Jones from kiosk to kiosk, waiting as he did interviews and attempted to play nice. McAdoo sidled up to Jones after one of his interviews and told him that Cenk Uygur, host of the popular online show *The Young Turks*, was filming his live show just down the hallway. Jones, who looked worn down from having to play professional, became wild-eyed and eager.

"We should go over," he said, a mischievous look on his face. "Show me where they are."

The Young Turks were broadcasting from a temporary set with couches, lounge chairs, and a coffee table. Uygur was discussing, with three other men, Trump's voting demographics when Jones crashed the set. "I'm going to come sit in your lap," Jones said, extending his hand to Uygur and stepping behind him. I approached the stage along with Dew and Francis.

This wasn't the first time Jones had appeared on *The Young Turks*. He had been a guest in previous years, though the two had opposing political views. The difference this time was that Jones hadn't been invited.

"Oh, Jesus Christ," Uygur said, reluctantly shaking Jones's hand. At first, he tried to be cordial, but that lasted only until Jones pulled out a shirt he was selling on Infowars. It featured an image of Bill Clinton, styled after Shepard Fairey's famous Obama "Hope" poster. Except instead of the word "Hope," it said "Rape."

Uygur snatched the shirt from Jones and crumpled it up. "You know who does this kind of shirt? First of all, a sick guy. Second of all—"

"Bill Clinton's not a rapist, folks," Jones interrupted with sarcasm.

"No, you know who's accused in court papers of being a rapist? Donald J. Trump," Uygur said.

Just then, Roger Stone—who'd been lurking in the crowd of onlookers—emerged and began heckling Uygur, calling him a liar.

"You're the world's biggest liar," Uygur shouted. "Didn't you admit you lied about Eliot Spitzer? Didn't you already admit that, you piece of crap?" He was referring to Stone's supposed involvement in the prostitution bust that brought down the New York State governor Eliot Spitzer, in 2008. Stone had claimed a major role in the scandal, though this was never confirmed.

Jones stood behind Uygur as he railed against Stone, pulling his shoulder, stirring the pot to ramp up the altercation. "Get up here, right now," Jones said to Stone, leaning back down to Uygur. "You're not afraid of him, are you? Get him in here."

"First of all, Alex, this isn't your fucking show," Uygur said. "And Roger, it certainly isn't *your* fucking show!"

Jones repeated that Uygur was afraid of debate, trying to goad him into bringing Stone onstage. He knew this would cause a stir—as evidenced by the swarm of people gathering around. Uygur wasn't oblivious to the spectacle; when his producers cut the live feed to his show, he demanded they start the stream back.

I stood at the foot of the stage, camera in hand, watching the absurdity unfold. But amid the frenzy, my gaze shifted to one of the men onstage. There, sitting next to Uygur, was Ben Mankiewicz— the grandson of Herman J. Mankiewicz (co-writer of the seminal film *Citizen Kane*) and the host of Turner Classic Movies. In fact, Ben Mankiewicz was my favorite host, the person who started and often ended some of the first viewings of what became my favorite films. Mankiewicz introduced David Lean's heartbreaking 1945 film *Brief Encounter* and Howard Hawks's 1938 film *Bringing Up Baby*. His face was followed by Humphrey Bogart and Lauren Bacall, Bette Davis and Joan Crawford, Robert Mitchum and Kirk Douglas, creating a Pavlovian response to some of the most exciting moments in my otherwise dull life. I was starstruck and felt a confusing sense of anticipatory wonder among the idiocy going on around me.

Jones, still behind Uygur, continued his childish antics—making bunny ears, pulling faces, baffled by Uygur's anger. To Jones, this wasn't real. It was all just a show, an exhibition.

One of Uygur's cohosts, Ana Kasparian, who had been absent during the debacle, appeared on the platform and addressed Jones. "Get off the stage, you fat fuck."

Jones, in response, accused the Young Turks of waging a "Jihad" funded by Saudi Arabia, and Uygur leapt up, ripping off his microphone and earpiece. "This is bullshit," he shouted, an inch away from Jones's face. "We're against Saudi Arabia, you dumbass! We talk about that all the time." Mankiewicz pulled off his jacket and held Uygur back while Ana pled with him to relax. "You don't know shit," Uygur continued. "What, do you think the lizard people are in charge?"

"No!" Jones said, defensive.

"The Bilderbergs?" Uygur pressed.

"Hey, you're pissed because we're kicking your ass," Jones said, referring to his viewership.

"Bullshit," Uygur shouted.

"We're being nice here," Jones said, the words drowned out by the chaos.

"Get the fuck off my stage!"

Then, Jimmy Dore, a former comedian who appeared on *The Young Turks* as the "Just Asking Questions" guy, walked on the stage with a mouth full of water and spit it in Jones's face.

Jones recoiled, astonished. "He just spit in my face," he said, sounding like he was trying to convince himself it had happened.

Event security arrived and escorted Jones away—the second time in twenty-four hours security had to pull him from a bad situation. Cameras circled, following him. "That is the craziest shit I've ever seen," Jones said with a hazy look of disbelief.

It took a second for him to regroup and remember why he'd started the scuffle to begin with. Attention. He straightened himself out, wiped the spit from his face, and headed back to the media area, where he was scheduled for more interviews, to start spreading his narrative of what just happened. This was precisely what Jones wanted, to sow enough chaos to become the story. But he knew if he confessed to being the instigator, his ploy would be foiled, so, instead, he played the victim.

"They set me up," Jones said, spinning his version of events to a talk radio host. He claimed a woman producer for *The Young Turks* had invited him onstage and encouraged him to "have fun." Even if everything had been caught on camera, his audience, along with the media who held his political views and wanted to cast conservatives as victims, would believe him.

Roger Stone chimed in. "This is very typical of the left," he said to a reporter. "When they can't argue with you on the facts, they start calling names and resort to violence. I don't think violence solves anything."

Jones was elated after the confrontation and wanted the crew to meet for an early dinner. The last thing I wanted after a chaotic event was food; my nerves shot, stomach in knots.

At the restaurant, Jones kept refreshing YouTube, upset *The Young Turks* live stream had more views than his. When he wasn't ranting about YouTube's supposed bias, he was asking the crew for feedback on the confrontation. We all adjusted to his narrative.

"They were the ones who invited you over," Dew said.

"It was a setup," I added.

"The video is all over the news," Buckley said. "Everyone knows they were the ones acting like maniacs."

After dinner, Jones wanted to head back to the convention, where Trump had officially secured the Republican nomination and was about to speak. We had only two tickets for the floor, and Jones asked me to go with him. The others seemed relieved.

There was a lull waiting for Trump to speak, so I checked my phone and noticed I had a text from Ronson.

> Hey! I just saw TYT footage. Jesus!! Where are you guys now? I'd love to come over.

Before I could respond, the lights dimmed and the crowd stirred. A spotlight appeared onstage and I heard gasps, turning to a feverish applause when an unmistakable silhouette appeared in front of the glowing orb. The speech lasted well over an hour, and Trump's words sounded like they had been ripped from the pages of Jones's imagination. He spoke of the attacks on police, terrorism in America, the dangers of illegal immigration. Jones was enraptured by the speech, staring up at Trump with reverence. After Trump said, "Americanism, not globalism, will be our credo," I looked over at Jones and saw tears streaming down his face.

"History is watching us now," Trump said. "It's waiting to see if we will rise to the occasion, and if we will show the whole world that

America is still free and independent and strong. To all Americans tonight, in all our cities and towns, I make this promise: We will make America strong again. We will make America proud again. We will make America safe again. And we will make America great again."

The crowd roared, but my eyes were fixed on Jones—now sobbing, his shoulders convulsing as he wiped ropy strings of snot from his nose. I couldn't understand it. Nothing Trump said resonated with me. Over the past few years, I'd witnessed police brutality against protesters in Ferguson, visited the communities Trump's supporters demonized, heard Muslims in San Bernardino call the terror attacks the antithesis of their faith. I'd spent weeks at the border, from Arizona to Mexico, having to fabricate stories to push bigoted exaggerations. Trump's world was Jones's world—a world I knew was a lie.

This was the moment Jones had been waiting for. In his mind, I believe he saw himself in Trump's place, once vilified, his ideas now manifested on the world's stage. If it all panned out, and Trump became the next president, Jones could see himself, his ideas, as part of the establishment, the one thing he'd spent the past twenty years fighting against. He could finally convince himself he'd won.

"He's the real deal," Jones said as we walked into the warm summer night, his eyes raw from tears. "I've never been more certain about anything. My god, I just can't believe we have a real shot at saving this country. The establishment is going to come after him even harder, and us too." He began to cry again, claiming he'd had an out-of-body experience during Trump's speech, that God had spoken to him and confirmed Trump was a legitimate, trustworthy person. He grabbed my arm. "You felt that too, right? What'd you think about being in there? It was historic."

"Um..." I stammered, trying to force the words out of my mouth. "It was...definitely...powerful."

I didn't believe God had spoken to Jones, and in my eyes, Trump was a wretched human being, a danger to our country, and one of the last people I wanted to see in the White House. But by that point, what I did or didn't believe was useless. My moral compass was off, I'd lost my way, and I could no longer trust myself.

Part Three
DISBELIEF

17

WAKING UP

During a speech Obama delivered in support of Clinton before the election, a fly kept landing on his face. While most people would see this as an annoying yet common occurrence, Jones transformed it into an insane headline. He claimed to have "intel" from sources close to Obama and Clinton who insisted they both smelled like sulfur. "They are covered in flies all the time because of their stench," he said. The reason, according to Jones—which he almost certainly made up on the spot—was their proximity to the underworld. "They're literal freaking demons from hell!"

When WikiLeaks released emails between Hillary Clinton and her 2016 campaign chairman, John Podesta, Jones reacted predictably. While the emails mostly contained mundane chatter, conspiracy theorists on 4Chan pounced, dissecting every word.

One email mentioned James Alefantis, a Democratic donor and owner of Comet Ping Pong, a pizzeria in DC. Alefantis had dated David Brock, a Clinton ally and founder of the media watchdog group Media Matters for America—one of the only sites monitoring and condemning Jones's rhetoric at the time. In this email, Alefantis considered organizing a fundraiser for Clinton's campaign. Conspiracists frantically searched Alefantis's social media accounts, using innocuous photos of children and basement construction to fashion a grand conspiracy claiming he, and Clinton, were part of a large network of pedophiles.

Another email revealed that the artist, Marina Abramović, had been invited to a fundraiser for Hillary Clinton. Abramović's art, often shocking and confrontational, was misunderstood as demonic, echoing the baseless fears of the 1980s Satanic Panic.

These unrelated pieces converged into a perfect storm, culminating in the infamous Pizzagate conspiracy. Armchair detectives scoured the emails, claiming coded messages about child trafficking lay hidden in discussions of food. References to hot dogs and pizza for parties were euphemisms for something far more sinister. Comet Ping Pong, once just a pizzeria, was suddenly the headquarters of a child sex trafficking ring.

Jones was out of town when the rumors first erupted, and one of his correspondents, Jon Bowne, posted a video about the emails. The next day Jones called, furious, and Dew put him on speakerphone. "How many times do I have to tell you all not to post anything calling out specific businesses or brands," Jones said, incensed. "Public figures are fine, but that's it. Take it down right now!"

Dew reprimanded Bowne and removed the video. However, viewers began accusing Jones and Infowars of covering up Pizzagate. As the backlash grew, Jones—ignoring his own supposed rule—began discussing Comet Ping Pong and its owner publicly, expanding the conspiracy's reach to a much larger audience.

Waking Up

In the months leading up to the election, Jones's obsession with Trump hit a fever pitch. He wanted us at every debate, determined to pound the pavement with as much positive coverage of Trump, and negative coverage of Clinton, as possible. Before the second debate in Saint Louis, he and Stone conspired to push the narrative that Bill Clinton had an illegitimate son from an alleged affair with his housekeeper. They even flew the man, Danney Williams, to Austin to appear on Jones's show.

It was clear they were exploiting him. Williams—shy and reserved—seemed uncomfortable with all the attention he was getting. Jones was eager to extract as much content out of him as possible, so he sent me downtown with Williams to shoot a "man on the street" segment where he claimed Clinton was his father. The interactions were confusing and awkward.

On the ride back, he shared with me that Stone had given him "media training," which he explained as talking points and a crafted story to sell the audience on his claim. I couldn't say if he believed he was Clinton's biological son—he admitted he'd never gotten confirmation with a blood test—but I did know this: Once the media dismissed the claim, Jones, and presumably Stone, discarded him as quickly as they'd ushered him in.

I just wanted the election to be over, for Trump to lose—something I was sure would happen—and for the travel schedule to ease up so I could finally consider my exit. Each time I reached a breaking point, Jones would offer a bonus, a raise, or heap so much work on me that I was too drained to think about leaving.

For the third and final presidential debate, I traveled to Las Vegas with David Knight. It had been two and a half years since we were in Nevada covering the standoff at Bundy Ranch. Back then, we were bright eyed and new to Jones's world, but now we were heavily relied upon employees. We had also grown despondent, miserable in our circumstances. Knight still aligned with many of Jones's views, but he despised him as a boss and a person. Despite our political differences, we bonded over the cumulative stress of working for Jones, resentful of how bitter and angry we'd grown along the way.

After the debate, as I boarded the flight from Vegas to Austin, I noticed Ronson's piece about the RNC had been released. I purchased the audiobook, *The Elephant in the Room*, and listened on the flight back. It was brief, but it hit me like a punch to the gut. For the first time, I was hearing criticism of Jones before he could spin it into another grand narrative of persecution. The smarmy bravado, the ridiculous conspiracy theories—it all felt painfully clear. I was flooded with shame at being tied to him, for having spent years in his orbit, feeding into his madness.

After the RNC, I texted Ronson to apologize for my lack of communication. I liked him and felt bad for ignoring so many of his attempts to connect with us. He was kind and accepted my apology, asking if I would keep him apprised of any plans Jones had before the election.

> Hey Jon, I'm traveling back after covering the debate last night and saw your latest work, The Elephant in The Room. I was barely able to download it from Audible before the plane took off. I've traveled all over the world for Alex: Bilderberg, Ferguson, Bundy Ranch, the latest nauseating Trump coverage, and a lot of times I'm conflicted with what I'm seeing out on the road. Anyway I won't get into that. I just wanted you to know I thought the piece you wrote was exceptional.

I sent the text in a hurry, not realizing the implications until Ronson responded. He thanked me for the compliment, but the following evening he sent another message.

> Btw—if you ever want to tell me about the conflicts you're feeling being out on the road I'd love to hear...

It seemed I was so consumed with the onslaught of day-to-day trauma—giving and receiving it—my subconscious was screaming for help from a friendly passerby. I set my phone down, choosing to ignore his offer, terrified of what I might say.

Election Day began like any other. Jones strolled into the office and beelined for the liquor cabinet. He filled a fresh white Dixie Cup with vodka, adding a splash of club soda, used his private bathroom to get changed into one of his tailored suits, and went to host his radio show. Already Jones was priming his audience for Trump's defeat, claiming the Democrats, Obama, and Clinton would commit voter fraud and a slew of dirty tricks to steal the election.

When the show ended, Jones returned to my office, filled his cup again—this time leaving out the soda—and asked me to ride with him to vote. He didn't appear drunk, but that wasn't a reliable gauge. It took more than most could handle to make him slur or stumble, especially during this chaotic period. He was still embroiled in a messy divorce, raking in more money than ever, and basking in unprecedented media attention thanks to his ties to Trump. Since his explosive performance at the RNC, speculation had bubbled up that Trump was pulling talking points from Jones.

Meanwhile, Hillary Clinton had taken the opportunity to slam Jones during a rally in Reno. She called him out by name, condemning his outrageous claims that the Sandy Hook tragedy was a staged false flag and the victims were actors. "I don't know what happens in somebody's mind," Clinton said, "or how dark their heart must be to say things like that."

For most, this level of condemnation from the presidential front-runner would be devastating, but Jones was elated. He pranced around the office for weeks, giggling and referring to himself as "Dark Heart," wearing the insult like a badge of honor.

I collapsed into the passenger seat of his Dodge Hellcat, a vehicle Jones adored like a lovesick teenager. Not in some lighthearted, cutesy way but as a full-blown romance. He once described his Hellcat as a woman, claiming that after he drove it, he needed to have a cigarette "like they did in old movies after sex."

Inside the car, Jones asked me to start streaming live to Facebook while he launched into his usual routine of brainstorming a headline. "Let's see," he said, taking a sip of his vodka. He placed the drink in the center console, the scent so strong from the cup and his breath that it filled the warm car. My internal sirens went off, telling me to get out, but by then, I'd gotten used to ignoring them.

He riffed through headline options. "Let's call it, 'Alex Jones Issues…,' no, no, 'Emergency! Voter Fraud…,' no, no, no…What do you think?" I hesitated, knowing from years of experience that my input didn't matter. He would stammer through all the buzzwords and phrases that had garnered views in the past—"RED ALERT," "BREAKING NEWS," "MUST WATCH," "BOMBSHELL," "POWERFUL"—until something felt right.

Finally, he settled on one. ALEX JONES DENIED RIGHT TO VOTE.

He cranked the engine and reversed so fast, the phone almost flew out of my hands. I waited until the office was out of view before starting the live video. As the years wore on and his notoriety grew, Jones became even more paranoid about keeping the location private. He had window decals put up every few months with new business names like Oak Shipping, Mountain Diagnostics, and Hill Country Supply, to throw rabid fans or adversaries off the scent.

As the stream began, Jones told the viewers he was on his way to the polls. For most of his career, he'd denounced voting as a scam, an illusion of choice, convincing his audience that the game was rigged. But this time was different; Jones had skin in the game.

"Some will say, 'Well the vote is a fraud, you admit they steal elections,'" he said, turning out of the parking lot. "We have to be involved in the vote to prove there's fraud to then try to improve the system and make it fairer. Just like Black folks had to fight for their right to vote and Christians fought with them."

He floored onto the frontage road, speeding faster as we reached the interstate. My stomach churned as I stared at the screen. Jones knew the polling place wouldn't let us film inside. It was the perfect setup, as it would allow him to claim later that he was denied the chance to vote for Trump, providing a thin foundation on which to base his accusations of fraud.

"Hey, get that city shot," he said, pointing out the window. As I pulled the camera off him, he reached for the white Dixie Cup and took a sip. *Is this really how I'm going to die?* I thought to myself, imagining the scene: Jones veering too close to the guardrail, ranting about George Soros and Hillary Clinton. Sirens echoing in the distance, flashing lights reflecting off oil-soaked pavement as he grabbed the camera and uttered his final words, "Hillary...rigged...the car." His listeners would have believed it. Years earlier, *I* would have believed it. I didn't want my life summed up by this experience—a pseudo sidekick to a narcissistic megalomaniacal lunatic—but the longer I stayed, the likelier that would be the outcome.

Fortunately, there were no sirens or flashing lights, and I was relieved when VOTE HERE signs began to appear. Jones had invited Cliff along for backup, and he pulled in as we exited the vehicle. A line stretched out the door of the polling place, in a local strip mall. Jones's plan worked. Outside, as he pontificated to the audience via live stream, a poll worker approached and said we couldn't bring a camera inside. Jones cried foul, saying it was a biased attempt to keep him from voting, and after minimal pushback, he decided to leave without casting his vote.

Walking back to the car, still taking sips from his white cup, Jones began slurring his words. He stopped a woman with a dog and bent down to kiss the animal on its mouth. When he learned the woman had voted for Hillary Clinton, he turned from a drunk weirdo into a misogynist prick. "See," he said, loudly addressing the camera so she could hear, "the civilization is built by men, and then it's overrun by people who can't wipe their noses. They sit here in Valhalla, and they piss on it because they hate it, because they didn't build it."

Across the parking lot, a Latino man in his late twenties, walking with his school-aged child, approached Jones to shake his hand. He unzipped his jacket and showed Jones he was wearing a Donald Trump shirt underneath. "Thanks for waking us up, man," he said in earnest. As soon as he walked away, Jones turned to the camera and whispered, "I think that guy was Latino... I don't know any Latinos that are actually for Hillary... I think the secret weapon is Latinos."

The two interactions, back-to-back, felt like they had come from the pages of a hackneyed movie script. As Jones wrapped up his commentary, the moment crystallized into a revealing snapshot of who he really was. "I'm bashing women, but these are dumbass women, man," Jones said. "I mean, let's just be honest, they are dumber than sacks of shit."

Cliff offered me a ride back to the office since Jones was having trouble walking by that point. He suggested giving Jones a ride too, but Jones refused. A moment later, he revved his engine, tires squealing as he sped out of the parking lot.

I knew how Jones would react if Trump lost the election. There would be an endless stream of emergency broadcasts, accusing Democrats of single-handedly destroying democracy. Hillary Clinton would be cast as the architect of a communist takeover. Civil war would be framed as an inevitability, peddled daily until either it happened, or Jones grew bored and shifted to the next impending disaster. In many ways, nothing would change.

But what I didn't know was how he would react if Trump won. I never thought it would happen. When the news broke late that night, I was sitting in my office with Gucciardi, who seemed to despise Trump too. Since Utah years earlier, we'd taken different paths. When Jones invited me out or asked me to join his family for the holidays, I avoided it. I had no interest in being his friend; I could barely stomach being his employee. Gucciardi, though, would mingle with Jones off the clock. They partied together, shared inside jokes, exchanged secret glances. Still, even with that connection, Gucciardi had to bend to Jones's will, keeping quiet about his apparent disdain for Trump.

We were both in stunned silence as we watched the chyrons scroll on TV news when suddenly, screams echoed through the hallway. It was Biggs, doing a victory lap around the office. "We did it," he shouted. "We fucking did it!"

I wanted to throw up, because on some level he was right. We weren't solely responsible for Trump's victory, but we had spent much of the past year, at Jones's request, helping him push his narrative. One lie at a time.

On the show, Jones looked happy Trump had won, toasting champagne with Stone. But afterward he walked into my office, despondent, fluctuating from rage to inconsolable sadness. He ambled over to the Stalin flag hanging on the cabinet door and began punching it. The door was already dented from previous bouts of violence, making a sad slapping sound as it ricocheted off its broken hinges.

After drinking all day, Jones was more intoxicated than I'd ever seen him. On the show he was slurring his words and had even knocked over his glass of champagne during an incoherent aside.

He stumbled from my desk to Dew's, then over to Tillman's, like a pinball floating in zero gravity. He muttered incoherently, grimacing with every hard blink, until he stammered out a request to go live on

Facebook. Buckley tried to talk him out of it, leading him to the other side of the building, but it didn't work. Jones staggered in the opposite direction, toward the nightly news studio. It was after 2 a.m., exhaustion had engulfed my despair, and I wanted to go home.

"Come on," Jones grumbled from the shadows. Buckley crossed his arms, but Dew grabbed a phone and asked me to turn on the studio lights. I threw my hands up, too tired to struggle. If he wanted to make a fool of himself, who were we to stop him? Buckley rolled his eyes and walked away, leaving us to deal with Jones.

"Now we are bound forever," Jones said, weeping on camera. "And if we don't deliver this plan, and free humanity, we will be bound to the ninth circle of hell." He sucked in air, gasping for breath, choking on his own drunken melancholy. "I've already run my course. I already know my entire life purpose has been completed." He stood up from the desk and unbuttoned his jacket. "I will continue on, but now I realize... I've won." He walked out of frame, out of the studio, and I didn't see him again for the rest of the night.

Before the election, there had been one morning when Jones seemed particularly low. "You all better hope Hillary wins," he said to Dew, Tillman, and me. The extraneous comment took us by surprise, as we hadn't been discussing the election. "Otherwise, I don't know if I'll be able to afford to pay everyone." He often used scarcity as a manipulation tool, but after witnessing his reaction to Trump's win, I wondered if he'd revealed his true insecurity.

Jones had existed on the fringes for so long, fighting against an elusive force. It was where he was comfortable, how he'd built such a profitable empire. Rumors were already circulating around the office—likely from Stone—that Trump would make sure Infowars had White House press credentials. Things were about to change; it would be much harder for him to stay in the shadows, and I think he was terrified.

Jones continued to drink, his behavior growing more frantic by the day, fueled by a manic need to shoot impromptu reports. He fixated on the idea of being banned from social media, convinced "they" were tampering with his views. He even claimed Trump had called to thank him for his role in securing the election. I knew Jones had spoken to Trump on the phone before, or at least he had pretended to in front of me on two separate occasions. But Jones had become so erratic, I'd started to wonder if he'd made it up. Trump used the same talking points as Jones, even repeating exact phrases, but I wasn't convinced their relationship was as intimate as Jones implied.

After Trump won, I pulled back, engulfed by a growing sense of impending doom, furious I'd stuck around so long. Strangely, that time felt reminiscent of when I first started listening to Jones. I was cynical, jaded, directionless, filled with animosity toward everyone and everything, especially myself.

I hadn't responded to Ronson's last message, and was surprised when, a month after the election, he reached out again.

> Hey! Just wondering how things are in the Infowars world post the election. If you ever want to talk about it I'd love to.

As I read his message, I thought back to what Jones had said three years earlier, while we dined with Vivian Kubrick in Dallas. "This is all providence," he'd told me. "Nothing happens by chance. All the decisions we make in life guide us to these moments."

Maybe my own providence wasn't about entering Jones's chaotic world, I thought. *Maybe it was about finding a way out.*

18

A GOOD MAN IS HARD TO FIND

Since the election, I'd been texting with Ronson, trying to find a time to meet. When I mentioned feeling "conflicted" about my experiences working for Jones, I hadn't planned on elaborating. The words spilled out in a moment of desperation, without considering the consequences. I didn't know what I'd say when we finally met, but it seemed like a step in the right direction.

Even after all that time, leaving felt impulsive. I had been isolated with a group of people for nearly four years, bound by a shared experience, like a shipwrecked crew reluctant to abandon their marooned island. I didn't know how to function outside of it. Any job skills I had developed were tailored for one individual—Alex Jones. I had learned to view the world through his lens, prioritizing his words, beliefs, and preferences above my own, out of fear, out of survival. At that point, I wasn't sure where he started, and I began.

Jones planned to cover Trump's inauguration in person. This meant he would broadcast his show from DC and would need equipment there to do it. For the RNC, Raymond had driven all the gear to Cleveland in the company RV, but Jones had since sold the RV and fired Raymond, the first person I'd met on my first day. He was a remnant of Jones's past, one of his oldest employees, but he was from another iteration of Infowars. The more Jones fixated on appearance and luxury, the less Raymond fit in.

Around this time, Jones also fired Jakari Jackson. For years Jakari had refused to cower to Jones. His defiance in California marked the beginning of a tense, often contentious relationship between the two. Like many of us, Jakari wanted to quit but hadn't yet found a way out. His dream was to move to Charleston, South Carolina, a city he first visited in 2015. The day after Trump announced his presidential run, a white supremacist took the lives of nine Black people at Emanuel African Methodist Episcopal Church in Charleston. Jones sent Jakari to report on the aftermath. While Jones demanded coverage of the Second Amendment and Obama's gun control stance, Jakari, instead, was overwhelmed by the community's solidarity in the face of hate. It left an indelible mark on him.

Two months after his firing, Jakari texted me a photo of him, smiling on the banks of the Cooper River. He had moved to Charleston. Below the picture, referencing the Otis Redding song he'd played on our drive through California three years earlier, he wrote: *Sittin' on the dock of the bay.*

I volunteered to drive the equipment to DC, presenting it as a selfless gesture. But I had an ulterior motive, one Jones couldn't know about. The real reason I'd offered to drive up early was to meet Ronson in secret.

Francis came along so I wouldn't have to make the trip alone. I had grown close with him, not just from shared experience, but because he was smart, funny, and I felt a sense of responsibility for him. He was a teenager when he was hired, and I feared he might get sucked into Jones's manipulative web like I had. I took a risk and confided in him about my meeting with Ronson. He was supportive but wary, not wanting to get involved in case Jones found out.

The drive from Austin to DC stretched over fifteen hundred miles and nearly thirty hours. It felt like a fever dream—driving through half the country to the nation's capital to witness Donald Trump's inauguration. Of all the outcomes I could've imagined when I began working for Jones, this was one I never would've guessed. That Trump would become president, aided by Jones's vigilant support, and I would be secretly meeting with Jon Ronson to blow the whistle on Jones's grand fraud.

After we'd arrived in DC, I walked the rain-slicked streets, heading to the hotel where Ronson and I had agreed to meet. My stomach was queasy from nerves, and I thought about turning around and calling the whole thing off. Instead, I took a deep breath and continued forward, walking through a revolving door into the hotel lobby. Ronson was seated near a fountain waiting for me. We ordered coffee at the hotel café and took a seat.

It wasn't long into our conversation when I realized the real reason I'd come there. I was looking to vent my frustrations to someone who had known Jones for a long time, to speak to a kind, levelheaded person who might be able to offer advice. I had decided to quit my job, but I was still scared of what the future might hold.

I shared stories about Islamberg, the lies we'd spread at the border, and my growing disillusionment with Jones and Infowars. Until that conversation, I'd felt overwhelmed with my dilemma. But in Ronson's presence, it all appeared much simpler. I had convinced myself I had to stay for my own well-being, because the alternative was nebulous and potentially catastrophic. I had distracted myself for so long that I hadn't even begun to do the one thing I could control.

Ronson listened patiently, giving me space to talk. I asked if I could pick his brain about the "writing world" to see if he could impart any advice. "I'm interested in moving in a different direction," I said. Writing was solitary, and I could use some time alone. As I told him about my experiences, he watched me with curiosity. "You know," he said, "if you're interested in writing, this is really what you should be writing about."

I'd never considered telling my own story. I was still asking Ronson to keep me anonymous if he used any of the information I'd given him. Stepping out of Jones's world was terrifying enough, but speaking openly about my experiences was another thing entirely. At that time, no one who left Infowars talked about what happened inside. We had been warned that anyone who spoke out would face serious repercussions. Jones wielded the non-disclosure agreement like a guillotine, threatening to release the rope and chop our heads clean off if anyone considered expressing dissent. And surprisingly, none of us questioned why he was so adamant about smearing people after they left and instilling a culture of secrecy.

I considered what Ronson said. He told me he knew people at the *New York Times* and the *Guardian* and would pass along anything I wrote. I was terrified by the prospect, but it was the first time I felt like leaving could serve something other than myself. If people knew who Jones really was, and the lies that sustained his conspiratorial world, maybe it would make a difference.

But my motivation wasn't purely altruistic. For years I had judged Jones's faults while overlooking my own. I didn't want to walk away from that chapter of my life feeling like it was all for nothing. I was ashamed of my weakness and complicity, and by choosing to speak out, even in the face of consequences, I might at least find it easier to live with myself.

As we wrapped up our conversation, I regretted that Ronson had come all the way from New York City to act as an emotional sponge for my problems. I cast about for something I could share so that he didn't have to leave empty-handed. Then a memory surfaced. A few months earlier, Buckley had told me the real reason Jones's family moved from Dallas to Austin when he was a teenager.

Jones's heroic version of the story involved him uncovering a nefarious operation where police officers peddled drugs to high school students. However, Buckley's version, shared with me after enduring mistreatment from Jones one too many times, painted a far less flattering portrait. According to his cousin, Jones wasn't a vigilante; he was a bully. As a kid, he terrorized his peers until a group of them decided enough was enough. Some of his classmates lured him to a party under false pretenses, only to brutally ambush him. Jones was beaten badly, left bloodied, and had to be hospitalized. His father, terrified for his son's safety, closed his dental practice in Dallas and moved the family to Austin, where Jones could have a fresh start.

Buckley's version explained Jones's obsession with conspiracies, his warped sense of justice, and his frequent tangents about physical violence. Cliff had told me that when Jones first moved to Austin, he was a loner, immersed in conspiratorial books. This story seemed to clarify everything.

Ronson was intrigued and promised to look further into it. Before we parted, he recommended I consult a lawyer about my NDA. If everything checked out, and I was still interested, he promised to help me tell my story.

It was raining when I stepped outside, so I ducked under an awning to make a call. My own mind was unreliable at the time, and I needed a second opinion. Lacey was the only person I fully trusted.

She took a deep breath and exhaled slowly. "Thank fucking god," she said. I could hear the smile in her voice. The time with Jones had been a heavy burden, not just for me, but for her too. After seven years together, our stretch in Austin had been the hardest. I lived in a constant state of anxiety, trapped in a cycle of stress and uncertainty. Each morning, I awoke knowing the pressure would only intensify, because that's what it meant to exist in Jones's world.

Lacey had to endure my internal tug-of-war between wanting to leave and the fear of what might happen if I did. The uncertainty. The second-guessing. I was miserable, and in turn, I was making her miserable. She needed me to find a way out, but she also knew I had to do it on my terms, in my own time. "Think through it," she said, "but it sounds like a great idea."

I walked back to the hotel in the rain, trying to put the meeting out of my mind, bracing for the chaos of the next three days.

Jones had plans to broadcast his show from an apartment he rented with a view of the Capitol, and he was already ruminating on how it would be an ideal vantage point if Trump were to be assassinated. We were right above Pennsylvania Avenue, where Trump would take the ceremonial walk from the US Capitol to the White House after his inauguration. This was when Jones predicted Trump would be the most vulnerable, where someone could perch out on a balcony, just like the one we were staying in, and take a shot at him. Given his enthusiasm, I couldn't shake the feeling that he welcomed the scenario.

My only other visit to DC had been in 2007 with my family, during the waning days of Bush's presidency. It was then I first began to grasp the chaotic world of politics, not long before I was introduced to Jones. Some were ecstatic about Bush's exit and Obama's historic entrance, though most people in my hometown were preoccupied with Obama's background, beliefs, and intentions—anything to divert themselves from their real concern with his skin color. Nearly a decade later and the city felt burdened by a viscous, oppressive atmosphere. Everything seemed ready for change, but this time, there was no sense of hope.

That night, Francis and I decided to have dinner at Comet Ping Pong, the pizza place roiled by conspiracy theories that Jones had played a major hand in promoting. A month earlier, a man had walked into the restaurant wielding an AR-15. Families were enjoying their meals and playing games when he stormed in, demanding to see the basement where he believed children were being held captive—though no such basement existed. The gunman, a loyal listener to Jones, fired shots, sending families diving for cover. Fortunately, the police apprehended the man, and no one was hurt. But Jones, as expected, spun the incident as a "false flag" to divert attention from his role in inciting it. Because of our part, we chose to have dinner there that night, eating and drinking more than our fair share, and purchasing merchandise. It wasn't much, but it was the least we could do.

When Jones arrived in DC, I noticed he kept wiping tears from his face and then flying into a rage over nothing. We spent much of the time walking around town, filming Jones as he rambled about the historic importance of the election. He'd hired five additional security guards, some of whom he claimed were former Blackwater mercenaries, and they looked the part, wearing their monochrome American flag hats, tactical earth-toned cargo pants, and black polo shirts, concealing weapons.

The night before the inauguration, I went out to dinner with Jones. Dew, Buckley, three of his security guards, and I accompanied him through the streets to an upscale Italian restaurant. He cried as we walked, muttering about something that was upsetting him. I kept my distance, unable to make out his complaints. In my paranoia, I briefly thought he had discovered my betrayal, that maybe Francis had ratted me out.

On the walk a group of guys recognized Jones and asked to take a picture with him. Jones obliged, looking miserable and red-eyed in the photo. They tried to engage him in conversation, but he ignored their comments and shuffled away. Dew stayed behind to speak with them—a sucker for arduous discussions, especially when the topic was conspiracy theories.

We sat down at the restaurant and ordered drinks. After fifteen minutes Dew still hadn't arrived. The waiter came to take our order and Buckley suggested we wait for Dew, but Jones wasn't having it. "If he's going to stand out there gossiping, he can buy his own dinner," Jones said, proceeding to order nearly the entire menu for the table.

After our second drink, Dew strolled in the front door. "About time," Jones huffed, telling Dew that we had already ordered and he'd have to find somewhere else to eat.

"I'll just fucking leave, then," Dew said, pushing the chair back from the table.

"Where are you going?" Jones said, confused.

"If you don't want me here, I'll leave," Dew said.

Jones looked shocked, suddenly preoccupied with rearranging the cutlery in front of him. "You think I really wanted you to leave? It was a joke..." He said the word "joke" like it had been lobbed at him for so long, he was pained a supposed friend would force him to use it. "Am I really that bad?"

Dew was in a precarious spot. In an instant, Jones had altered the dynamic, turning himself into a victim so he wouldn't feel the need to apologize. Dew backtracked, changing his tune, saying he had misunderstood the whole situation.

"Am I that terrible of a person?" Jones asked, more to himself than any of us, unlatching a Rolex from his wrist. He turned it over in his hand and then held it across the table. "Take it," he said to Dew, the silver glinting in his palm. Dew refused, but Jones insisted. He stood from his chair, groaning as he stretched over the table and placed the watch in front of Dew. "Take it," he said again, his voice soft with feigned generosity. Dew picked up the watch, holding it as if at any moment it might come to life and bite clean through his hand. "Try it on," Jones said. I looked over at Dew as he snapped the watch on his wrist. It reminded me of a picture of my younger sister as a toddler, trying on my mother's comically oversized high heels.

The watch—a Rolex Submariner in white gold—hung from Dew's wrist, as he inspected it from every angle. "Thanks," he said, promising to take care of it and give it back before we left the restaurant.

"It's yours," Jones said. "I don't want it back. I'm giving it to you."

Dew looked shocked. We were all dumfounded by this gesture. He pinched it tight to his wrist to see what it would look like once he got it fitted. The watch was nice, it was a Rolex after all, but it still didn't look right on him.

"Would a bad guy do that?" Jones said.

"What?" Dew said, looking up at him, confused.

"Give you a Rolex off his own wrist. Would a bad guy do that?" Jones's voice was stolid, like he wanted a certain response but didn't want to give the impression he needed it.

Dew laughed and said no, in his estimation that's not something a bad guy would do, which seemed to satisfy Jones.

The white tablecloth was covered in empty plates once filled with arugula and artichoke, prosciutto and melon, Bolognese, carbonara, amatriciana, sirloin, and mussels. Bottles of cabernet sauvignon and pinot noir were corked and emptied.

At the end of the meal, Jones got a text message. He breathed a heavy sigh before tossing his phone on the table and burying his head in his hands. He had been checking his phone more neurotically that night—fishing it from his pocket with speed, scanning the screen, and then sluggishly returning it. Usually, he would be looking at Infowars or his social media accounts, obsessing over the grandiloquence of headlines, but this time he was waiting to hear from his wife.

Jones had found out his new girlfriend was pregnant, and they had gotten married before the trip to DC. That morning their doctor had discovered the unborn baby might have microcephaly, a rare condition in which the infant has a smaller head than normal.

"What did I do to deserve this?" Jones asked, tears dropping on the empty plate in front of him. "I'm a good person."

Suddenly the incident with the Rolex made sense. With each rhetorical question, he worked himself into a deeper desperation until he was wailing in the restaurant, overcome with sadness. "I'm going to have a kid with a... with a... peanut head!"

Buckley tried to console Jones, telling him the diagnosis wasn't certain, and even if it happened, it wasn't because he deserved it. But Jones wasn't listening. He kept insisting that the only mistakes he'd ever made were with women and alcohol, and that wasn't enough for God to hurt his child. "I don't deserve it," he said, sucking in air between sobs. After a few moments his crying had slowed, but under his breath, like he couldn't believe the unfairness, he kept muttering "peanut head... peanut head... peanut head."

The following morning, he was in higher spirits, or was at least trying to be. It was Inauguration Day, and he was determined to keep it together. We met Roger Stone outside the entrance to the Capitol grounds wearing a top hat and a three-piece suit. It felt fitting. Trump's inauguration in many ways was a three-ring circus, and Stone had dressed the part.

We were streaming back to Jones's live show, and Stone began talking about how he'd been poisoned a few days earlier. He claimed a doctor had determined someone attempted to poison him with polonium before the inauguration. It was like he and Jones were cut from the same cloth, incapable of existing without crafting stories to draw more attention to themselves.

The expectation, for those of us circling the drain of an extreme internet-generated reality, was that the streets of DC would be a hellscape of violent protests and carnage. But that didn't happen. A few fights broke out, windows were smashed out of a Starbucks and a bank downtown, but the chaos and those participating in it were few and far between.

After parting ways with Stone, we walked around for a bit, and when nothing interesting happened around us, Jones decided to go into the US Capitol grounds, where the inauguration was soon underway. We were only able to secure a single ticket, so Jones went on his own. At the gate, Buckley followed behind him like a mother sending her child to grade school after summer break. "Do you have your phone?" Buckley asked.

Jones felt around in his pockets and pulled it out. "Got it," he said, holding it up for Buckley to see.

"What about your wallet, in case you need your ID?"

At this, Jones turned toward the entrance and marched off. "I have everything I need," he grumbled over his shoulder.

It was evident Buckley cared about Jones and seemed to have his best interest in mind. But I can't say the same for Jones. He treated Buckley like he treated everyone around him—needing their care and concern but resenting and hating them for it. As far as I could tell, Jones only knew how to have the kind of relationship where he was at the center.

We lingered near the gate for the duration of Trump's inauguration, waiting for Jones to return. An hour or so later he did, wanting to join the live show to discuss his experience inside. As we connected to the studio, people passing by recognized Jones and surrounded him. Men, women, and children approached to get a photo or shake his hand. Even an on-duty police officer came over and asked for a picture, looking nervous and starstruck.

The crowd that gathered reflected the audience he'd accumulated during his year-long association with Trump. I thought back to the early public outings with Jones. The fans who surrounded him back then were eccentrics, weirdos, the kind of people you imagined in front of a desktop computer with tin foil over the windows, watching hoax moon landing videos and searching information on chemtrails. It was easy to spot one of those people. But now Jones was reaching a whole new audience—white suburbanites in cargo shorts.

As the crowd grew, Jones went from discussing how Trump was invoking American ideals to delivering an impassioned performance reminiscent of a street preacher. He spoke with conviction, declaring that while a person doesn't get resurrected—unless it's Jesus or Lazarus—a country can come back from the dead. The crowd huddled close, listening with bated breath to the utter nonsense spewing from Jones's mouth. And then, like any good street preacher, he began to cry.

"I'll be honest with you, I want to get in a room by myself and hit my knees and start crying." Unlike the night before, when he cried for real, these were crocodile tears. A woman cheered, urging him on. He shifted from tears to fervent shouting, warning that evil would retaliate, and they had to remain vigilant. He claimed that Infowars, his guests, his listeners, Matt Drudge, and himself were the ones leading the charge against this perceived threat, acting as the blueprint to dismantle their enemies. Now everyone around us cheered, and I was shocked by the number of middle-aged women, clamoring to touch his hand.

Jones was overwhelmed by the crowd and disappeared. He loved getting attention but he hated giving it. I don't know where he went, but when I met up with him later that evening, his mood had improved. His wife had called with good news. After further testing, her doctor believed their child's risk of having a birth defect was much lower than originally anticipated.

That evening, Jones invited me to a steakhouse. I met him, Buckley, and the five security guards at the Capitol Grill off Pennsylvania Avenue. Before Jones, steakhouses were a rare indulgence. But *with* him, they became routine, and I can't pretend that part of my reluctance to leave wasn't tied to the lifestyle. Being in Jones's inner circle was often straight from the pages of Dante's *Inferno*, with each successive ring more hellish than the last, but at least the food was good. The metaphorical bread and circuses were actual bread and circuses, and the fall of the Roman Empire was the end of democracy and objective truth in America.

As the world burned, we ate and drank and suffered under the ire of a despotic ruler. Only in *our* catastrophic scenario, we had helped strike the match and seemed to welcome the raging inferno we'd created.

After dinner, Jones stumbled outside, where the Capitol gleamed in the distance. "Let's go live on Facebook," he slurred. Buckley tried, as always, to stop him, but Jones had been broadcasting his drunken ramblings during the entire trip, and it was no use.

"That's the people's house," Jones said. "Hey, guys, let's do this, let's march down to the Capitol. Let's get some exercise after gobbling steaks at the Capitol Grill . . . which God gave us. Listen, we're humbled by how great America is. I mean, look, we're not on power trips but this is a damn great country." I was surprised by how quickly he moved, given how inebriated he appeared. He looked and sounded the kind of drunk that only made sense immobile. His face drooped like a sad basset hound and his mouth seemed swollen, like an allergic reaction to the garbled nonsense coming out of it, but he had no problem walking a straight line.

"People that want to be peaceful to us, want to be our friends? We're your friends," he said. "If you want to take us over like the Islamicists, you're gonna get your ass kicked. Okay? You want a fight, you got one." This would have been a spot-on impression of a drunk family member revealing their bigotry after too much eggnog over the holidays if these weren't the talking points Jones had grown accustomed to using daily.

"I'll tell you, I'm so humbled and honored, I can hardly even talk right now," he said, hardly able to talk. "Look, everybody wanted us to march on Washington. I always heard, 'March with guns.' I said we're going to march with information. And it's happening. Look!"

Jones kept stopping his diatribe to carefully swallow, like he was about to throw up. He handed the microphone to the security guys and Buckley, forcing them to vamp as he stepped off camera to try and collect himself. He circled us like an inebriated shark, grabbing the microphone anytime he wanted to grumble some unintelligible quip—threatening to fight those who disagreed with him, and debating if January 20 (Trump's inauguration) should replace July 4 as the new Independence Day—until finally he lost focus and went to urinate behind a row of portable toilets.

On the walk back, he spotted a group on a third-floor balcony overlooking the Capitol. "That's CNN," he said. We were too far to read any logos, but it didn't matter. "We won, you bastards," he shouted. The silhouettes on the balcony turned toward us. "We beat you. You thought you'd win, but *we* won." Jones laughed maniacally, shouting "America" as he pounded his chest. "You tried to piss all over us, but we were victorious. Fuck you! We're the new media, we're the renaissance. Your gods have fallen, and it's only the beginning, you chicken-necked fuckers. Burn in hell!"

As we neared, the people on the balcony came into view. They had drinks in their hands and were pointing and laughing at us. It wasn't CNN. It wasn't even a news outlet. It was a dinner party.

We were scheduled to leave the next afternoon, but I rose early and made my way downtown one last time. The streets were already crowded for the women's march, a direct response to Trump's rhetoric on reproductive rights, health care, and workplace equality. Across the country, similar marches unfolded, but DC was the epicenter, the National Mall transformed into a sea of pink hats and banners. I was in awe of the tens of thousands of people filling the streets. It was an exercise of collective resistance, and it dwarfed any demonstration I had ever seen.

While most protesters moved in solidarity with those around them, I overheard one woman complain that men were in attendance. "Don't they know this isn't about them? Get the fuck out of my way," she said, shoving past a guy on the sidewalk. My first reaction was to pull my phone out and record her. Jones would love it. He could play the clip on his show for weeks, framing it as proof these women were motivated by a hatred of men, using this minor outburst to dismiss an entire movement.

But I stopped myself. This was one person, an outlier, who had no bearing on the unity and significance of the moment. My reasoning had become so corrupted that my immediate response was to exploit the situation. This wasn't the kind of person I wanted to be—cynical, judgmental, focused on everything but my own hang-ups. Ever since I watched Jones wander through the California redwoods in a documentary eight years earlier, my mind had been rotting from the inside out.

Nearby, Jones mocked the marchers, calling the women "dumb" and the men "beta male cucks." He asked me and Francis to come film him. I ignored his call, but Francis agreed to go. I'd tried to pull him from Jones's ideas, but unlike me, Francis hadn't stuck around out of fear. He was there because he had become a believer.

As I watched Jones on the live stream, calling people names, shouting at the protesters, I saw him in a new light. The man who once seemed so complex had turned out to be something much simpler. Something that Lacey had seen years earlier. He wasn't a hero, or even a villain, but a flawed human being who was a victim to his own narcissistic inability to see beyond himself.

19

MONSTERS

Ronson and I stayed in touch. He reached out about the chaos of our coverage in DC, noting the overtness of Jones's on-screen intoxication. While independently verifying the story I'd shared, he confided that he was tracking down people who knew Jones before his family left Dallas. "It's a great challenge," he said.

When we returned from the inauguration, I made an appointment with a lawyer. I knew I wanted to tell the truth about Jones and his world, but I was concerned with the legal ramifications. Four years earlier, on my first day at Infowars, I had been so unconcerned with the NDA, I had only scanned it, ignoring the particulars, failing to even keep a copy.

I went to Lydia and asked if she could provide the document for my personal records. I knew it was a risk—if Jones heard, he would go ballistic. But as it turned out, I had no reason to be nervous; she was happy to hand it over. I got the sense Lydia had lost her patience with Jones and the environment he fostered.

The law office was in downtown Austin, its narrow windows offering a faint glimpse of the tree-lined street outside. When I mentioned Jones, the attorney's eyes narrowed. It was obvious he recognized the name. Surrounded by fudge-colored walls, I watched in anticipation as he read over the NDA. After a few minutes, he placed the stack of papers on the table, removed his glasses, and rubbed the bridge of his nose, buying himself a moment to think.

"It's my job to protect you," he said, leaning back in his worn leather chair. "I have to consider what's best for my clients. You understand that, right?"

I nodded my head.

"As your lawyer, my advice is simple: You can't do this. It's too much of an unnecessary risk."

The silence was deafening as his words hung in the air. I told myself it was the obvious response, unsure what other outcome I expected. But then, just as I thought the matter was settled, he shifted forward in his seat.

"However, as a human being who has to live in this country, my advice is..." He paused, glancing down at the NDA, then back to me. "You *have* to do this."

The room stilled again. I couldn't tell if he was pleading with me, advising me, or simply acknowledging the inevitability of my choice. He shared that he and his wife spent their evenings glued to the news, anxious about the future of the country. If I wanted to write about my experiences, he was in full support. It was a big risk, but it was mine to take.

I reached out to Ronson and let him know I had met with a lawyer and decided to write something. I also told him he could use my name on the record if he chose to release anything from our meeting in DC.

He responded with a text, asking if I planned to quit before I published the story.

> Yeah, that's my only dilemma. As you know I'm ready to get the hell out of there. Would love to have some writing prospects before, just to pay the bills, but the risk seems worth it now to jump ship if I get the opportunity to publish this story. But yes, I'll leave before. I will be declared an enemy as soon as I put anything out (haha sounds so ridiculous—like I'm leaving the church of scientology or something)

For the first time since I started working for Jones, I sat down and began examining the past four years. It quickly became clear this would be a more challenging endeavor than I had anticipated. My mental state was a disaster. I was too entrenched in the experience to gain any clarity, and realized I couldn't move forward while still in that environment.

In the weeks after the inauguration, I began searching for another job. The thought of giving up my financial security was daunting. The previous year I'd made $92,000 without saving a dime, living beyond my means to cope with my unhappiness. I wasn't even sure what jobs I qualified for anymore. Holding a camera and editing videos made me physically ill. I associated those skills with a profound sense of shame and guilt, and I couldn't imagine continuing that as a career.

Lacey had landed a job at a fashion start-up in Austin, where I applied but never heard back. I felt lost and aimless, much like I had in film school. The difference was, this time, I had Alex Jones on my résumé and, worse, on my conscience. After four years of hard work, stress, and heartache, I was burned out and ashamed of who I had become, trapped in a cycle of second-guessing every decision to the point of paralysis.

In the meantime, I was still working for Jones, and things had only gotten worse since the inauguration. He spent much of his airtime praising Trump, and in doing so, he had effectively endorsed his ideas. Now he had to highlight the positives of Trump's first months in office, which was a departure from his usual rhetoric. Jones needed Trump to succeed to maintain credibility with his audience, but he also had to keep them afraid if he still wanted them to tune in and buy his products.

At 7 a.m. one Saturday morning, Jones called me in a panic. "This is it," he said, breathless. "They're going to assassinate Trump. I feel it in my gut." I stood in the kitchen, groggy, having stumbled in there to avoid waking Lacey. "I'm getting ready to head to the office to shoot an emergency report," he said. "You're on call this weekend, right?"

Jones had become so frantic that we now scheduled someone to be available at all hours.

I got to the office at 7:30 a.m. and set up the studio. I didn't hear from him again until he texted a voice memo at 1:16 p.m.

"Hey, bro, as usual I'm running late. I got to get the kids to my parents and stuff, so just try to complete the clips you already have." I didn't have any clips or know what he was talking about. "I'm going to tie it into Islam and how the left is tied to the most radical forms of Islam, and, you know, cutting the hearts out and murdering the people and how they're covering up the rapes in Europe. And then, uh, just basically tying it into all the satanism and all the occult stuff."

None of it was surprising. Every story was tied back to some bigoted talking point about Muslims or trans people, or how abortion was a satanic ritual. Over the next few hours, he continued texting me Infowars articles he planned to use for the report.

Sitting there, waiting, was the most pathetic I'd ever felt, and yet, I was like a beaten dog still hovering by the dinner table hoping for scraps, waiting for the carrot or the stick.

Jones stumbled in at 4 p.m., nine hours after he had called, smelling of alcohol and only half interested in the report. He lingered in his private bathroom for what felt like an eternity, and when he finally emerged, he meandered into my office, trying to make small talk. But I wasn't listening. I still had to edit and upload this "emergency" video—what felt like nothing more than an excuse for him to escape his family over the weekend.

Noticing my lack of enthusiasm, Jones became suspicious. "What's going on with you?" he asked, his tone shifting. I thought he was continuing the idle chatter, but when I gave a half-hearted answer, he pressed for more. "Seriously, you seem like something is wrong."

I brushed it aside, saying I was tired and maybe a little burned out.

"You need to get laid," Jones said. "A little something on the side to de-stress. I'm telling you it'll make a world of difference."

"I'm all right," I shot back at him, staring at the ground, afraid if I made eye contact, I might lunge at him, or laugh in his face. He was such a cliché. There were times when it seemed like Jones had learned how to be a man by emulating high schoolers, still stuck at the party where he was ambushed and beaten up.

As "providence" would have it, a week later during a live broadcast of Jones's show, he recounted the story of why his family moved from Dallas to Austin. He was emotional, having been drinking, and his tone was charged.

"I'm going to give you the greatest message from the day I began," he said, painting a vivid picture of his teenage years, recalling parties where police officers allegedly sold drugs to children.

As he spoke, Jones gazed into the distance, recalling an auditorium assembly at school focused on drug testing. Sitting in the Infowars studio, he gestured toward an imaginary stage, like he was a kid again. "I stood up and I said, 'I was at a pool party; he was selling cocaine and ecstasy last week.' They took me in an office, rammed my head in the wall, and told me, 'We're going to kill you and have Black people with footlong dicks rape you in the ass tomorrow if you don't shut up.'"

Tears streamed down his face as he fought to hold back his emotions. With a mix of pride and sorrow, he explained how he had reached out to his father, whose connections helped them escape the town's toxic grip. He spoke passionately, saying, "The difference is, I wanted justice. And I wanted to be a good person. And I wanted to stand up for what was right. And I wanted to change the world...and I did change the world. And you changed the world. And we don't have to let evil people run things anymore. We don't have to turn things over to them. All they've done to me, and all the things they've done to my family... It's beyond any movie."

I clipped the video and sent it to Ronson. He asked if I thought the tears were genuine. There had been countless instances when Jones had feigned emotion for the cameras, yet something about this moment struck me as authentic. I wasn't sure if it was tied to the story, or if something deeper was going on with him.

A few weeks later, Francis and I were summoned to a meeting where Jones informed us he'd received a legal letter from James Alefantis, the owner of Comet Ping Pong. Alefantis was demanding a public retraction and apology over the Pizzagate conspiracy theory Jones had amplified on his show. He instructed us to comb through his past broadcasts, identifying every mention of Pizzagate to forward to his lawyer. If we were thorough, he promised us a $5,000 bonus each.

Despite the legal maneuvering, Jones still intended to issue a retraction. It wasn't out of contrition but concern over the time a legal battle would take. The last thing he wanted was to be tied up in meetings with lawyers instead of proselytizing to his millions of listeners.

Francis, anxious that Jones might discover we'd dined at Comet Ping Pong while in DC, raised it as a sort of mea culpa. He insisted we hadn't talked about it publicly, and no one else knew. I was revolted by his sycophantic groveling, knowing that, had it been a year earlier, I would have done the same thing.

But Jones didn't care. He never believed the Comet Ping Pong conspiracy anyway. The only reason he started talking about it, insisting it was a child-sex ring, was because his listeners accused him of covering it up. Jones cared only for his platform, his audience, and his money, and making sure no lawsuit would take that away from him.

I reached a point where I avoided him at all costs. I began arriving late, timing my entrance for when he was hosting his live show, and I stayed away from my desk afterward to dodge his usual bathroom trips. If I heard his voice nearby, I'd duck into a supply closet or lock myself in the bathroom until he moved on. For the longest time I had sought his approval, and eventually, I got it. Now I didn't care. I had gone from his star employee to the office ghost.

Jones posted a lackluster apology on his website, acknowledging his role in spreading the Pizzagate conspiracy, and in the end, the lawsuit was dropped. It felt as though luck was always on his side; nothing seemed capable of bringing him down. And even if someday it did, he was like a cockroach—no matter what, he would always bounce back.

My job search dragged on until one evening, while complaining about my situation, a friend of Lacey's—someone she'd met while teaching a summer art program—offered a lifeline. Molly worked at a company that managed social media accounts for small businesses. She offered to recommend me for an entry-level position if I could reshape my résumé to downplay the previous four years of my life. It wasn't a guarantee, and I'd have to accept a significant pay cut if I landed the job, but I was desperate. Determined, I revised my résumé, highlighting my skills while sidestepping my past, and waited for a response. That week, Jones filmed a report where he unleashed an obscene, homophobic rant directed at a US representative from California, and a few days later, I got the new job.

It was a 75 percent pay cut, but I didn't care. I had never been less concerned about money in my life. This was my chance to break free, and I seized it without hesitation. That same day, I handed in my resignation to Dew, telling him I would be leaving in three hours. He reminded me it was customary to give two weeks' notice, but there was no way I could spend another day in that office. I had given Jones, Dew, and everyone else there enough of my time.

Less than forty-eight hours after quitting, I received a phone call from Jones. When I answered, my voice shaky, I dug my thumbnail into my arm, trying to sound calm, inhaling through clenched teeth.

"Let me tell you a little secret," Jones said. "I don't want to do this anymore either."

"What do you mean?" I asked.

"I don't want to do it anymore," he said, "and I got all these people working for me, and you know, then I feel guilty. You think I want to keep doing this? I haven't wanted to do this for five years."

When I quit, Jones had already gone home for the day, so we hadn't spoken in person. I'd been naïve to think it would be that simple.

"Look, I'm going to be really honest with you," Jones continued. "I get in a hole sometimes. I wouldn't call it depression, it's more like everything falls away around me for like five minutes, and then I just feel totally horrible. Do you understand what I'm saying?"

"Mm-hm, yeah," I said, unsure where this was going.

"And then I feel like I'm not doing enough 'cause I'm in this war," he said. "I didn't use to be like this, and I'm a drunk and everything."

As I sat there, I couldn't help but think this display of vulnerability was a ruse, a manipulative sleight of hand. I guessed his main concern was losing power and control. Jones offered to double my pay, suggested I work remotely, and even proposed funding a feature-length film of my own. I told him it wasn't about money and turned him down. That made him angry.

"I'm just saying this is a place where you can fucking grow and do big things if you fucking took the challenge by the horns and decided to be a fucking alpha male," Jones said. "Instead of fucking changing the environment you're in, and deciding we're doing important work, you take the negative and let it rot in your brain, like *we* are the negative, instead of us countering the negative. When you're shooting fucking bullets into a negative wall, it's gonna be splattering, there's gonna be pieces of negative everywhere..."

I didn't know how to respond, and I was barely able to follow his logic. After almost forty minutes of pandering, manipulating, and attempting to convince me to second-guess my decision to leave, he asked to call back the next day. He wanted to come up with a plan moving forward, anything to keep me from completely shutting the door.

Even though I was no longer beholden to Jones, I couldn't be honest about how I felt. I was to blame for my actions, unequivocally, and yet I resented Jones for creating an environment of rage, fear, and confusion. I resented him for making me do the things I did, for creating an environment where everyone was too afraid to speak up, for constantly making me doubt myself and my choices. I wanted to say these things to Jones, but I didn't. Instead, I lied, agreeing to continue the discussion later. The next morning, he called numerous times, and then again that evening. I let the calls go to voicemail.

"I just wanted to finish the conversation we had last night, and I just wanted to pick your brain about stuff I can make better," Jones said. "I agree, I want to get where I don't get upset about stuff. And I want to find out what else, if you could just tell me off record, what's going on around the office, so I can work on it. I've got to quit working as much, and I've got to pull back. So I don't blame you not wanting to stare into the abyss sometimes, 'cause you can become the abyss."

The last comment was a reference to the German philosopher Friedrich Nietzsche, from the book *Beyond Good and Evil*. The aphorism goes, "He who fights with monsters should look to it that he himself does not become a monster. And if you gaze long into an abyss, the abyss also gazes into you." But the opposite happened to me. Being surrounded by constant anger and hostility forced me to reckon with my own beliefs. I didn't want to hate people who were different than me, those whose lives consisted of distinct circumstances and experiences devoid of my opinions and criticisms. I wanted to be better.

20

MADE IN AMERICA

After I quit, I began having nightmares about being trapped inside the office. I would wake up drenched in sweat, gasping for breath, a wave of relief washing over me as I realized it was all in my head. I didn't see Jones in person again for three years. During that time, I started therapy, battled depression, and began the long journey of working through the trauma and taking ownership of my actions.

In 2018, over a year after I left, I received a call from Francis. An Infowars employee had died in a motorcycle accident. This employee (who would hate having his name memorialized in a book about Alex Jones, so I won't include it) had agreed to be a reference for me while I was searching for a job, and we kept in touch after I quit. He, more than anyone else, managed to exist in Jones's world without being wholly consumed by it. A few days later, I attended his funeral and saw some of my old coworkers for the first time since leaving. I recognized the exhaustion on their faces, listened to them complain about still working for Jones and tell me how lucky I was to have gotten out.

Another former colleague had left Infowars too, but Joe Biggs would take a darker path. After a falling out with Jones, he had become a prominent figure in the Proud Boys, a group that branded themselves as "Western chauvinists" and were notorious for their anti-Muslim and misogynistic rhetoric. Biggs entered the US Capitol on January 6, 2021, during the insurrection, and was later arrested and convicted by a jury of multiple felonies, including seditious conspiracy and conspiracy to obstruct an official proceeding. On August 31, 2023, he was sentenced to seventeen years in prison. A little over a year later, after Trump won the presidency for a second time, Biggs's sentence was commuted, and he was released from prison.

It was surreal to think that we had once shared the same space, gone to the same places, echoed the same rhetoric, and yet walked away from those experiences with radically different perspectives. Biggs and I had both entered Jones's sphere in search of something. We'd come, each in our own way, hoping to alter our fate. While I'd sought a sense of direction and purpose, Biggs had yearned for something more elemental. In the Army, he'd hoped to find connection and family, then he'd looked for the same thing at Infowars. Eventually, he'd turned to the Proud Boys. If I had to guess, he's still searching, somewhere.

At the funeral, I was equally overcome with sadness and relief. It was tragic losing a friend. This employee had always talked about wanting to quit working for Jones, but he had children and struggled to find a job making enough money to support his family. At the same time, I was grateful to no longer be weighed down by the chaos of that world.

Jones wasn't at the funeral, but a year later, Ronson released the story that stemmed from our secret meeting in DC for an episode of *This American Life*.

He spent that time traveling to Jones's hometown and interviewing those who knew him as a young man. One of his former classmates said that Jones would bite open pens, fill his mouth with black ink, and claim he was the devil. Another former classmate said that Jones was aggressive and threatened to rape her. Ronson discovered that Jones's version was a total fabrication, another one of his cinematic creations that skewed reality in favor of propping himself up as the hero. The man who would one day wield truth like a weapon was not born in battle; he was born in defeat.

After it aired, which was the first time I had publicly spoken about my experience working at Infowars, I received a text from Jones.

> Hope you are doing well. All my best! Alex

This was followed by a voice recording, and in true Jones fashion, his manipulative propensity was on full display:

> Once you open the door up to talking about me, it's always going to be more, more, more. "Give us this. Give us that." So, I just think you should be honest with yourself about the people you're involved with. Remember, it's never going to be enough. Whatever you say, whatever you think is fair and balanced, is never going to be enough. Because they're deceivers, they're very bad people. I just hope going down this road—because it's like heroin, you're going to need a bigger and bigger fix—that you just don't think of me as the bad guy, and you start projecting whatever is going on in your life onto me. I can tell you run this

stuff through your head a lot, and I wouldn't stare into the abyss too long, lest you become the abyss. But I'm not mad at you, Josh. I care about you, you're a talented guy... I'm just not going to be your villain.

In 2018, Jones began to reap the consequences of his actions. After years of listening to Jones claim the Sandy Hook tragedy was a "completely fake" hoax, the victims' families fought back, filing lawsuits against Jones in Texas and Connecticut. They had suffered for years, being harassed, threatened, and stalked because of Jones's rhetoric. In 2021, the courts issued default judgments against Jones after he failed to comply with their orders to produce evidence. In October 2022, a jury awarded an unprecedented $1.5 billion in damages to the families.

But that wasn't the end of his story. After the verdict, Jones declared personal bankruptcy, a move seen by many as a ploy to delay or avoid paying the families. His company, Free Speech Systems, followed suit, citing hundreds of millions in debt owed to the victims. Despite this, Jones remained defiant. He continued broadcasting from the Infowars studio, railing against the courts, the media, and what he described as a "deep state conspiracy" to silence him. Meanwhile, the families had yet to see the money awarded to them as legal battles over his assets dragged on amid growing suspicion that he had hidden wealth in shell companies or siphoned off funds.

What might've destroyed someone else only marked the beginning of a new chapter for Jones. Whether he retained his assets, the Infowars brand, or even the studio where I spent four years, I knew he wouldn't stop. He had already built a backup network, a new studio, and an online store, claiming they were owned by a third-party sponsor and therefore beyond the court's reach. Like a phoenix rising from the ashes of his own ruin, he would find a way to continue spreading his twisted version of reality, no matter the harm it caused or the people he left in his wake.

For years I watched Jones utter and promote things for which, against all odds, he was never held accountable. Countless families in Muslim communities like Islamberg lived in fear after false accusations, their children growing up under the shadow of threats and suspicion. Migrants at the Southern border were reduced to symbols, cast as villains in a story they never chose to be a part of. Survivors of mass shootings, public health workers, and grieving parents across the country found themselves targeted and harassed simply for existing within the narratives he twisted. Jones tried to frame Sandy Hook as an exception in his career when, in fact, it was the rule.

I'd hoped the simple act of removing myself from that world would be enough to rid me of my anger and regrets, and it did for a while. But the questions kept piling up: Why did I stick around for so long? What drew me to these ideas? How could I atone for my mistakes?

One thing was clear: I hadn't made it out on my own. Through the unraveling, the confusion, and the long paralyzing stretches of uncertainty, Lacey was there. She became the anchor who helped me break free from Jones's orbit, and the reason I'd progressed in the aftermath. It was Lacey who suggested therapy. Lacey who asked the hard questions when I stopped asking them myself. She never tried to drag me out or force me to confront what I wasn't ready to face, even though she had every right to. Without her, I'm not sure I would've made it out at all, at least not intact.

But finally, for the first time in my life, I wasn't following someone or something. I was no longer an open vessel, impressionable and willing to attach my sense of self onto a story or an idea that attracted me in the moment. I couldn't say I fully understood who I was, but I knew, without a doubt, who I wasn't.

In 2019, after two years of writing, rewriting, and giving up numerous times, I finally published an essay in the *New York Times Magazine* titled "Mr. Jones and Me," detailing part of my experience working at Infowars. Following the release, I was interviewed for documentaries and news specials seeking insight into who Alex Jones really was. I was approached by Leonardo DiCaprio's production company and spent nearly a year developing a film script with Jonah Hill set to play Jones.

During the Sandy Hook trial, I was deposed and did what I could to support the families. In the nine years since I walked away, I've met people who showed me real kindness and treated me with respect, despite my past. But when it came to Jones—and most of my former coworkers who remained in his orbit—I cut ties completely. When the *New York Times* reached out to him during the fact-checking process, he sent me two final texts.

> Hope you have good legal representation.

And

> I am going public.

That was the last I heard from him. Though it wasn't the last time I saw him.

Four months later, as Covid-19 ravaged the world, Jones—living his ultimate fearmongering fantasy during a pandemic—staged a protest at the Texas State Capitol. Since I lived nearby, I decided to make my way downtown. As I watched from a distance, a mask tightly fitted to my face, hundreds of protesters gathered around Jones. "This is twenty-first-century war," he shouted into a megaphone, referring to the lockdown. The protesters cheered as colorful signs flittered in the air: WE ARE NOT PRISONERS. REBELLION IS ESSENTIAL. FREEDOM IS GREATER THAN SAFETY. Even a few children held placards reading DOWN WITH CORONA-PANIC, and SHUTDOWN THE SHUTDOWN, while a toddler sat next to them in a stroller waving an American flag.

As I watched, I thought back to the years I'd spent idly behind a camera. I wondered if any of them had seen the videos I'd filmed, the reports I'd edited, the lies I'd helped disseminate.

When Jones first hired me, I knew only a handful of people who were aware of him. But after I quit, I realized that had changed. My parents had friends who idolized Jones, coworkers who listened to his show on a regular basis, community members in positions of power in state and local government who were captivated by his rhetoric. My hometown district elected Marjorie Taylor Greene as their representative—a frequent guest on Jones's radio show. The same ethos that fueled Jones for decades had become ubiquitous.

At the rally, Jones's voice cut through the applause. "God bless you all for standing in defiance of this tyranny," he said. "Choose freedom, choose America, not fear, not propaganda." As the crowd cheered—oblivious to the irony of Jones advocating the rejection of fear—I made eye contact with a man standing nearby. "Can you believe this?" he asked with a grin, whistling and waving a sign reading GIVE ME LIBERTY OR GIVE ME DEATH.

"Yes," I said, thinking back to my first day at Infowars, where I saw those same words, LIBERTY OR DEATH, hanging on a sign in the hallway. "Unfortunately, I can." His smile faded as I turned to walk away. Jones began chanting "Texas!" and then "USA!" as the crowd joined in, many of them watching, as I once had, through the cameras on their phones.

ACKNOWLEDGMENTS

The world changed as I wrote this book. First as I lived it, then as I tried to understand it, and again as I shaped it into something worth reading. The rhetoric grew louder. The lines between truth and performance blurred further. What once felt urgent could feel outdated within months, or weeks, or by the time this reaches your hands.

Thank you to those who make books their life's work, and who dedicated a portion of that life to this story. I'm grateful for the time and craft you all offered so generously. Thank you to Ethan Bassoff, my agent, for your quiet confidence and sharp instincts; to Gail Ross and Howard Yoon, who saw the shape of this book before I could; to Maddie Caldwell, whose clarity and precision pulled this manuscript back from the brink more than once; and to Amar Deol, who took the handoff without hesitation and carried the work forward like it mattered. My thanks as well to those who edited, typeset, and helped launch this story into the world—Megan Muralles, Morgan Spehar, Bob Castillo, Joan Matthews, Carolyn Levin—and to everyone at my publishers, Grand Central and HarperCollins UK.

To Jon Ronson, Charlie Warzel, Elizabeth Williamson, Anna Merlan, and Dan Reed—thank you for treating me like a person, not a subject. Your kindness landed deeper than you know.

To Dan Friesen and Jordan Holmes of Knowledge Fight, whose

in-depth analysis of Alex Jones helped me contextualize and better understand my own experience in his world. Without their insight, I might never have seen the full picture.

To my closest friends, who I am eternally grateful for: Matt Herndon, Jeremy Smithey, Saad Hanif, and Zachary Feinerman. To Taylor Holland, one of the first to read this story, and a consistent reminder not to take myself too seriously.

To Jacob Meszaros and Russell Hollander for seeing the story in me and being willing to walk through it for a while.

Thank you to my in-laws, Kenny and Kelly, for your unwavering support. Your steadiness and example have meant more than I've said.

To my parents, without whom neither this book nor the writer of it would exist. Thank you for everything. To my mom, for always listening—longer than anyone should have to—and for teaching me the power of honest communication. To my dad, who made integrity and service to others look simple, and who treated emotion as something worth making room for. To my sisters, Jenni and Leah—the first who showed me how far the world can stretch, and the second who showed me where it always leads back. To my grandmother Glenda, who filled my hands with more books than I could finish and encouraged me to keep writing. And to my aunt Edie—thank you for reminding me, often and without apology, that people are generally exhausting. To my family, whom I love: Arthur, Louise, Donald, Christy, Chris, Christen, Christiana, Chrisaren, Devin, Stephanie, Ronnie, Braxton, and Brynley. And to Owens and Betty Jean.

This book took years, and for much of that time, it felt impossible. Thank you to those who told me to keep going, and to those who told me it was okay to stop. Some days I'm still not sure which of you I should've listened to.

Finally, to Olive and Midge, my forever companions. And to Lacey, my partner in every sense, my everything. I could never have done this without you.

ABOUT THE AUTHOR

From 2013 to 2017, **Josh Owens** was a video editor and field producer for Alex Jones and his media company, Infowars. After nearly four years on the front lines of a radical new form of media, he quit and began speaking out against conspiratorial thinking and reactionary opportunists. He has written about his experiences at Infowars for the *New York Times Magazine* as well as CNN, and has been interviewed for his expertise on Alex Jones and Infowars' tactics in dozens of media outlets including the *New York Times*, Vice News, the *Atlantic*, PBS, Bloomberg, and others. He has appeared in the HBO documentary *The Truth vs. Alex Jones*, about Sandy Hook, and was the consultant for the *This American Life* episode titled "Alex in Wonderland." He is currently a writer, and this is his first book.